CW00504920

British History in P

General Editor: Jere

Matthew Roberts *Political Movements in Urban England, 1832–1914*
David Scott *Politics and War in the Three Stuart Kingdoms, 1637–49*
G.R. Searle *The Liberal Party: Triumph and Disintegration, 1886–1929 (2nd edn)*
George Southcombe & Grant Tapsell *Restoration Politics, Religion and Culture:*
Britain and Ireland, 1600–1714
John Stuart Shaw *The Political History of Eighteenth-Century Scotland*
W.M. Spellman *John Locke*
William Stafford *John Stuart Mill*
Robert Stewart *Party and Politics 1830–1852*
Alan Sykes *The Radical Right in Britain*
Bruce Webster *Medieval Scotland*
Ann Williams *Kingship and Government in Pre-Conquest England*
Ian S.Wood *Churchill*
John W. Young *Britain and European Unity, 1945–99 (2nd edn)*
Michael B. Young *Charles I*
Paul Ziegler *Palmerston*

British History in Perspective
Series Standing Order
ISBN 0–333–71356–7 hardcover
ISBN 0–333–69331–0 paperback
(*outside North America only*)

You can receive future titles in this series as they are published by placing a
standing order. Please contact your bookseller or, in case of difficulty, write to
us at the address below with your name and address, the title of the series and
the ISBN quoted above.

Customer Services Department, Macmillan Distribution Ltd,
Houndmills, Basingstoke, Hampshire RG21 6XS, England

Restoration Politics, Religion, and Culture

Britain and Ireland, 1660–1714

GEORGE SOUTHCOMBE & GRANT TAPSELL

First published 2010 by
PALGRAVE MACMILLAN

Palgrave Macmillan in the UK is an imprint of Macmillan Publishers Limited, registered in England, company number 785998, of Houndmills, Basingstoke, Hampshire RG21 6XS.

Palgrave Macmillan in the US is a division of St Martin's Press LLC, 175 Fifth Avenue, New York, NY 10010.

Palgrave Macmillan is the global academic imprint of the above companies and has companies and representatives throughout the world.

Palgrave® and Macmillan® are registered trademarks in the United States, the United Kingdom, Europe and other countries.

ISBN-13: 978–0–230–57444–1 hardback
ISBN-13: 978–0–230–57445–8 paperback

This book is printed on paper suitable for recycling and made from fully managed and sustained forest sources. Logging, pulping and manufacturing processes are expected to conform to the environmental regulations of the country of origin.

A catalogue record for this book is available from the British Library.

A catalog record for this book is available from the Library of Congress.

10   9   8   7   6   5   4   3   2   1
19   18   17   16   15   14   13   12   11   10

Printed and bound in Great Britain by
CPI Antony Rowe, Chippenham and Eastbourne

For Clive and Felicity: tutors, colleagues, friends

Contents

CONTENTS ix

List of Figures

Every effort has been made to trace the copyright holders, but if any have
been inadvertently overlooked, the publishers will be pleased to make the
necessary arrangements at the first opportunity.

Preface

The dedication of this book indicates the extent of our debts to Clive Holmes and Felicity Heal. It also reflects the fact that they are cherished friends. This book arises from a series of lectures we first delivered in Oxford during the academic year 2004/5 when we replaced Clive and Felicity during their periods of research leave. Besides the direct and indirect tuition we have been privileged to receive from them over the last 14 years, and the very welcome job opportunities that they provided, we are particularly grateful to Clive for providing us with such a superb model for our work in his analytical study *Why was Charles I Executed?* Our admiration for this has only increased as we wrote this book and found ourselves grappling with all the issues of concision, argument, and organisation that he had so brilliantly overcome. As all those who know them can testify, Clive and Felicity are scholars and teachers who believe in helping others. We hope that this book goes some way to continuing their example for a period slightly beyond their core interests.

George Southcombe would like to thank Jen who has been, and always will be, brilliant. His parents, John and Judy, have made everything possible, and his Gran has always been there for him. The following provided support and inspiration along the way: Ian Archer, Susan Brigden, Elizabeth Clarke, Patricia Clavin (who first suggested that we should write a book for Palgrave), Jane Garnett, Perry Gauci, Ralph Hanna, Joanna Innes, Matthew Kempshall, John Morrill, Natalia Nowakowska, Matthew Owens, Malcolm Parkes, Mark Philpott, Robert Saunders, Nigel Smith, and Benjamin Thompson. Naomi Hirst, Clive Holmes, Matthew Jenkinson, and Nicholas McDowell all read material and provided careful and helpful commentary on it.

Grant Tapsell would like to thank his parents, Peter and Joan, for expressing the bracing hope that his second book would be more accessible than his first. Living with Catherine Wright has been a constant joy, even when her keen historian's eye forced re-writing and further reflection. John Saxton and John Morrill's friendship and example continue to be both influential and inspirational. He is also grateful to John Reeks, James Smith, and Ruth Venney, all former students at the University of St Andrews, who offered careful and constructive critiques of several chapters.

We are very grateful to the British Academy for electing us both to Postdoctoral Fellowships at crucial points in our careers, and Grant Tapsell continues to appreciate the supportive environment provided in his current academic home at St Andrews. Lord Egremont kindly granted permission for us to quote from the Petworth House Archives. Rosie Borland, Maya Evans, and Jonathan Fitzgibbons all heard these chapters as lectures when they were undergraduates, and have then and since taught us a great deal. Anna Bayman, Leif Dixon, and Alex Gajda have supported us and fired our ideas. All errors that remain are our own. We can blame them on nobody else, least of all each other.

Abbreviations

BL	British Library
Bodl.	Bodleian Library, Oxford
CSPD	*Calendars of State Papers Domestic*
EHD	Andrew Browning (ed.), *English Historical Documents Vol. VIII: 1660–1714* (1953)
EHR	*English Historical Review*
HJ	*Historical Journal*
HMC	Historical Manuscripts Commission
JBS	*Journal of British Studies*
JEH	*Journal of Ecclesiastical History*
Morrice, *Entring Book*	Mark Goldie (gen. ed.), *The Entring Book of Roger Morrice 1677–1691* (6 vols, Woodbridge, 2007)
NLI	National Library of Ireland
NRA	National Register of Archives
ODNB	*Oxford Dictionary of National Biography*
P&P	*Past & Present*
Pepys, *Diary*	Robert Latham and William Matthews (eds), *The Diary of Samuel Pepys* (11 vols, 1970–83)
Reresby, *Memoirs*	Andrew Browning (ed.), *Memoirs of Sir John Reresby*, (ed.) Andrew Browning, new edn with an introduction by W.A. Speck and Mary K. Geiter (1991)
RO	Record Office
SCH	*Studies in Church History*
SHR	*Scottish Historical Review*
TRHS	*Transactions of the Royal Historical Society*
UWB	University of Wales Bangor

All books were published in London unless otherwise stated.

Introduction: Why Study Restoration History?

Charles II's reign was 'a disgrace to the history of our country'. Such was the verdict of Charles James Fox in the early nineteenth century. Fox had peculiar insight into the rule of a duplicitous, libertine king. He had been named after the 'Merry Monarch' and was a direct descendant of the king on his mother's side. The similarities between the two Charleses did not end with their names or shared ancestry. Fox became a Regency rake of some infamy and his own moral dissoluteness means that his assessment of Charles II, while that of a hypocrite, was based on an understanding he had gained from direct experience.[1] A century later the Tory Oxford academic C.R.L. Fletcher, who stood at the very opposite end of the political spectrum from the arch-Whig Fox, painted an even more damning portrait of James VII and II. James was 'a bad, cheap copy' of Charles I, one who lacked 'the dignity and courage of his father in adversity' and was just 'bad, unromantic and a fool'.[2] Both Fox and Fletcher were writing within a venerable historical tradition in which ethical lessons were drawn from the past, and in which great figures were described in order to provide either exemplars or warnings to the authors' contemporaries. The warning offered by the later Stuarts was stark. Their example demonstrated with exceptional clarity the dangers posed to a nation by the prevalence of vice within its political elite. The writings of Fox and Fletcher confirmed what those readers steeped in the classical tradition knew already: corruption at the centre spread outwards, coursing through the veins of the body politic and enfeebling all its limbs. The personal failings of rulers and leading ministers, it was firmly believed, would fundamentally undermine public life and prompt national decline.[3]

For Charles and James's subjects visible signs of such decline were not hard to find. Oliver Cromwell and his military forces had played a major ᴧe on the European scene, surprising contemptuous statesmen in Paris, Madrid, and elsewhere who had become used to thinking of the islands off the North-west corner of the continent as impotent and irrelevant. But while Cromwell's godly forces had comprehensively beaten their nearby rivals in the First Anglo-Dutch War (1652–4), Charles II faced the humiliation of crushing defeat in the second (1665–7). It was impossible to put a positive gloss on a war that saw the Dutch fled, led by Admiral de Ruyter, sail up the Medway in June 1667, burn out the royal shipyards, and tow away the king's flag-ship, the *Royal Charles*. Before 1660 that vessel had been known as the *Naseby*, after the battle of 1645 at which royalists had been humbled by parliamentarians. Re-naming the ship had not recreated military success. For many in future generations this humiliation remained burned as a mark of shame on the face of the nation. When Rudyard Kipling came to illustrate the Restoration period in his verse contributions to C.R.L. Fletcher's populist *History of England* in 1911 it was this incident which he recalled. Kipling, in full jingoistic mode, pointed to the way in which it illuminated the inevitability with which martial decline followed moral decline. Putting bitter words into the mouths of English sailors, Kipling wrote

> Mere powder, guns, and bullets,
> We scarce can get at all,
> Their price was spent in merriment
> And revel at Whitehall,
> While we in tattered doublets
> From ship to ship must row,
> Beseeching friends for odds and ends –
> *And this the Dutchmen know!*
> No King will heed our warnings,
> No Court will pay our claims –
> Our King and Court for their disport
> Do sell the very Thames!
> For, now De Ruyter's topsails,
> Off naked Chatham show,
> We dare not meet him with our fleet –
> *And this the Dutchmen know!*[4]

Even after historians replaced the tendency to moralise with a more dispassionate approach, the Restoration period continued to be the poor relation of early modern studies. While some exceptional scholars carried out research in this area, theirs was a minority pursuit, the results of which were dominated by biographies of leading politicians.[5] In part, this relative neglect was the result of what went before the Restoration: the origins of the civil wars, and the profound upheavals of the 1640s and 1650s, naturally excited massive scholarly attention. But it was also due to the problematic position of the later seventeenth century within the still whiggish meta-narrative of constitutional and intellectual developments. The explicit moralising may have gone, but there remained an underlying distaste for the Restoration. It was a squalid interlude between interregnum and Enlightenment. A corrupt court had replaced an innovatory republic; an intolerant national church had destroyed Oliver Cromwell's cherished liberty of conscience. It was not only late seventeenth-century English history that was unfashionable: the national historiographies of Scotland and Ireland characterised this period in decidedly retrograde terms. The former was dominated by the severe religious repression of Presbyterians – the 'killing times' enshrined in the martyrological writings of Robert Wodrow.[6] The latter focused on the development of a Protestant ascendancy in Ireland built on the economic dispossession and political displacement of a Catholic majority.[7]

So why study Restoration history if its core themes appear to be moral turpitude, military impotence, and religious repression? In the last 30 years, it has emerged from the intellectual ghetto. Central advances in the historiography have been driven by dramatic reconceptulisations of the position of the Restoration within the longer term history of Britain and Ireland. Jonathan Clark incorporated the period within a 'long eighteenth century' stretching from 1660 to 1832, which was typified more by the continuing strength and influence of established churches than enlightened ideas.[8] Others have reconfigured the Restoration era within a seventeenth-century experience dominated by recurring themes of crisis and instability prompted by persistent fears about 'popery and arbitrary government'. According to Jonathan Scott, 'England's troubles' did not end in 1660.[9] Analogous trends can be seen in Scottish and Irish historiography where older preoccupations with Jacobites and oppressed religious groups have been supplemented and enriched by wider discussions of political cultures, social groups, and core institutions.[10]

Within these debates over periodisation, historians have also redefined the key issues and areas for research. Different phases of older scholarship offered varying arguments as to why 1660 marked the end, or the beginning of the end, of religion as a central factor in political affairs. Those committed to showing that the Enlightenment represented an anti-religious impulse, and the rise of modern, rational scientific enquiry, could point to the apparent contrast between radical puritan sentiments suffusing the speeches of Oliver Cromwell as Lord Protector in the 1650s, and Charles II founding a Royal Society designed to stimulate understanding of the natural world and the human body in the 1660s.[11] Other scholars celebrated the connections between Puritanism and liberty. In the 1640s, these had led to military resistance to a perceived tyranny of monarchical power and clerical pretension; the execution of the 'tyrant' Charles I; and the abolition of both episcopacy and the House of Lords. In the maelstrom of these events, and continuing into the 1650s, radical authors poured out ideas creating a literature which continues to inspire academics and left-wing politicians alike. All this was swept away by the return of the monarch in 1660.[12] These historiographical positions, which were not mutually exclusive, thus produced a picture of the Restoration period as increasingly secular. In reaction against these arguments perhaps the greatest single historiographical advance in recent years has been the demonstration of the continued importance of religion as a driving force of politics in this period.[13]

Restoration historians have also started to integrate the insights to be gained from an approach which revolutionised analysis of the early seventeenth century, especially during the 1980s and 1990s: the new British history. Insular English history was challenged by the argument that the interconnections between the Stuart monarchs' three kingdoms were a major part of the explanation for the conflagrations which ripped through the isles in the mid-century.[14] If anything it is surprising how long it took for scholars of the later period to engage in 'British' analysis, but there are signs that this will become as important a component of future work on the late seventeenth century as it remains for early Stuart specialists.[15]

The final major area of historiographical expansion has been the investigation of the social depth of politics. The early domination of the field by biographical accounts of leading politicians cast light onto the politics of the royal court and parliament but they were much less useful when it came to investigating politics outside of these closed arenas. Politics 'out of doors' has thus been a vibrant part of recent writing, with detailed analyses now available of crowd activity, women's participation in public life, and disputes in the localities rather than metropolitan centres.[16] Crucial to much of this broadening out of the scope of political history has been increased interest in the history of communication. A mass of published pamphlets, poems, broadsheets, and sermons contributed in a myriad of ways to Restoration life; indeed, it has even been argued that the physical form and visual style of printed works helped to shape the structure and course of political debates.[17]

This summary of the issues which now most exercise historians has perhaps given a false impression of consensus. While there may be a growing sense of what we should be investigating, there remains considerable debate over what the rapidly accumulating scholarship teaches us. The sheer amount of material which has been produced can seem intimidating; the nuances of the debates on the above issues can appear bewildering. What these debates have shown conclusively is that Restoration history is worth studying in its own right and as an integral part of chronologically broader themes and debates. Through it we can examine the attempts of a society to overcome memories of civil war and religious crisis. We can see attempts to reach back before the civil wars to older ideals of government from the Elizabethan and Jacobean period. And we can see that the events of this era vitally contributed to the assumptions and world view of the generations that came to maturity in the period after another profound trauma in national life: the revolution of 1688/9. We wrote this book in the hope that it might help newcomers to navigate their way through this terrain. Like all navigators, we have not simply mapped the territory but plotted our own path through it. As such, this book does not aim just to detail debates but to contribute to them.

Chapter 1: What was Restored in 1660?

In 1644, the poet and polemicist John Milton wrote of how he saw in his 'mind a noble and puissant Nation rousing herself like a strong man after sleep, and shaking her invincible locks'.[1] The civil war had opened up opportunities for England to awaken and fulfil God's purpose. Milton would later write defending the execution of Charles I, asserting the legitimacy of an act which removed the country from the bondage of tyranny. But in 1660, the hopes which had been raised to dizzying heights in 1644 lay broken, and Milton did not seek to conceal his contempt for most of the English people. Overtaken by a 'deluge of ... epidemic madness' they threatened to bring England to 'a precipice of destruction'. Even the few for whom he retained any hope seemed to be 'chusing them a captain back for *Egypt*'.[2] He wrote these words in a pamphlet designed to propose a remedy, to halt a process which his own imagery suggested was inexorable. He failed. The captain he feared, Charles II, was restored to the thrones of England, Scotland, and Ireland soon after he published.

As Milton recognised few others would interpret these events as he did. *Some* did express their discontent, albeit rather less elegantly. On 1 May 1660, for example, one Thomas Blacklocke in the Red Lyon Inn, Southwark exclaimed that 'if ever the Kinge come into England, He shold come in a Wheel-Barrow, and his Breach shold be stucke full of Nettles'.[3] However, the very fact that a record of such statements now exists was normally the result of somebody loyal to the Crown being offended enough to report the speaker. For most the Restoration was a joyous occasion, monarchy the natural government of Britain and Ireland. The diarist John Evelyn like Milton viewed the situation through the lens provided by biblical history. But whereas Milton saw England being returned to bondage, Evelyn wrote that

6

it was the Lords doing, *et mirabile in oculis nostris*: for such a Restauration was never seene in the mention of any history, antient or modern, since the returne of the *Babylonian* Captivity, nor so joyfull a day, & so bright, ever seene in this nation: this hapning when to expect or effect it, was past all humane policy.[4]

Charles and his advisers, showing an awareness of the importance of public opinion which would continue throughout his reign, capitalised on the mood of celebration. Charles triumphantly entered London on 29 May 1660. His return had been postponed in order for it to coincide with his 30th birthday, which was to be metaphorically linked with his kingdoms being born again.[5] As an *Act for a Perpetuall Anniversary Thanksgiving on the nine and twentyeth date of May* recorded this was: 'the most memorable Birth day not onely of his Majesty both as a man and Prince but likewise as an actual King, and of this and other His Majesties Kingdomes all in a great measure borne and raised from the dead on this most joyfull day'.[6] Charles's way into the capital was paved with flowers, tapestries adorned the streets, and the fountains flowed with wine.[7] What Milton regarded as a return to slavery was thus for many other observers a return from a period so dark that it could be likened to death itself.

But when they awoke, bleary eyed and hungover, on 30 May, Londoners might well have asked themselves what exactly they had been celebrating. The return of the king, certainly, but on what terms? What was restored in 1660? The answer to this question has two parts. First, and most obviously, an analysis of the political settlement as it was worked out between king and parliament in the early 1660s is required. But secondly a more conceptually sophisticated examination of why, despite the ways in which this settlement was relatively favourable to the monarchy, Charles II's polities remained unsettled is necessary. This unsettled state was dramatically shaped by the impact of the Revolution. We trace this impact in three key areas – print and popular politics, constitutional debate, and religion. The themes introduced here are expanded upon in the chapters that follow and provide our book's unifying argument.

Restoration

In constitutional terms England was to be returned to a point reached in 1641.[8] This meant that the legislation passed in the early, heady days of the Long Parliament – where those who would become Parliamentarians and

Royalists, Roundheads and Cavaliers, still often spoke with one voice on central issues – remained on the statute book. Charles I, albeit unwillingly, had given his assent to these measures which asserted that in theory no future king could rule with the admixture of blinkered authoritarianism and unchecked innovation which he had demonstrated from 1629–40. The fiscal expedients of the personal rule, based on a novel interpretation of age-old rights, all remained abolished. The prerogative courts of High Commission and Star Chamber which had convicted and brutally punished the puritan 'martyrs' Henry Burton, John Bastwick, and William Prynne were not resuscitated.[9] The only key piece of legislation dating from this time which was substantially altered was the Triennial Act. The Cavalier Parliament's Act (passed in 1664) retained the Long Parliament's requirement that a parliament be called every three years but, unlike the earlier Act, it did not set out any mechanisms by which parliament could be called should the king fail in this duty.

The Restoration thus represented a moment of belated triumph for those who in 1640 and 1641 had wanted to clarify the boundaries of kingly power but who had not sought to capitalise on the king's weakness in order to drive forward further reformation.[10] But it was also, ostensibly at least, a triumph for the monarchy. None of the more radical legislation of the years of civil war and interregnum was kept on the statute books. Parliament finally resolved what Clarendon called the 'great bone of contention during the late ware' in passing measures which placed the militia under Charles's sole control.[11] In addition, virtually all of the armed force on which power in the interregnum had rested was disbanded, and Charles was to be allowed a standing army with the important proviso that he had to pay for it.[12] The financial settlement, it is true, did not solve the problems of chronic underfunding to which early modern English monarchs had been subject. It was adjudged in September 1660 that government required £1,200,000 a year, and without its previous fiscal rights and given the inadequacy of income from land and customs, alternative funding had to be decided upon. The possibility of a land tax was discussed, but the first attempt at a solution which was pleasing to both the Crown and parliament – which, with much of its membership drawn from the gentry, had landed interests at its heart – was found in the grant of an excise on alcoholic beverages. When this failed to meet the necessary amount, a Hearth Tax was voted in 1662. Even then these measures did not at first provide the requisite amount for government, and the king was forced to rely on parliament for extra grants.[13] But while this financial settlement set some limitations on monarchical power, if only because of the initial inadequacy of its provisions, it put Charles in no worse a position than his predecessors. Also, by relying on the excise rather than a land tax, it ironically created a system that would ultimately provide the Crown with a strong economic foundation from which to withstand the challenges of the late 1670s and early 1680s.

Thus at first the answer to what was restored in 1660 seems to be a relatively simple one: virtually everything that did not seem to the nobility and gentry represented in parliament to be related to Caroline arbitrary rule. It was to be as if the civil war and interregnum had never happened. The legislation that enshrined this, the Act of Indemnity and Oblivion, was passed in August 1660. The act declared that everybody – with some named exceptions – who had been involved in 'all and all manner of treasons, misprisons of treasons, murthers, felonies, offences, crimes, contempts and misdemeanours' in the name of the Royalist or Parliamentarian cause between 1 January 1638 and 24 June 1660 would be granted pardon and indemnity.[14] The act also attempted to force the nation to participate in an act of collective amnesia, and to obviate the languages of political conflict that had developed. Any of those labels that had denoted different sides in the civil war were declared anathema, removed from the political lexicon of England.[15] In a speech to parliament of September 1660, Edward Hyde, Earl of Clarendon, Lord Chancellor and, apart from the king, the leading figure in politics from 1660–7 spoke with anger of those who sought to keep the memory of the civil wars alive in their labelling of others. He extended his opprobrium to those guilty of thought-crimes, who brewed evil thoughts within them, occasionally allowing their minds' construction to be shown on their faces. Charles himself

> hath given us a noble and princely example, by opening and stretching His arms to all who are worthy to be His Subjects, worthy to be thought English men, by extending His heart with a pious and a grateful joy to finde all His Subjects at once in His arms, and himself in theirs: and shall we fold our arms towards one another, and contract our hearts with Envy and Malice to each other, by any sharp memory of what hath been unneighbourly or unkindely done heretofore? What is this but to rebel against the Person of the King, against the excellent Example and Verture of the King, against the known Law of the Land, this blessed Act of Oblivion?[16]

Remembering was figured as rebellion. In conjunction the legal fiction that Charles II's reign had commenced immediately after his father's execution in 1649 was set down, and the statutes of his reign are still numbered as if he had ruled from that moment. England had no longer been without a monarch for 11 years.

And yet, unsurprisingly, minds were not wiped blank. Indeed, some of the actions of the Restoration government were actually in conflict with any sustained attempt to erase the past. A number of individuals were excepted from the Act of Indemnity and Oblivion and 13 who had signed Charles I's death warrant, or who had played a leading role in his trial, were executed at Charing-Cross.[17] In the horrifying Grand Guignol theatre of an early modern execution for treason, the gathered crowds witnessed the hanging, disembowelling, and quartering of these men. Their senses were assailed: Evelyn who 'saw not their execution' nonetheless described how he 'met their quarters mangld & cutt & reaking as they were brought from the Gallows in baskets on the hurdle', whilst the inhabitants of Charing-Cross petitioned the king asking that there should be no further executions there because 'the stench of their burnt bowels had so putrified the air'.[18] The heads of the traitors were displayed prominently, their dead gazes cast over London reminding its inhabitants of the past in all too obvious a form. Even more strikingly than this, the phrase 'digging up the past' was literalised in a particularly grotesque way when it was ordered that the bodies of Oliver Cromwell, Henry Ireton, and John Bradshaw should be exhumed. In an act of symbolic revenge they were hanged, dressed in their winding sheets, on the anniversary of the regicide 30 January 1661. Their heads were then put on spikes outside Westminster Hall. For almost 20 years Oliver Cromwell's head looked down upon London. Oblivion? Hardly. The chief statesman of the 11 years that officially did not exist was ever present during the 20 years in which all Londoners were meant to forget that he had ever been alive. But it was, of course, not only the actions of the Restoration government that kept the past at the forefront of people's minds. The interregnum was unforgettable. The past indelibly affected the present: the major political issues; the political languages used; and the political and religious decisions taken; all of these things bore the marks of the experiences that had preceded 1660. Just as Cromwell's head watched over Restoration London, so the Restoration as a period was watched over by the ghosts of the civil war and interregnum, and they were ghosts who refused to lie down.

This is key to understanding why, despite the apparent strength bestowed upon the restored monarchy by the settlement, the period remained turbulent. The Restoration was fundamentally affected by the English Revolution. The concept of the English Revolution is a controversial one, but its use is appropriate here. While the arguments supported by the teleological underpinnings of Whiggism and Marxism crumbled in the face of the detailed archival researches of revisionist historians, recently the notion of an English Revolution has been rescued from obsolescence partly because it has been redefined. The English Revolution is now seen less as a social and economic event and more as a cultural and intellectual process. As the erstwhile president of the United States, John Adams, had commented upon a very different revolution: 'What do we mean by the Revolution? The war? That was no part of the Revolution; it was only an effect and consequence of it. The Revolution was in the minds of the people'.[19] The English Revolution too was in the minds of the people. We turn now to its impact.

The Impact of Revolution I: Print and Popular Politicisation

It was inevitable that the experience of civil war would catalyse the development of popular politicisation. Irrespective of the reasons why men initially chose sides (or chose not to choose sides), as the war progressed they came to think more about what their role in the polity entailed and to what kind of polity they wished to return. This is most obviously true of the members of the New Model Army – who had the weight of arms to transfer their thoughts into action – but it is also true of the neutralist Clubmen beloved of revisionist scholars.[20] The war was also one fought in words. Indeed, it had been heralded in words, and ideological division in politics out-of-doors both before and during the war had been driven in part by the written word. This was related to an event which is emblematic of the concept of cultural revolution. The abolition of the Courts of Star Chamber and High Commission in 1641 had profound consequences. Censorship, the application of which relied on these courts, collapsed, and the numbers of printed works, already rising rapidly, soared. Figure 1 demonstrates this explosion in striking graphical form (Figure 1).

From 1588–97 on average 260 books were published per year. In 1641, 2042 were published and in 1642, this figure had risen to 4038.[21] From 260 to 2042 in less than half a century: an almost eightfold increase. Vast numbers of these works were polemical and political and responded to the contemporary crises (one remarkable statistic is that of the 1500 pamphlets produced between 1641 and the outbreak of civil war in August 1642, one in six was concerned with the Irish rebellion).[22] Print had been enshrined as an immediate medium, a mechanism for the fast and public

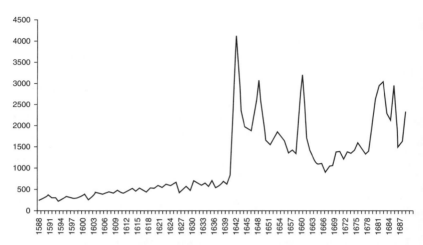

Figure 1 'Annual Press Output, 1588–1688', from Joad Raymond, *Pamphlets and Pamphleteering in Early Modern Britain* (Cambridge, 2003), p. 164. Cambridge University Press.

expression of variant political and religious views. Charles II had to contend with this fact when he was restored, and he recognised the potency of print. On 19 May 1662, he gave his assent to *An Act for preventing the frequent Abuses in printing seditious treasonable and unlicensed Bookes and Pamphlets and for regulating of Printing and Printing Presses*. The wording of the Act left no doubt as to the rationale behind it. The 'well-government and regulating of Printers and Printing Presses' was a 'matter of Publique care and of great concernment'. This was particularly because 'by the general licentiousnes of the late times many evil disposed persons' had 'been encouraged to print and sell heretical schismatical blasphemous seditious and treasonable Bookes Pamphlets and Papers'. They continued to do this 'to the high dishonour of Almighty God the endangering the peace of these Kingdomes and raising a disaffection to His most Excellent Majesty and His Government'.[23] Charles was keen to show that his own interests cohered with those of parliament. He made explicit the link not just between the possibility of future turmoil and the freedom of the press, but also what he saw as the link between past events and this freedom:

> Mr Secretary *Morice* acquaints the House, from his Majesty, That, next to the Bill for settling the Forces of the kingdom, his Majesty held, that the Bill, now depending, for regulating the Press, and to prevent

the Printing of libellous and seditious Books, did most conduce to the
securing the Peace of the Kingdom; the exorbitant liberty of the Press
having been a great Occasion of the late Rebellion in the kingdom, and
the Schisms in the Church ... [24]

This is a remarkable statement. The armed forces and the printing press
were the most important issues for Charles to have settled. The metaphor
often used of printed material in this period, 'paper bullets', seems to
have been real enough in Charles's mind. But as another cursory look at
the graph shows it proved impossible to restore pre-1641 levels of control
over the printed word. The lid had been taken off and it was impossible to
force it back on. Through many different expedients dissenting religious
and political voices found ways to be heard, and in the years of the Exclusion Crisis they were helped by the fact that the Licensing Act lapsed, and
the emergent Whigs were in no hurry to reapply it. Thus the restored
world of Charles II was one in which the printed word was used to fuel a
growing public forum for political debate. This is not to claim that print
was the only motor driving the development of politics out of doors, and
we will examine others in more detail in Chapter 7. But it is to emphasise, contrary to several recent attempts to diminish the significance of
print, that 1641 and the years after witnessed a profound change in the
use and reception of the printed medium and that this was something
which Charles II had to contend with, knew he had to contend with, and
at various points in his reign failed to contend with.

The Impact of Revolution II: Constitutional Debate

The second complex legacy of the English Revolution was constitutional.[25]
The reality of the situation was that the overwhelming popularity of the
Restoration hid a morass of tensions. These tensions were inherent in the
forces which had coalesced in the crisis year of 1659.[26] As England threatened to slide into anarchy, ideologically disparate groups co-operated
tactically to bring about stability. For some this meant the return of monarchy from the start, whilst others came to believe this as events unfolded.
Presbyterians and Anglican royalists found a common cause in the fight
against radical sectarianism, and, in a move with more than a touch of
historical irony, members of the army that had played the central role
in bringing about the execution of Charles I were now fundamental in
restoring his son.[27] The taciturn general George Monck led troops from

Scotland, crossing the Tweed in January 1660, and ensured the return of members 'purged' in 1648 to parliament in February. Originally sphinx-like in revealing his intentions, Monck came to recognise that the logic of his actions pointed to a Stuart restoration, and he set about ensuring that he would profit from that eventuality.[28] The Convention Parliament assembled in April, and its make up gives an indication of the different constitutional perspectives prevalent among those who would oversee the initial stages of the Restoration. It included those members whose intransigent insistence on treating with the impossible Charles I had led directly to Pride's Purge – men like Denzil Holles and Sir Harbottle Grimston, who were dubbed the 'Presbyterian knot'.[29] But whilst these men's actions had been reprehensible to an army that by late 1648 thought of Charles I as a man of blood (the 'capitall and grand Author of our troubles' who needed to 'be speedily brought to justice for the treason, blood and mischiefe, he is therein guilty of'[30]), they had a firm sense of the fetters which should be put upon the monarch. Their view of monarchy, as we have seen, did not win out in the Restoration settlement, but it illustrates nicely the opinions that some continued to hold towards the institution of monarchy. And these were opinions that could easily lead to conflict.

The potential for conflict that pertained despite the relative unanimity with which Charles was welcomed back was a symptom of the failure during the civil war and interregnum to resolve key constitutional questions, and the way in which the experience, and subsequent memory, of those years had sharpened those questions. The events that most starkly raised questions about the position of the monarch, and which were burnt on to English memories were those of the king's trial and the regicide of 30 January 1649. This demonstration that kings could be brought to account for their actions had a somewhat counter-intuitive impact on Restoration politics: it could be used as a way of bolstering monarchical power. A cult of Charles king and martyr thrived.[31] Those who were critical of the Crown could quickly be branded with the label of potential regicides. During the Exclusion Crisis – when, following revelations of a popish plot, attempts were made in consecutive parliaments to remove the Catholic James, Duke of York from the succession – those who sought to limit the backlash against both the present and future monarch recalled the regicide as the ultimate example of what had happened last time certain MPs had become too sure of their own importance. As one pamphleteer who tried to rebut such tactics complained:

These are the men who exclaim against our Parliaments proceedings, in relation to the Plot, as too violent, calling these Times by no other Name but that of 40 or 41. when to amuse as well his Sacred Majesty as his good People, they again threaten us with another 48.[32]

Also, as this quotation reveals, references were not simply made to 1648 (for those living in early modern England the year was taken to start on 25 March, so they would have thought of Charles as having been executed on 30 January 1648); the years preceding the outbreak of civil war could be used similarly to smear those who acted in an oppositional way. Indeed, the cry that '41 would come again was perhaps the most commonplace of the claims made. So quotidian was its use by loyalists that it became the subject of satire. So it was that the vitriolic, loyalist polemicist Roger L'Estrange could be portrayed as a dog simply and bestially barking out the slogan 'Forty One' in the 1681 print *The Time-Servers*. As both this print and the pamphlet quoted above demonstrate polemic based on recalling the 1640s was sufficiently damaging for its targets to try to tackle it head-on. They attempted to emphasise the scaremongering tactics of their opponents. But such attempts to render these attacks impotent through satire could only be partially effective, and it remains the case that in the emerging Restoration war of words these two powerful linguistic weapons were in the armoury of the monarchy.

Nonetheless, whilst the fears of a return to civil war permeated political discourse in a way which could strengthen the monarchy, other elements of Restoration political discourse which had been profoundly shaped by the 1640s and 1650s were loci of controversy. In particular the relationship of monarchical authority to the law, one of the cruxes in the events which had led to war, was a contested area. This was in part at least because the idea that the king was the fountain of justice, and central to a constitution which safeguarded the fundamental legal rights of the subject, was at some level shared across political divides. This is best illustrated through an analysis of some of the grounds on which the return of the monarch was legitimised. The central figure is again Clarendon, for whose political thought the law provided a lodestar.[33] The interregnum had been illegal – its constitutional forms had provided no safeguards to the English subject. In this line of thinking, Oliver Cromwell as Lord Protector had been granted a position which, despite resting on England's first written constitution, was essentially meaningless within the only constitution that mattered – the ancient constitution.[34] The law, so the argument went, did not recognise the title, and impose obligations upon its holder, because the law ran in the name of the king. As such, Cromwell could rule in a more arbitrary, unbounded way than any king.[35] The Restoration returned England to a recognisable legal situation. In May 1661, Clarendon praised the fact that 'we have our King again, and our Laws again, and Parliaments again'.[36] He placed great weight on those who were required to ensure that the king's justice was implemented – informing Serjeant Thomas Twisden at his swearing-in as a judge that their conduct should lead to 'such reverence of the laws, and such an estimation of the persons who justly execute those laws, that they may look upon those who could pervert the laws at home, as enemies of the same magnitude, as those who would invade the country from abroad'.[37] Clarendon's thinking was echoed from pulpits across the land. George Morley, Bishop of Worcester and dean of the chapel royal said in his sermon at the coronation on 23 April 1661:

> For a *Despotical* Monarch governs his Subjects as a *Master* doth his *Servants, arbitrarily* according to his *own will* and pleasure, whether it be Right or Wrong; But a P*olitical* Monarch governs his Subjects as a F*ather* doth his *Children*, by Equal and Just Lawes, made with their *own consent* to them, The *former* is the Government of the T*urk* and M*uscovite*, the *later* is, or ought to be the Government of *all Christain* K*ings*; I am sure it is of *Ours* . . . [38]

In printed panegyrics too, various authors sought to assert Charles's lawful authority. Charles Cotton wrote:

> And it may be worthy your Majesties Princely consideration, and best thanks to Almighty God, that your way was laid open by your peoples love, and not forced by your own just Vengeance, that your Throne is established in the Judgements, and supported by the voluntary and united Strength of your People, fixt and riveted to the Centre of your Laws, not floating in Blood, nor raised upon heaps of Ruine, but built upon its true and ancient Foundation . . . [39]

Thomas Fuller attempted to make the point in verse. Having drawn a comparison with Edward the Confessor, Fuller proceeded to make the lessons for Charles clear:

> The *COMMON LAW* to him the English owe,
> On whom a *better gift* You will bestow:

That which He *made* by You shall be *made good*,
That *Prince* and *Peoples* rights both understood,
Both may be *Bankt* in their *respective station*;
Which done, no fear of future *Inundation*.[40]

In these examples, it is possible to discern the different inflections which the legal-constitutionalist discourse could be given, and to identify the spaces which it opened up for debate. Tensions arose over the question of defining the king's precise position in the polity, and because his legitimacy was based on his role within the law the question remained to be asked of him, as of his father before him: what should be done if the king ruled in an illegal, arbitrary manner? The political situation thus retained some of those tensions that had partially caused and been present throughout the civil war and interregnum, but the catalyst for the fracturing of these tensions was not simply constitutional, it was religious. And in order to understand this, it is necessary to turn to the final legacy of the Revolution: the growth of myriad religious groups during the civil wars and interregnum.

The Impact of Revolution III: Religion

As part of the revisionist enterprise, it became fashionable to downplay the significance of the experiences of these groups. As the researches of John Morrill and Judith Maltby, among others, have shown, the majority of English men and women adhered to a popular religion which remained predominantly based on an understanding of the Church of England that was neither puritan nor wedded to the controversial forms of Archbishop Laud, but was instead organised around the rhythms of the prayer book and the liturgical year.[41] This proved resilient in the face of the various attempts made during the mid-century to establish a different kind of religious settlement.[42] But outside of this tenacious prayer book Protestantism, a torrent of other religious ideas was flowing. The membership of some groups grew, whilst others, most famously the Quakers, trace their origins to the interregnum. Presbyterians, Independents, Particular Baptists, General Baptists, Quakers, Muggletonians, Grindletonians, Diggers, and Ranters all formed part of the religious landscape of England.[43] Some groups did not survive the interregnum (and some have argued that at least one never existed at all) but others did.[44] Whilst dissenters were never to make up a large proportion of the English population (around

6.2 per cent by the early eighteenth century), this fact belies their ultimate importance.[45] When Charles II returned, the religious composition
of England had dramatically changed – as recent commentators and some
at the time stressed the religious upheavals of the interregnum might
be seen as a 'second Reformation', ultimately more important than the
sixteenth century in forming England's religious complexion.[46] The question was raised of what sort of church would be restored. Charles, in the
Declaration he issued from Breda before he returned, seemed to offer a
glimpse of hope to those who would not welcome the return of a restrictive Church of England: 'we do declare a liberty to tender consciences,
and that no man shall be disquieted or called in question for differences
of opinion in matter of religion, which do not disturb the peace of the
kingdom'.[47] Furthermore, it seemed in the debates over the church that
occurred between 1660 and 1662 that the largest group, the Presbyterians, were to be comprehended within the Church of England. But these
hopes were soon dashed. In May 1662, Charles gave his assent to the Act
of Uniformity. The terms of this Act were unacceptable to many of the
clergy and ensured that by the end of August 1662 around 2000 men had
been ejected from their posts.[48] A series of astringent acts were passed
that sought to fetter dissent. But the religious legacy of the revolution was
such that these groups had too many adherents, who were too committed, for them to collapse in the face of persecution. Instead, the problem
raised by the existence of large-scale dissent became one of the key political issues of the day that would arguably be instrumental in the formation
of parties.

Conclusion

The three themes outlined above run throughout our book. We are concerned to show both the ways in which the Restoration period differed
from previous periods, but also to show that the period only makes sense
within the context of the seventeenth century as a whole. In doing this,
we are indebted to one of the most significant historians of the period, at
the same time as subtly departing from him. Jonathan Scott has argued
that post-Restoration developments 'are almost xerox copies of events,
structures and issues of the early Stuart period' and that 'The Restoration ... succeeded too well, for it restored not only the structures of
early Stuart government, but subsequently its fears, divisions and crises.'[49]
Scott's provocative phrasing precludes too much in the way of change to

be compatible with the thesis we have set out (and indeed Scott's powerful defence of the concept of the English Revolution sits uneasily with his own argument).[50] However, behind his over-excitable language rests an important perception: the seventeenth century as a whole was wracked with fears of popery and arbitrary government, and attempts to assuage these fears lay at the heart of that tumultuous century's successive crises. If our book is provided with thematic coherence by the three issues discussed in this chapter, its conceptual coherence is to be found in our analysis of the significance of this discourse. As we will see Andrew Marvell's sentiment that 'There has now for divers Years, a design been carried on, to change the Lawful Government of England into an Absolute Tyranny, and to convert the established Protestant Religion into down-right Popery' was widely felt.[51] However, the fact that many would have disagreed with what he *meant* by these words illuminates how debate over the location of the threat of popery and arbitrary government was at the centre of the political conflicts we analyse.

In answer to the question of what was restored in 1660 we need to be clear, as Scott is, that the issues which had driven the country to war remained unresolved. But we also need to be clear that the political world of Charles II was fundamentally different from that of his father, and that the attempts to resolve the political and religious issues would be carried out in this new world. That the English revolution never happened was, and remains, the stuff of Royalist dreams; that it did happen was to forge the shape of Charles's living nightmares.

Chapter 2: Why were Dissenters a Problem?

On 9 January 1661, Samuel Pepys was awoken in the morning at around '6 a-clock by people running up and down' saying that there were armed fanatics in the streets of London. He rose from his slumber and went down to the street where he found his neighbours 'in arms at the doors'. Noting this, he went back into his house and retrieved his sword and pistol, not because he was feeling particularly courageous, but because he did not want to appear scared in front of his fellow Londoners. It is a good thing that he was not called to action, because although he marched out with a gun, he did not have any charge for it.[1] So what caused Pepys to wave his curiously pacifist pistol? The answer is a Fifth Monarchist rising led by a cooper called Thomas Venner. The Fifth Monarchists had been prominent for a period during the interregnum. Their understanding of the prophecies in Daniel and Revelation had led them, in common with other millennial thinkers, to expect the imminent establishment of the 1000-year Fifth Monarchy of Christ on Earth. But unlike these other thinkers, they posited a key role for human agency in wiping away the corrupt powers that be and in ushering in the millennium.[2] As the manifesto of Venner's rising, typically interlacing biblical quotation, citation, and interpretation, recorded:

> it is lawfull for the true spiritual Seed, the legitimate Heirs of the promises and the World, Rom. 4.13. To RISE UP against the carnal, serpentine, accursed seed, who are the destroyers of the Earth, Rev. 11.18. To possess the GATE of their Enemies, to binde their Kings in Chains, and their Nobles in Fetters of Iron.[3]

According to Pepys, Venner and his crew marched through London, beat the trained bands, and forced the king's lifeguard to flee. They cried: ' "King Jesus, and the heads upon the gates!" ' a reference to the heads of executed regicides who had been exempted from the Act of Indemnity and Oblivion, and which now dismembered from their bodies overlooked the city (see Chapter 1).[4] It was Venner's second attempt at a rebellion and it did make greater advances than his first, but ultimately it still failed.[5] However, in Venner's rising we might think we have found an answer to the question: why were dissenters a problem? They were, it would seem from this incident, politically radical terrorists given to open violence. But the more this claim is probed the less sustainable it becomes. How many made up the marauding and terrifying horde that according to Pepys 'broke through the City gates twice'? Pepys thought at first they numbered at least 500.[6] He soon found, to his astonishment, that there were 31 (modern estimates now put the actual figure at around 50).[7] It was emphatically not a mighty force. This example suggests that dissenters cannot accurately be described as a dangerous and potent threat to civil society that needed to be crushed. Around 50 men led by a cooper who had shown himself to be an inept rebel leader once before hardly had revolutionary potential.

It is clear when tackling the question, why were dissenters a problem, that a more sophisticated answer is required. To that end we will explore events like Venner's rising not to prove their inherent strength, but rather to show the impact that they had on how dissenters were perceived. Furthermore, it will be important to discuss the question of how religious dissent became central to growing political divisions, and fuelled the political process that led to the development of parties. Finally, we will turn to the insights offered by an analysis of nonconformist culture that is methodologically indebted to literary and art historical methods. In this last section of the chapter, it will be suggested that a close reading of much nonconformist literature suggests that they used cultural forms – poetry, pamphlets, and the woodcuts associated with them – in order to make points that might be defined as broadly oppositional to the established Church and government. Thus, ultimately it will be shown that one of the reasons that dissenters were a problem is because they insisted, through the works they produced, on continuing to make themselves a problem for the Restoration Church and state.

Political Violence

First, it does remain true that some dissenters plotted to rise in arms against the iniquities of the Restoration regimes, and some of these risings even made it into reality. As has already been shown, around 50 men in London could cause remarkable unrest, and the reaction to Venner's rising suggests the fears that it had engendered. It was met with a show of extreme force as under noble leadership 700 of the Life Guard entered London.[8] Richard Greaves has demonstrated that a series of other conspiracies coloured the political landscape of Restoration Britain and Ireland.[9] Some certainly showed a great deal of imagination. The Tong plotters of 1662, for example, had lofty aims. Trustworthy republican members of the Rump Parliament were to be brought back and the monarchy, House of Lords, episcopacy, and Book of Common Prayer were to be done away with for good. This situation would be safeguarded against the recurrence of the counter-revolutionary developments of the interregnum. As one of the witnesses against the conspirators explained, the republican governing body 'should not have power in things of an Ecclesiastical nature, to impose any thing upon the consciences of the People' and 'it should be high Treason amongst them to assert the interest of a King, House of Lords, or single person'. Finally, as long as these and certain other crucial measures were kept in place 'it should be high Treason to disturb them'.[10] At one swoop an eternal republic would have been put in place – any backsliding into monarchy or protectoral government was to be guarded against, any who like Cromwell took it upon themselves 'to disturb' the proceedings of parliament would be treated as traitors. All this was, of course, so much fantasy. The plot was weakened by disputes occurring among the conspirators about the best ways in which to proceed, and in any case they had been infiltrated by spies. Vital figures were arrested before any rising could commence.[11] In many ways, the denouements of the Tong plot and Venner's rising are emblematic of what most of those who attempted armed insurrection could expect: their plans were either stillborn or strangled at birth. The conviction that society could be changed for the better was never backed with the necessary force of arms. Even Monmouth in 1685 who convinced c. 3000 men – among them a number of dissenters – to rise in his cause could not mount a serious challenge to the government.[12]

If the would-be insurrectionaries were possessed of startling imagination, then it is also the case that a certain amount of the subversive caballing recorded was the product of the fevered and paranoid imaginations of government agents. Mythologies could develop easily concerning the weaponry and numbers available to the 'fanatics'. The State Papers of the period contain some remarkable statements about the strength of dissenting forces. In an intelligence note probably dating from 1664, for example, details are recorded of the frequent meetings of principal Presbyterians in London, who supposedly had a widespread intelligence system and boasted that 'they have intelligence of all matter that passe in ye court'. When they learned that the king intended to raise three more regiments of horse, they laughed at the number and claimed that they had 'assurance of 50000 men in London'.[13] So it was that the Restoration regime was kept in a climate of fear, with radical dissenters apparently under the bed, threatening violent insurrection. Informers roamed the streets, seeking to cash in on the paranoia.[14] It is in the development of this climate that the main importance of the various plots lies. By interspersing the early years of the Restoration with various ill-fated and foolish plots, a small number of radical dissenters kept the regime reminded of the subversive elements within the country, and whilst this was not the only cause of the persecution of dissenters, it did harden pre-existing attitudes.[15] Thus Venner's rising confirmed the worst suspicions of those who would sit in the Cavalier Parliament. The Cavalier Parliament, which contained a large number of MPs who might be thought of as intolerant at the best of times, had an array of other suspected radicals rounded up and incarcerated, and it was to be the Cavalier Parliament, as is discussed later, that introduced a host of persecutory legislation.

The first reason that dissenters were a problem is thus that a radical caucus was able to heighten government fears of a more substantial revolutionary force just waiting to spring itself upon an unsuspecting England. But this is only at best a partial explanation, and it does not explain why there was debate over the position of dissenters within the polity. For if everyone was agreed that they were largely a fervid, dangerous, and violent group, then nobody would have bothered articulating arguments which sought to defend them. In order to understand why the issue of Church and dissent became central, it is necessary to examine the debates over church government that ensued at the time of Restoration, and the later developments which saw not only the growth of persecution, but also the development of arguments against this persecution.

Church and Dissent

The second part of the argument begins with Charles in Breda before his triumphant return. As we saw in Chapter 1, Charles declared a 'liberty to tender consciences'.[16] It seemed then that there might be some hope for those groups which gained strength during the civil war and interregnum.

The Presbyterians were particularly hopeful not for toleration, but for comprehension within the Church. (Toleration refers to the acceptance of different forms of worship existing outside of the Church; comprehension refers to the acceptance of a group within the Church.) The debates on the nature of the Church started even before the king returned in 1660, and it did seem at first as if progress was being made. In May 1660, Clarendon's agent Dr. Morley 'prevailed with' Edward Reynolds and Edmund Calamy (two leading moderate Presbyterians) 'to comply as to episcopacy and the liturgy with little alteration', although at this stage they could not undertake the same for their co-religionists.[17] Here it seemed that agreement might have been reached on two of the issues on which any church settlement might have foundered: the nature of church government and the nature of the liturgy. At this moment, due to their apparent willingness to compromise, there did appear to be a real possibility that Presbyterians would be encompassed within a broad church settlement. This in itself provides a key to understanding Restoration Presbyterianism. Restoration Presbyterians should largely be seen as the heirs of the early Stuart puritans, rather than being wedded to a specific Presbyterian style of church government as would be found in Geneva and elsewhere in seventeenth-century Europe.

It did not seem that Charles would renege on his promise in the Declaration of Breda, and indeed following a discussion at Clarendon's London residence in October 1660, the king issued the Worcester House Declaration. This provisional measure ceded a great deal to the Presbyterians 'until such a Synod may be called, as may without Passion or Prejudice give Us such farther Assistance towards a perfect Union of Affections, as well as Submission to Authority, as is necessary'. Bishops were not to ordain or censure without the 'Advice and Assistance of the Presbyters'; in order to ensure that each diocese (some of which were extremely large) was administered effectively, suffragan bishops were to be appointed; a meeting of 'learned Divines' including equal numbers of Presbyterians and conformists was to be set up to 'review' the prayer book, to make any changes considered necessary, and to create 'some additional Forms ... suited unto the Nature of the several Parts of Worship' so that ministers could choose whichever form they wished; ministers would be dispensed from carrying out certain ceremonies which were repugnant to their consciences (thus those ceremonies which Presbyterians found so objectionable – kneeling to receive communion, the cross in baptism, bowing at the name of Jesus, and wearing the surplice – would not be enforced); finally, neither 'the Subscription required by the Canon' nor the 'Oath of Canonical Obedience' would be required of those who in conscience could not accept them.[18] This was part of a programme written expressly in terms to appeal to the zealous, fearful for the future of the international protestant cause:

> And let us all endeavour, and emulate each other in those Endeavours, to countenance and advance the Protestant Religion Abroad, which will be best done by supporting the Dignity and Reverence due to the best Reformed Protestant Church at Home; and which, being once freed from the Calumnies and Reproaches it hath undergone from these late ill Times, will be the best Shelter for those Abroad... [19]

But despite the efforts of some, this Declaration was not turned into legislation, and for all of the early hopes, comprehension did not happen.

At the Savoy House Conference of 1661, which was called to debate the church settlement, Richard Baxter, the most prominent Presbyterian, did not help matters by his insistence that the prayer book should be completely revised. This proved a non-starter and, even though the Anglicans themselves had differing views on the liturgy, it was little altered in essentials.[20] But it was a large number of the members of the Cavalier Parliament that formed the major barrier to a relatively broad religious settlement. The naturally reactionary temperament of many MPs, stoked by the recent memories of Venner, led them into a narrower vision of the Church of England. In April 1662, they accepted the new prayer book, and on 19 May, the royal assent was given to the Act of Uniformity. Before the feast of St Bartholomew on 24 August 1662 ministers had to give their assent to two statements which placed many Presbyterian consciences under what was ultimately an insupportable weight. First, before their congregations ministers 'had to declare ... unfaigned assent and consent to all and every thing contained and prescribed in and by ... The Booke of Co[m]mon Prayer ... and the form or manner of making ordaining and consecrating of Bishops Preists and Deacons'. Secondly, they had to subscribe that they did 'declare that it is not lawfull upon any p[re]tence whatsoever to take Armes against the King' and that

> there lies no Obligac[i]on ... from the Oath comonly called the Solemne League and Covenant to endeavour any change or alteration of Government either in Church or State And that the same was in it selfe an unlawfull Oath and imposed upon the Subjects of this Realme against the knowne Lawes and Liberties of this Kingdome.

In addition, only those ministers who had been ordained by bishops would be recognised. The Act also imposed conditions upon those involved in education at all levels. All those who would not (or as they believed, could not) bend their consciences to the letter of the statute would be deprived.[21] These conditions meant that by that fateful day, remembered to posterity as Black Bartholomew Day, 1909 men had been ejected in England and a further 120 in Wales (some had been deprived before 1662).[22]

The workings of the Lord had rarely seemed more unfathomable, as the Vicar of Montacute, Somerset wrote to the Earl of Bedford's chaplain:

> I hope the cryes of many 1000 soules in England for the bread of life will pierce the heavens (there being neere 2000 ejected ministers), and that God, who hath now hid his face, will not contend for ever, but will repent Him of the evill, to which end the Lord purge away the iniquity of the daughter of Sion.[23]

Joseph Baker, echoing the prophet Jeremiah whose words would be fallen upon with increasing frequency by nonconformists living after this great ejection, wrote to Richard Baxter: 'How many poor souls (alas) that are now straying, & stumbling upon the dark mountains!'[24] Others looked forward to the divine punishment of those who had carried out this wicked deed. George Eubanke, in his farewell sermon, said: '*Herod* did but cut one mans head off, and he is gone to Hell for it. Oh what an Hell mayest thou look for, who hast got so many heads, and drunk the blood of thousands of the Saints and faithful servants of the most High?'[25] Whether it was met with anger, sorrow, or fantasies of retribution, the fact remained that from a clerical body of around 9000, a significant proportion had been pushed outside of the Church. Dissent had been thrust upon them.

However, it is important that the problem of dissent is not conceived of as having simply been created by a narrow and intolerant church settlement. The Act of Uniformity, of course, just applied to those ministers who had been acting within the Church of England. These were predominantly Presbyterians, only 194 of those deprived can be identified as Independents and only 19 as Baptists.[26] For those who had always found the idea of a state church anathema the decision to dissent had been a choice taken long before the Act of Uniformity. Whilst 'magisterial' Independents had accepted the idea of an Erastian church under Cromwell, and some took livings or at least a form of state funding, a large number always remained suspicious of any such settlement; the majority of Baptists never reached any level of accommodation with the state Church, and no Quaker ever did.[27] These were not then reluctant dissenters in the Presbyterian mould. It is also worth noting that even if Presbyterian hopes for comprehension had succeeded that would not have led ineluctably to other dissenting groups being treated with more tolerance. Presbyterians at this stage saw no reason why these obviously error-ridden groups should be given any concessions. Indeed, after their ejection it was a cause of great annoyance and profound distaste to many Presbyterians that they should be categorised with such radical groups as the Quakers. But it is clear that in 1662 and after, with blood in their nostrils, the intolerant members of the Cavalier Parliament increased the level of persecution for all nonconformists. A series of vicious acts were passed in addition to the Act of Uniformity. The Quaker Act (1662) imposed penalties upon those who held 'that the taking of an Oath in any case whatsoever although before a lawfull Magistrate is altogeather unlawfull', and who refused to take such an oath, or tried to convince others not to take an oath. It also made any religious gathering of five or more Quakers over the age of 16 illegal.[28] The Conventicle Act (1664) banned any meetings of five or more people from outside one household who practised religion 'in other manner then is allowed by the Liturgy or practise of the Church of England'.[29] The Five Mile Act (1665) set down an oath that bound its taker to reject the legitimacy of taking arms against the king, and not to 'endeavour any Alteration of Government either in Church or State'. Any ejected or otherwise dissenting ministers who did not take the oath were not to come within a five mile exclusion zone surrounding any town or any place where they had ministered since the Act of Oblivion.[30]

By the end of 1665, the legal bonds had thus been tightened around dissenting action, although actual persecution was patchy throughout the period and often depended on local circumstances and the national political temperature.[31] One of the reasons that dissenters continued to prove a problem was that they refused to collapse in the face of this legislative onslaught. Many remained strong. The Welsh Fifth Monarchist, Vavasor Powell, for instance, walked as a free man for less than a year under Charles II, and yet he remained constant in his faith – drawing solace from the act of translating Jeremiah's lamentations.[32] But it was not just in their refusal to disappear that dissenters proved a problem, it was in the political debates which their existence triggered.

As Tim Harris has made clear, the issue of Church and dissent was not simply a focus for debate between churchmen and dissenters. Some, whilst not Nonconformists themselves, wanted a broader Church with, perhaps, a degree of toleration outside it. These were met in the lists by others who wanted to protect a restrictive church settlement.[33] The debates took place in a variety of forums, including parliament. Thus far the impact of the conservative, intemperate, and reactionary attitudes of some members of the Cavalier Parliament has been highlighted, but to represent the entire parliament in this light would be to caricature it in a deeply misleading way. In actuality an examination of the 859 members who were at one point in the Cavalier House of Commons shows that over 300 can safely be thought of as having some sympathy with dissent.[34] The triumph of persecutory legislation may make it seem that these voices were drowned out, and yet many of the religious debates had been hard-fought and divisive.[35] After the fall of the Earl of Clarendon in 1667, debates were renewed over the nature of the religious settlement, and Gary S. De Krey has rightly named the period 1667–73 the first Restoration Crisis. It was a crisis over religious conscience and the limits that could be put upon it. Parliament considered comprehension and toleration bills during these years, and in the sites of popular politics the debates over conscience raged.[36] After this period, where an individual stood on the question of Church and dissent was a central part of their political identity. Rather than proceeding to show the emergence of these debates chronologically, the precise nature of the issues at stake will be brought out by examining the languages that participants in the debates used.

The debates over Church and dissent interlocked with the dominant political discourse of the period: popery and arbitrary government. The importance of this can be illustrated first by an episode that took place in the ever-expanding world of politics out-of-doors. In the furore that hit the streets of London after the passing of a second, more restrictive, Conventicle Act in 1670, two Quakers, William Penn and William Mead, were arrested for unlawful assembly and disturbing the peace.[37] Initially four intransigent jurymen refused to follow their eight fellows in bringing a conviction. On five occasions, the jury was told to leave the courtroom and come to a decision. Harangued from the bench, members of the jury were informed that they would be incarcerated until they had returned an acceptable verdict. When the jury eventually returned a verdict of not guilty, it was decided that its members should be fined and kept in prison until payment was made. Interference with the jurors pointed to arbitrary government, and this meant popery. This was made clear in the report of the trial produced by the Quakers in which the prosecutor was recorded as imagining what was required to deal with those like the defendants: 'it will never be well with us, till some thing like unto the Spanish inquisition will be in England'.[38] Dissenters and their allies believed that such hopes were widespread amongst their enemies. The desire to persecute was thus represented as a popish and arbitrary desire, and this argument was given historical ballast. Again and again the point was made that England's last Catholic ruler had also been a persecutor. Fears of a return to the reign of Queen Mary retained potency in an England that had partially been led from Catholicism into Protestantism by the bloody tales told of that reign by John Foxe in his *Book of Martyrs*.[39]

However, the discourse of popery and arbitrary government could be used by those who opposed dissenters as well. To take a broad example, Quakers were often branded with the label Jesuit. Many indeed were imprisoned on these grounds. This was not just a case of trying to hang all of the evils of the world around the neck of your enemy; it was based in the actual way that defenders of an intolerant Anglican Church saw Quakers. Quakers did not take oaths, their loyalty to the state was untestable, they were in this like Jesuits. And if they were in this like Jesuits, then they were popish, and to allow them to flourish was to invite popery into the kingdom. Nor was the claim that Quakers were popish mere rhetorical venom; many Quakers were tried under legislation originally intended under James VI and I to quell a Catholic threat.[40]

It is important, however, that it was not simply Quakers who could be portrayed in this way. The Quakers could easily be viewed with disgust even by other dissenters, and thus their persecution and vilification alone would not necessarily have become the focus of major political dispute. But all dissenting groups were vulnerable to accusations of popery and this increased the potential which such claims had to increase the volatility of the political situation. The attack on dissent in these terms is well illustrated by the print *The Committee; or Popery in Masquerade* (1680) (Figure 2).[41] This engraving by an unknown artist was provided with a verse by Roger L'Estrange.[42] It is a print which betrays an obsession with the past and an obdurate refusal to enact the erasure of the civil war and interregnum from historical memory. For the artist and L'Estrange the dangers that the present king faced were those that had either brought his father to the scaffold, or had emerged as a result of that cataclysmic moment. Thus the forces which they believed to be arrayed against the king in the present are related to their mid-century antetypes. The print presents the full panoply of religious identities and radical sects that emerged in that turbulent period, in order to equate them with the dissenters of Restoration England and their supporters. Lodowick Muggleton, a leader of the idiosyncraticMuggletonians is placed next to a

Figure 2 *The Committee; or Popery in Masquerade* (1680). © The Trustees of the British Museum.

Ranter, a Quaker, and an Anabaptist. An Independent and Fifth Monarchist engage in debate, whilst James Naylor – the Quaker whose pathetic recreation of Christ's entry into Jerusalem in 1656 had led to his horrific mutilation – is placed next to a naked Adamite. At the centre of this motley crew is a member of the largest group of Restoration nonconformists, a Presbyterian. For the artist and L'Estrange, despite the fact that this group of nonconformists was hardly homogenous, all of these men were dangerous dissidents bent on the destruction of the monarchy and society. Any who supported them were similarly dangerous. The subversive political intent of this group is made clear, again with reference to the civil war era. Archbishop Laud and the Earl of Strafford are shown being placed behind chains, whilst the bust of Charles I upended on the ground figures the regicide without having to take the indecorous step of displaying it realistically. The Bible and Magna Carta lie thrown on the floor. The alleged dangerous social consequences of dissent are also portrayed. A man stands with a horse in 'The Colchester Wedding' whilst an Elders' Maid is placed next to the dog Swash. Both couples are drawn from work first published by the Royalist John Berkenhead in the mid century. According to Berkenhead, these individuals – a Colchester Quaker and the Presbyterian maid Jane – had engaged in bestiality. This charge of sexual perversion was recalled as a way of further smearing nonconformists.[43]

The events of the civil war and interregnum were thus shown to have a present application. The artist created a powerful visual polemic by emphasising the radical religious heritage of dissent and associating nonconformists and their supporters with the forces which dismantled the Caroline state. The bloody years of civil war, the regicide, and the rise of radical sects could all, according to this pictorial argument, come again. But more than this, these fears are articulated within the terms of popery and arbitrary government. The Pope shouts down from the top right hand corner 'Courage mes enfans', and the title proclaims that the religious groups presented are but popery in masquerade. Why? They aim, as papists do, at the overturning of the English state. As their treatment of Magna Carta reveals, these people also intend to impose arbitrary government.

The two opposing theories of tolerance and intolerance could be expressed with many different gradations and subtleties, but ultimately it was these two theories which provided the intellectual underpinnings of the first political parties.[44] Tory hatred of dissent was matched by Whig loathing for a narrow, persecutory Church, but both were sure that their views on this subject were part of a larger conflict. For whilst Tory and Whig fears lay ostensibly in the same things, they differed over where they located those fears. The debates over Church and dissent were thus also debates over how to identify the threat from popery and arbitrary government. That this threat was felt so deeply, that the definition of its true nature was a matter of such urgency, and that debate over it raged so fiercely help to explain why partisan conflict developed in the first place, and why it continued for so long.

Dissenting Culture

So dissenters were a problem because they were central to a controversy that led to increased political conflict and polarisation. However, within this controversy they should not simply be seen as the passive victims of Tory prejudice, and this observation presages the third component of the argument. Dissenters were a problem because through the cultural artefacts that some of them produced they presented themselves in an oppositional way to the persecuting authorities. They thus did not suffer in silence but were vocal in their attacks on those who sought to suppress them. In short they insisted on making themselves into a visible problem. Before proceeding with this analysis two caveats might be offered. First, not all dissenters produced cultural material, and of those that did not all produced oppositional material. Some preferred to turn away decisively from the affairs of the world and to develop a powerful, spiritual, internalist aesthetic which allowed them to bolster their inner strength through devotion rather than action. However, this aesthetic has perhaps been emphasised too much at the expense of the material examined here.[45] Secondly, oppositional does not necessarily, or even usually, mean republican, although the opponents of comprehension and toleration often found it convenient to make this connection. Indeed, throughout much of the 1660s and 1670s, the king seemed sympathetic towards dissent, and nonconformists often sought to get him to make good on the promises he made at Breda in the face of the anti-dissenting legislation passed by his parliaments. A striking example of this is to be found in a work published in 1660 that railed against those in the localities who persecuted the Quakers. The authors wrote of the violence done to them that this 'molestation tends to the violation of the Word of the King, solemnly given, That we should not be disquieted nor called in question for our Religion, which doth not disturb the peace of the Kingdom'.[46]   The   emphasised sections almost quote the Declaration of Breda, in which the king had proclaimed: 'we do declare a liberty to tender consciences, and that no man shall be disquieted or called in question for differences of opinion in matter of religion, which do not disturb the peace of the kingdom'.[47] But they subtly and forcefully change it, 'no man' becomes 'we'; 'matter of religion' becomes 'our Religion'. The Quakers here turned the Declaration into a specific document that referred to them. They claimed that Charles had made a special promise to them, and that he should not renege on this. It is a polemical argument, but it also demonstrates very clearly that their hopes at this stage lay with the king.

The oppositional culture developed by dissenters took many forms, both visual and written. Figure 3 shows a woodcut from the 1662 work of the Lincolnshire General Baptist Thomas Grantham. In 1662, Grantham was imprisoned and this woodcut was the opening illustration of the pamphlet that he produced in prison, *The Prisoner against the Prelate*.

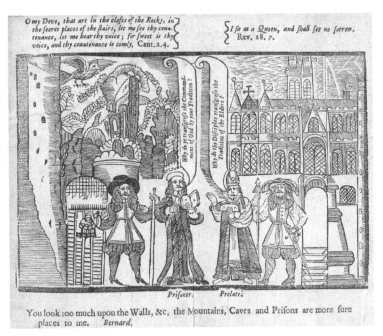

Figure 3 Thomas Grantham, *The Prisoner against the Prelate* (n.p., *c.* 1662). Bodleian Library, University of Oxford, Vet. A3f. 286, frontispiece.

This woodcut encapsulates the argument of the pamphlet. On the left hand side, Lincoln gaol is depicted and before it stands the gaoler, and the prisoner – a simply robed, moustached minister, who holds a book (presumably the Bible). The prisoner asks, '*Why do ye transgress the Commandment of God by your Tradition?*' The right hand side of the woodcut depicts Lincoln cathedral, set against a dark sky. In the foreground stand the prelate and an armed guard. The prelate is dressed in robes and mitre. '*Why do thy Disciples transgress the Tradition of the Elders?*', the prelate asks. The epigram for the right hand side is from Revelation 18.7 and it reads: '*I sit as a Queen, and shall see no sorrow.*' On seeing this picture for the first time the reader is thus made aware of the fundamental question to which the following work provides an answer: is it wrong to transgress the commandments of God in order to follow tradition, or to transgress the traditions of the elders in order to follow the commandments of God? This was a central question all dissenting groups faced. Should the traditions of the national Church, and the legitimacy claimed for them on the basis of their longevity, be traduced if they appeared to go against the word of God? Did the claims of conscience override those of obedience to the state Church? The contrast between the light and natural beauty on the prisoner's side with the dark and imposing form of the cathedral further compounds the reader's sense that the prelate represents the polar opposite of the prisoner and thus of the commandments of God; the prelate is one of those who still walks in darkness. The quotation on the prelate's side refers to the ultimate symbol of evil: the whore of Babylon described in the Revelation of St John. It records her revelling in complacency. But the chapter the verse is from shows this to be hubristic, and it looks forward to her destruction. The prelate is thus being constructed as the whore of Babylon, glorying in his assumed power in the face of impending destruction – it is hard to think of a more damning indictment of the Anglican Church. It is thus quite clear here that this image does not bespeak any quietist internalised spirituality, but a direct and forceful attack upon the established Church which insults it in the most potent terms possible.

Turning from visual to literary culture we encounter one of the most remarkable poets of the seventeenth century, Robert Wild. Robert Wild was a Presbyterian and after Black Bartholomew's Day he used poetry as a means of making points about the religious situation and of attacking the mechanisms which were used to silence nonconformists. Wild's verse was written in a deeply scurrilous, scatological, and satirical vein – it is difficult to imagine poetry more removed from internal spiritual considerations. This was popular, public poetry with a vengeance (and it *was* popular selling in vast quantities to a wide audience). This is Wild, for example, on the subject of what fills the press:

> Methinks the Man who stuffs the Weekly Sheet,
> With fine New-Nothings, what hard Names did meet.
> The Emp'ress, how her Petticoat was lac'd,
> And how her Lacquyes Liveries were fac'd;
> What's her chief Woman's Name; what Dons do bring
> Almonds and Figs to *Spain*'s great little King:
> Is much concern'd if the Pope's Toe but akes,
> When he breaks Wind, and when a Purge he takes[48]

Wild's point is that the press allowed by the government wallowed in the minutiae of Roman Catholic celebrity lifestyles. He made the further point within this poem that whilst the government allowed this sickening display, it also silenced loyal Presbyterian voices. This is a theme in much of Wild's work and he saved special opprobrium for the Surveyor of the Press, who oversaw censorship, Roger L'Estrange whom he christened 'Crack-fart'.[49] He also grew ever more disillusioned with the Anglican Church that had ejected him, memorably imagining it as Judas, or as made up of ill-educated illiterates who sign with crosses.[50] In Robert Wild's verse then, a nonconformist might be seen expressing himself in colloquial and robust terms. Literature was not a means to sublimity for him, but a form of action which could be used in an attempt to reconfigure the religious settlement.

Others too sought to harness the power of the written word for their cause. The Quakers' history is often written as if 1660 marked a decisive turning point at which the radical glories of the 1650s (which had seen naked Quakers interrupting services and James Naylor's extraordinary demonstration) were transmuted into pacifism and quietism. In fact, they continued to use print to berate the persecuting authorities. Around 1674, for example, the Lincolnshire Quaker John Whitehead hollered from the pages of a pamphlet addressed to the bishops:

> ... *ye have both against Reason and Truth proceed d against us in you Courts,*
> *and censured us, over whom ye have no Power, and excommunicated us, who*
> *never were of your Church, and persecuted some of the Lord's People unto*

Imprisonment, and kept them in Prison by your Writs of Excommunication till Death . . .[51]

This is a direct address concerning the wrongs done to the Quaker movement, which emphasises the dramatic increase in legal action taken against the Quakers since 1660, and the unreasonableness and irreligion of those who have acted against them. Whitehead had thus not retreated inwardly as the Restoration period progressed. He had come out fighting.

For Whitehead, as for Grantham, persecution had to be met not simply with stoical withdrawal but with outrage and public condemnation. True religion had always been persecuted, but dissenters were quick to combine the sense that their sufferings were a mark of their righteousness with descriptions of the retribution that would eventually be meted out to their enemies. The Quaker Mary Mollineux in 1668 wrote of 'a Glorious Day' to come:

> Then shall her Tyranizing Foes
>   Receive just Punishment,
> Who did her Children dear expose
>   T'Exile and Banishment.
> These shall return to her again,
>   With Sacred Songs of Joy;
> But those shall Roar and Howl for pain,
>   And to the Mountains cry,
> Fall on us, hide us from the Wrath
>   Of the Lamb's Anger[52]

Words like these, should they come to the attention of dissenters' enemies, sounded less like a desire to leave everything in the hands of God than a threat of political violence. Given that these enemies knew from the 1640s and 1650s how the saints could come to rationalise taking extreme actions themselves as the conduits of God's justice, it is perhaps not surprising that they did not read such words as the harmless dreams of a defeated people.

Conclusion

Prince Hamlet, himself a curious religious figure, famously asked 'Whether 'tis nobler in the mind to suffer/The slings and arrows of outrageous fortune/Or to take arms against a sea of troubles/And by opposing end them'.[53] It has been a common mistake of historians to assume that these were the only two options open to Restoration dissenters, either to turn to passive quietism, or violently to protest. There was another way: they could turn to culture as a means of intervention. In many ways, this is unsurprising. A number of dissenters had served in the parliamentary army, and all of the early Restoration dissenters had witnessed the collapse of a regime predicated on military power. That they for the most part eschewed violence was not necessarily a sign that they had stopped being concerned with the affairs of the world; it might just have been a sign that they realised that physical force had little chance of working. In a variety of different forms, and literary genres, dissenters could attack, berate, and argue with those in the Anglican establishment who sought their destruction.

The debates concerning Church and dissent which were so important in this period were thus in part driven by this vibrant nonconformist culture. However, this culture also had the effect of making dissenters more visible, and indeed the quantity in which it was produced suggested that they were far more numerous than in reality was the case. It was a culture intended to combat persecution, and it made the sufferings of dissenters very clear. But ultimately it could not control audience response. Thus what to one reader appeared justifiable outrage to another looked like the threat of sedition. If the cultural evidence examined in this chapter is read through the eyes of high churchmen and those who supported them, then it is no wonder that dissenters appeared to be a problem. In articulating their grievances dissenters confirmed the fears of their enemies. That, of course, does not mean that silence would have been a better option.

Chapter 3: What was at Stake in the Exclusion Crisis?

There is no strong reason to believe that MPs in the seventeenth century were any less vain and pompous than their twenty-first century successors. So we should not be surprised to find sweeping statements and hyperbole issuing naturally from their mouths. In November 1680, many MPs were quite clear about the signal importance of what they debated when considering a bill to exclude James, Duke of York, from the succession to the throne on the grounds of his avowed Catholicism. According to Sir Nicholas Carew, 'I think all is at stake'. Hugh Boscawen articulated the opinion of many when arguing that, 'we are now come to that pass, that we must be either Papists or Protestants'. Colonel Titus poured scorn on the notion that the House of Commons should proceed 'moderately' by investigating legal expedients to limit James's future regal powers rather than exclusion. He vehemently pressed the widespread view that Catholics under a future Catholic king would not act moderately towards Protestants: 'For our souls, we are heretics, they will burn us, and damn us. For our Estates, they will take our lands, and put Monks and Fryars upon them. Our Wives and Children must beg, and this is the Moderation we are like to expect from them.' With James as king, Colonel Birch asked rhetorically whether 'we shall not have Idolatry set up'? Sir Richard Graham reflected the high temperature of proceedings when he proclaimed that 'This affair is certainly of as great moment as ever was in an English Parliament'.[1]

However tempting it might be to ascribe such words to the fevered imaginations of MPs caught up in a passionate debate, it is easy to find similar worries expressed in unpublished texts and published polemic. Horrified opponents of Exclusion unburdened themselves in their private writings. By the close of the third Exclusion Parliament in March 1681,

Sir John Reresby felt that 'The truth was that the question was not now
whether the Duke [of York] should succeed or not, but rather whether
it should be a monarchie or a commonwealth'.[2] The very fabric of government and order appeared to be fraying in the face of renewed fears
of civil war. From the opposite perspective, the author of the published
pro-Exclusion pamphlet *An Appeal from the Country to the City* conjured
up a graphic composite picture of the nation's fate under Catholic rule,
which initially played on the common belief that the Great Fire of London
(1666) had been started by Catholics, before invoking fearful memories
of Protestant martyrdoms under Mary Tudor during the 1550s:

> Imagine you see the whole Town in a flame, occasioned this second
> time, by the same Popish malice which set it on fire before. At the same
> instant fancy, that amongst the distracted Crowd, you behold Troops
> of Papists, ravishing your Wives and your Daughters, dashing your lit-
> tle Childrens brains out against the walls, plundering your Houses, and
> cutting your own throats, by the Name of Heretick Dogs.... Also cast-
> ing your eye towards *Smithfield*, imagine you see your Father, or your
> Mother, or some of your nearest and dearest Relations, tyed to a Stake
> in the midst of flames, when with hands and eyes lifted up to Heaven,
> they scream and cry out to that God for whose Cause they die; which
> was a frequent spectacle the last time Popery reign'd amongst us.

For any readers not yet hiding under their beds, the writer of the *Appeal*
went on to describe the abuse of Protestant churches, Church of England
clerics being torn apart, and the destruction of all trade in the metropolis. Overall, 'what the Devil himself would do, were he here upon Earth,
will in his absence infallibly be acted by his Agents the Papists'. Nor was
this presented as a distant possibility: 'without a miracle our apparent
ruine is at hand, the Sword already hangs over our heads, and seems
to be supported by no stronger force than that of one single hair, his
Majesties life'.[3]

Whether we see this as scaremongering, or a principled attempt on
the part of the author to awaken his contemporaries to their imminent
danger, these arguments were given powerful visual expression in a print
published in the run up to the Oxford Parliament of 1681 whose activity we have already seen Sir John Reresby decrying. As the banner along
the top of 'A Prospect of a Popish Successor' (Figure 4) proclaims, the
inevitable result of a Catholic monarch would be 'Hell-bred Cruelty',
'Popish Villany', 'Strange Divinity', 'intended Slavery', and 'Old Englands

40

Figure 4 *A Prospect of a Popish Successor* (1681). © The Trustees of the British Museum.

Misery'. The left-hand of the two central figures, 'Mack', half devil, half Irish Catholic is shown burning Protestants at the stake, and setting fire to London. The right-hand central figure is another monstrous amalgam, this time of a cleric who is half Church of England bishop, half pope, and is portrayed driving Protestant dissenters out of the church with his crosier, whilst other priests ride the church towards Rome under the approving gaze of a flying devil. With heavy sarcasm, the caption under 'Mack's' burning brand reads, 'This is a hopefull Successor is it Not'? The urgent necessity of excluding Charles II's Catholic heir seems straightforward.

Yet in the face of such lurid contemporary imagery and rhetoric a number of recent historians have offered three ingenious lines of argument that call into question precisely what was at stake in the period between revelations about a Popish Plot in 1678 and the dissolution of what we now know to have been the last of Charles II's English Parliaments in March 1681. First, Ronald Hutton has argued that there was no Exclusion 'Crisis' at all because Charles II always had things under control. He held all the constitutional trump cards: the Restoration period was still very much one of personal monarchy, in which kings ruled as well as reigned, and Charles could prorogue or dissolve parliaments at will in order to break the momentum of his political opponents. He could also choose where parliament would sit, as he notoriously did in March 1681, when he called Parliament to royalist Oxford, removing it from the increasingly fractious and unsettled capital. Since the monarchy's critics relied on Parliament as a forum for their views, the Crown's powers meant that in reality they never had a chance of success; they simply could not sustain a political campaign that the monarchy found obnoxious.[4]

Jonathan Scott has offered a second critical perspective. He does not deny that there was a 'crisis' in this period, but questions whether the issue of 'Exclusion' was really central to it. For Scott this crisis was not so much about who succeeded to the throne after the death of Charles II, but how the later Stuart monarchy used its prerogative powers, as much in contemporaries' here and now as in their distant future.[5] This, then, was a particular part of the longer term 'crisis of parliaments' in the early modern period, one in which MPs and peers self-consciously sought to protect their present status and future existence.[6] This view of a 'Restoration crisis' found qualified, but immensely detailed, support in Mark Knights' reading of the polemical discussion and understanding of the political situation throughout England. What MPs and constituents clashed so vigorously about was a range of issues subsumed under the shorthand title particularly associated with the politician–poet Andrew Marvell: 'popery and arbitrary government'.[7] Although far from unimportant, 'exclusion' in these accounts becomes one part of a much wider political and religious jigsaw.[8]

A third challenge to older scholars' focus on the 'Exclusion Crisis' has emerged from a large-scale shift in the historiography of the Restoration period. As late as the mid 1980s there was a general view that the Restoration period was less interesting than the early Stuart period, partly because there seemed to be fewer overt crises. That was what made the Exclusion Crisis so striking. It was the exception to an emerging picture of 'political stability' that would be given shape by the Glorious Revolution and its aftermath.[9] But recent researches – notably those by Gary De Krey – have identified numerous Restoration crises: crises about conscience and counsel in the mid and late 1660s, about prerogative power and religious settlement in the early to mid 1670s, and about standing armies in the 1690s. The whole concept of political stability looks problematic, not least because religion – far from rapidly falling out of public life around 1660 – remained a vital and divisive part of the political landscape.[10]

Taking these arguments into account, then, might suggest that the answer to what was at stake in the Exclusion Crisis was either nothing, because no such crisis existed, quite a lot, but not exclusion in particular, or something, but perhaps not more than during other parts of the wider Restoration period. By contrast, in this chapter we will argue that there was a crisis, one that was not simply a political fraud perpetrated by a gaggle of over-excited MPs; that although Exclusion may not have been the only issue at stake in these years, it was centrally important because of the way it focused religious and constitutional fears; and that the stakes were enormous because this crisis overshadowed all others since 1660. In order to make these arguments, it will be necessary to show that Exclusion called into question the whole system of government as its proponents sought a fundamental reshaping of the church-state that had been created in the Restoration settlement of 1660–2 (see Chapter 1). Precisely because the issues involved were so significant, the Exclusion Crisis succeeded in polarising the nation, entrenching a series of political and religious binary opposites in unprecedented ways. The outcome of this period was a bitterly divided polity in which partisanship had hardened into rival Whig and Tory groups that would be of great significance for the future.

The Road to Exclusion

The decade leading up to the Popish Plot revelations of 1678 witnessed deepening fissures within the English polity. These were the result of growing anxieties about Charles's political and religious agendas, and their likely impact on both foreign policy and domestic politics. Ministers came and went, but this served only to highlight the critical significance of the Stuart dynasty's fondness for France and high regard for Catholicism. Rather than championing the interests of his people, Charles came to be seen by many as trampling on them.

Clarendon's fall from power in 1667, a scapegoat for the failed second Anglo-Dutch War, opened up a new era in politics. Instead of appealing to an older ideal of legally bounded monarchy and harmony between king and parliament, subsequent ministers looked to further their royal master's agenda of friendship with France abroad and religious indulgence at home. Christened the 'Cabal' after their initials – Clifford, Arlington, Buckingham, Ashley Cooper, and Lauderdale – these men were not pious Anglicans like Clarendon, but closet Catholics, Presbyterian sympathisers, or irreligious debauchees. Although a popular Triple Alliance (1668) superficially brought the Stuarts together with the great continental Protestant powers of Sweden and the Dutch Republic, Charles's Francophilia was too strong to be hidden for long. By the Treaty of Dover (1670), the king established an open diplomatic amity with Louis XIV, the European monarch he most admired, but who appeared to most of Charles's subjects to be a chronic threat to European Protestantism. In the words of Andrew Marvell, Louis was 'the Master of Absolute Dominion . . . the declared Champion of Popery'.[11] Secret clauses to this treaty – which nevertheless attracted much speculation at the time – even went so far as to promise Charles's conversion to Catholicism and Louis' military help to establish that faith across the Stuart kingdoms. Words were translated into deeds when England cooperated with France in a war against the Dutch Republic that came perilously close to destroying that state in 1672. Although the Dutch were widely disliked for their sharp business practices, republican ideology, and tolerationist tendencies, few wished to see one of the pillars of European Protestantism annihilated and an overmighty king of France left in control of the whole North-west European littoral facing England across just a few miles of water.

These disturbing foreign events were carried out against a backdrop of Charles's attempts to use his royal prerogative powers to recast the church-state that had been entrenched against his wishes in 1662. His Declaration of Indulgence of 1672 exempted all non-Anglicans from the penalties prescribed under the Clarendon Code. Although Charles endeavoured to put a benign spin on this, claiming that he had 'found a good effect of it by securing peace at home when I had war abroad', parliament was vehemently hostile. Forced to call it into session to secure badly needed funds, the king had to endure repeated instruction from MPs and peers self-righteously standing on their dignity as the 'great counsel' of the realm. They told Charles bluntly that he had 'been very much misinformed' if he thought his prerogative allowed him to suspend penal statutes, 'since no such power was ever claimed or exercised by any of your Majesty's predecessors'. Only parliament could overturn statute law, as they had already maintained in 1662 when rejecting an earlier royal push for indulgence. The king was forced not just to back down on the Declaration, but also to agree to a new Test Act (1673) that required all public office-holders to swear the oaths of allegiance and supremacy, to take annual communion within the Church of England, and to make a declaration against the core Catholic doctrine of transubstantiation.[12] Overall the policies propounded during the Cabal period led some observers – not least leading clerics like the archbishop of Canterbury, Gilbert Sheldon – to conclude that the king could not be trusted to support the Church of England as by law established.

Many contemporaries felt that the events of the early 1670s administered a deep-seated shock to the body politic. In particular, the Test Act 'outed' the Duke of York, the heir to the throne, as a Catholic. As the diarist John Evelyn wrote with palpable horror, this 'gave exceeding grief and scandal to the whole nation, that the heir of it, and the son of a martyr for the Protestant religion [i.e. Charles I], should apostatize. What the consequence of this will be, God only knows, and wise men dread'.[13] This revelation crystallised a widespread suspicion that the Stuarts closely sympathised with Catholics. Those near the centre of politics had long worried that their period of exile in Catholic Europe during the Commonwealth and Protectorate had proved intellectually infectious for Charles and James. As one of the lords of the treasury, Sir Edward Dering, argued in 1681, especially from 1672 'the nacion began to thinke that the court enclined to favour poperie and France'.[14]

Charles was not unaware of the problem. The obvious solution was to cast down the Cabal and from 1673 appoint a vociferously Anglican chief minister in the form of Thomas Osborne, created Earl of Danby. Danby's mission was straightforward: to expiate his predecessors' political sins from the government's collective conscience. He was quite clear about the need to rebrand Charles's government as a Protestant ministry, writing in October 1673 that he aimed 'in all things to promote the Protestant interest both att home and abroad'.[15] Such an approach did bear fruit, especially when he was instrumental in arranging the marriage of James's eldest daughter, Mary, to William of Orange, one of the leaders of the European Protestant cause, in November 1677. Seven months earlier he had written a memorandum to Charles designed to show up his own importance. The language is revealing. Danby claimed that he had been 'instrumentall' in Parliament

> in making men beleeve not only your sincerity to the Protestant religion, but that your concernes for France were no other then as they might bee most usefull to the interests of your owne people, and that you would never suffer its greatnesse to goe beyond those due bounds which might consist with the safety of England.[16]

In other words, Danby rather boldly argued that he was successfully defending the king's tarnished reputation.

The years from 1673 to 1677 certainly saw a rise in crown prestige, but this was not unambiguous and ultimately merely exchanged one problem for another. The political nation transferred its dislike from a collection of ministers clearly acting in ways inimical to the Church of England to a single minister who seemed in danger of becoming over-mighty. As lord treasurer, Danby controlled the purse-strings and expended large sums of money buying support from MPs. The emergence of a 'court party'[17] threatened to undermine the whole system of English government in the opinion of many MPs and peers who were no less jealous of their parliamentary privileges than their early Stuart predecessors, indeed were in some prominent cases the same people.[18] One of the articles of impeachment brought against Danby in 1678 complained that he had 'wasted the King's treasure' by giving out 'unnecessary pensions and secret services' worth £231,602 in just two years.[19] It was for this reason that the Cavalier Parliament that had sat since 1661 became labelled the 'Pensionary Parliament'. To those critical of the government and steeped in the language of classical political thought, the waters of state had stood still for too long and had inevitably corrupted. This was particularly frightening because of the totemic status that Parliament enjoyed in the English political system. Men juxtaposed free Parliaments with the arbitrary will of princes. But what if princes succeeded in subverting parliaments by bribery? Then they would be able to rule as they pleased, whilst maintaining the superficial norms of English government. Nor did Danby seem only to be making advances in the Commons. His close co-operation with the bishops in the House of Lords raised the hackles of many who recalled the heyday of clerical pride and pretension during the Laudian 1630s.[20] Thanks to a combination of bribed MPs and tame bishops Danby seemed to be on the brink of becoming an 'omnipotent figure'.[21] Most frighteningly of all, Charles chose to maintain an army after the Peace of Nijmegen (1678) rendered it obsolete for the anti-French war Parliament had intended. Long-standing English fears of a standing army combined with distrust of a slippery king and a domineering chief minister. Some ambitious politicians, notably the former Cabal member Anthony Ashley Cooper, Earl of Shaftesbury, sought to have the Cavalier Parliament dissolved and a new parliament called, one which might both be free of Court influence and also more amenable to their own. Memories of the euphoric joy that had greeted Charles on his return in 1660 seemed very dim indeed by the later 1670s. The political and religious fears that were so powerful by 1678 point to another growth of mutual distrust between Stuart sovereign and English subjects to match those evident in the early Stuart period.[22]

Perceptions of Crisis

By 12 November 1678, a well-placed commentator on political affairs, Sir Robert Southwell, was able to draw breath and take stock of the recent tumultuous events: 'there has been a strange coincidence of things to raise the present indignation to the height it is'. For Southwell, the emerging crisis was the product of a combination of long-term political factors – specifically 'the long stream of discontent' about the degree of indulgence shown towards Catholics – particular individuals and incidents, and the extent to which 'the present horror of things feared throughout the kingdom in one day' could easily be made to map onto previous English history, 'the evidence of what had formerly passed'.[23] Exclusion thus emerged from an unfortunate combination of bad political management, bad luck, and bad memories; in sum, a toxic mix of anxiety about social disorder and acute anti-Catholic sentiments.

Who were the individuals who contrived to mesh together recent political discontents with the more distant past? In the autumn of 1678, Titus Oates, one of the great liars in British history, swore that there was a popish plot to kill the king, largely incited by hopes for a better future under the Catholic James. There was little that was new in this. Allegations of popish plots had been a commonplace of the Restoration era, bringing brief flurries of activity and little else. But Oates was lucky. In October 1678, the London JP (Justice of the Peace) he first swore his evidence before – Sir Edmund Berry Godfrey – was found murdered. Most assumed that Catholics, probably Jesuit priests, were to blame. Subsequent searches of Catholic homes turned up nothing until a number of letters were found in the possession of Edward Coleman, James, Duke of York's former secretary. These were written to Jesuits – most significantly Père la Chaise, the confessor of Louis XIV. Then in December Ralph Montagu MP, formerly ambassador to France, stood up in the House of Commons and revealed details of negotiations through which the government had sought financial subsidies from Louis XIV.[24] Danby was deeply incriminated. All the worst fears of contemporaries seemed to be confirmed. Catholics were covertly active in the most frightening way. They had friends in high places who looked to James, Duke of York, for a happy Catholic future. And Danby, for all his veneer of pious Anglicanism, had been heavily complicit in undermining Parliament: if money was received from France, there would be no need to call it. The nation was left in uproar. In October 1678, the popish plot was 'so far credited' in Oxfordshire 'that no man thinks himself secure because of a general massacre which is here reported to be designed by the conspirators'.[25] Accounts seeped out to the furthest corners of the realm of the 'monstrous shape' of a plot that would subvert 'our religion, lawes, and properties', and lead to 'a tyrannicall arbitrary government by an army'.[26] The following month both houses of Parliament voted unanimously that 'there hath been and still is a damnable and hellish plot contrived and carried on by the popish recusants for the assassinating and murdering the King, and for subverting the government, and rooting out and destroying the Protestant religion'.[27] Political opinion reacted so sharply to events that Charles was forced to dissolve the Cavalier Parliament in January 1679, after 16 sessions and almost 18 years.

Yet far from lowering the political temperature, according to one provincial writer, 'All people in these parts are much surprised at the dissolution of the parliament, and are apt to talk very hot'.[28] Elections to three parliaments between the spring of 1679 and 1681 whipped up fears to fever pitch. By June 1679, Daniel Finch urged his uncle, Sir John, to return from an overseas trading mission because of the vital need for 'men of conscience and integrity'. In Finch's view, 'never were men's fears from abroad and from within greater than at this present' time.[29] Things only got worse. In September 1679, the Buckinghamshire gentleman Sir Ralph Verney was told by one of his correspondents that 'Never was a civil war feared more than now'.[30] By January 1680, the sardonic Earl of

Halifax wrote to his brother from London that 'Our world here is so over-run with the politicks, the fools' heads so heated, and the knaves so busy, that a wasp's nest is a quieter place to sleep in than this town is to live in'.[31] Although it could be claimed that after a very troubled seventeenth century Englishmen might have been given to panic, it is still significant that even veteran authors with long memories were deeply troubled. Algernon Sidney had been a politically active radical politician since the 1640s. But by early 1681, he could write that he had never seen 'men's minds more heated than at present'.[32] Such high emotions had a polarising impact: they made many fundamentally distrustful of the king and his court, but they also left many reflecting on parallels with the early 1640s when Charles I's government had imploded under massive popular pressure. Mob activity, mass petitions, and tumultuous local elections became the disturbing norm.

Fear played a hugely important role in influencing political choices: those who believed that the greatest threat came from imminent Catholic despotism emerged by 1680/1 as 'Whigs', whilst those who dreaded Protestant sectarian zeal and social anarchy rallied to the Crown's defence as 'Tories'. Division begat further division as partisans vilified each other's positions and sought to lay exclusive claim to political, religious, and moral rectitude. 'Tory' originally referred to Irish Catholic bandits, and was deliberately chosen as a term of abuse to impugn the religious position of the Crown's supporters, and to emphasise the fact that James had several high profile Irish friends, notably Richard Talbot (see Chapter 6). 'Whig' smeared the Crown's critics by associating them with Presbyterian rebels in Scotland, a charge which aimed to draw attention to the prominent role of English nonconformists within their ranks. Far from being loyal subjects as the large majority claimed, dissenters were thus pigeon-holed as the descendants of king-killing rebels in the 1640s (see Chapter 2). Faced with determined partisan politicians, and deluged with highly charged pamphlets from the presses, it proved difficult for moderates to protect a pacific middle ground. English political discourse became ever more sharply etched in black and white opposites.

The Centrality of Exclusion

The MPs who drafted the Exclusion Bill did not mince their words. James was 'notoriously known to have been perverted from the Protestant to the popish religion'. The consequences of this were twofold. In the first place, it gave 'great encouragement' to the 'popish party' to destroy Charles II and his government. And secondly, 'if the said Duke should succeed to the imperial crown of this realm, nothing is more manifest than that a total change of religion within these kingdoms would ensue'. These perceived consequences of James's religious faith reflected the view that Catholics were committed to killing 'heretic' princes, and that Catholic monarchs would never respect the rights of Protestant subjects. The bill went on to exclude James 'by authority of this present Parliament' and to stipulate that if in the future James tried to exercise the power of king, he would be guilty of high treason, as would anyone who sought to abet his activities. James would also be deemed guilty of high treason if he entered the realm after 5 November 1681 – the anniversary of the Gunpowder Plot – and parliament pre-emptively indemnified anyone who fought against or otherwise sought to capture him under those circumstances. James was to be treated for the purposes of the succession as if he were naturally dead, the Crown passing at Charles's demise to the duke's eldest daughter, Mary, Princess of Orange. To ensure that the bill's clauses were never forgotten, it was to be read at every judicial assizes and quarter sessions throughout James's lifetime, and also from the pulpits of all churches on Easter and Christmas Day.[33]

This was a remarkable document, one whose 'tenor...is...so harsh...against the Duke that many were amazed to hear it'.[34] The Exclusion bill constituted a swingeing assault on the line of succession, paying no deference whatsoever to the divine right of kings, a key ideological buttress of the restored monarchy. It was a damning indictment of James's perceived lack of 'throneworthiness', one that exposes the extent to which a wide section of contemporary opinion regarded rule by Catholics as inevitably disastrous. As the MP Sir John Knight put it during an exclusion debate in May 1679, it was 'impossible that the Protestant religion should be preserved under a popish prince' since the two faiths were 'as inconsistent as light and darkness'.[35] Yet others passionately disagreed with exclusionists' arguments. Parliament had no right to meddle with the succession: James had an indefeasible hereditary right to succeed his brother based on proximity of blood. God had willed this series of events, and to try and interpose human law and authority would be a defiance of Providence even more than it was an affront to the established constitution of the kingdom. Opponents of Exclusion came to rely on a very different rhetoric of 'arbitrary government' from that used by James's critics. Rather than seeing the primary threat in alleged crown activity, anti-exclusioners insistently recalled the events of the 1640s and

1650s to show up how 'arbitrary' parliaments could be. According to one pamphleteer, Exclusion was

> that Anarchical Bill lately fram'd by some turbulent Zealots of the House of Commons against his Royal Highness, wherein they peremptorily assume to themselves a Sovereign and Despotical Power of Deposing Princes, and disposing of Kingdoms, as their spirit moves them; and withal most impudently affirm, that this has been the ancient custom of Parliaments.

This was a powerful critique that insinuated that Exclusionists' actions were akin to papal claims to depose heretical princes. Under 'a Cloak of Religion' James's critics were really pursuing a ruthless and ambitious agenda of their own, one that would elevate parliament above the Crown in a perversion of the ancient constitution. They were 'cunning Politicians' who 'will have a new model of Government' involving an 'Omnipotent Parliament' possessing an 'Absolute and Independent power'.[36] It was this kind of sentiment that underlay Reresby's fear by 1681 that the struggle was actually about whether the kingdom should be a monarchy or a commonwealth. Rejecting medieval precedents for parliamentary involvement in deciding who would succeed to the throne, anti-exclusioners argued that such interference had inevitably led to civil war across generations and was always ultimately 'overthrown with blood'.[37] Less negatively, some also chose to extol their faith in James personally, claiming that he was a man of his word and that he had promised not to threaten the Church of England. Although such arguments would within a decade be proved worthless that does not invalidate the sincerity with which they were made.

Exclusion was thus an immensely important divisive force within parliament. But its true strength was much augmented by the way in which other, broader, issues increasingly latched onto it, like barnacles on the ship of state. By far the most important of these was the politics of religion. Two key issues stood out: what was the proper role of bishops in secular affairs? And should Protestant dissenters be welcomed within the pale of political society or be regarded as dangerous incendiaries? At root both issues were different dimensions of the all-powerful debate about 'popery and arbitrary government'. The bishops had seemed to be a politically renascent force alongside Danby in the mid 1670s, and they attracted bitter criticism when trying to protect him against impeachment charges during the Exclusion period. The bishops' anti-Exclusion, pro-James, stance cemented their perceived position as malign influences within the body politic, not least as their votes in the House of Lords were vital. As Southwell remarked in May 1679, 'there is a very evil spirit abroad in reference to the Bishops'.[38] Popular cries of 'no bishops' became a feature of the crisis,[39] allowing anxious contemporaries the gory pleasure of remembering the huge petitions demanding 'root and branch' reform of the Church of England in the run-up to the civil wars.[40] But there was no organised sentiment during the Exclusion period for an abolition of episcopacy, even if later Tory propaganda tried to claim that this had been a key plank of the Exclusionists' programme. As one polemicist put it, the Whigs had 'with the Sacred Solemnity of a Sacramental Vow' committed themselves to 'the utter Extirpation of Prelacy, and the Royal Race of the *Stuarts*'.[41] Whigs wanted prelates to spend more time acting as pastors and less as politicians apparently bolstering the Stuarts' arbitrary pretensions.

Protestant dissenters also re-emerged in the Exclusion period as a hugely controversial force in politics precisely because of their often vociferous participation in the debates about James's succession. In March 1679, for instance, Exeter was convulsed by violent elections, with a pro-dissent JP, William Glyde, allegedly appealing to 'the rabble' to help him stand against a self-regarding 'loyal party' whom he smeared as closet Catholics. The 'loyal' candidate, Thomas Carew, was threatened with burning by the crowds around the poll, a disobedient vehemence he imputed to the long-term influence of dissenting preachers in the area 'poisoning and depraving the people's loyalty and obedience to the government both of Church and State'.[42] Although bitterly partisan, Carew here pointed to a significant truth: nonconformists were extremely active supporters of pro-Exclusion MPs who were usually sympathetic to calls for the reform of the Church of England. Moves to 'comprehend' more Protestants within the established church by broadening the boundaries of the settlement of 1660–2 were an integral part of parliamentary affairs at this time.[43] Indeed Gary De Krey has gone so far as to call this period 'a crisis about reformation'. Dissenting authors emphasised the iniquity of persecution, and spoke up for their right to conduct their religious lives according to their own consciences. Some argued that clericalism was the greatest threat to English liberties in the whole constitution. Ambitious clerics were trumpeting the powers of the monarchy from the pulpits in craven efforts to secure promotion, and in the process were misleading the prince into arbitrary government.[44]

Such arguments called forth a bitterly hostile response from hard-line Anglicans who thought that widening the boundaries of the Church of England would in fact weaken it, and let in popery by the back door. According to this school of thought, dissenters should be called 'fanatics': for all their talk of moderation and unity they were in fact the desperate descendants of the men who had put Charles I to death. As the anonymous author of the pamphlet *The Character of a Fanatick* put it in 1681, a fanatic

> Puts on Religion, as a Cloak ... and so makes his Impostures with Holiness to the Lord: Thus *Absolom* pretends a Sacrifice, when his business is Rebellion; and *Herod* a Worship, when his design is Murder: Nor with much wonder, the *Florentine* [i.e. Machiavelli] hath taught him, He that would gain by Deceit, must first acquire a Credit, by ... a shew of Integrity.[45]

This kind of intolerant language reflects the deeply held convictions that were at stake during the years of the Exclusion Crisis. The whole future shape of the Church of England seemed up for debate, both in terms of the powers afforded its hierarchy and the breadth of its comprehension. Such conflict was only possible because of the way in which these issues intersected with the central problem of the succession.

The Impact of Exclusion

Exclusion was a parliamentary bill but it was also a national event. Three general elections in quick succession prompted widespread political contestation, built around clashing principles and rival personalities. After travelling from the West Country to London in September 1679, Sir Robert Southwell

> observed everywhere in the countries [i.e. counties] a strange agitation in the spirits of the people; their minds warmed in a great part by contention and animosity in the elections for the Parliament, where not only inclination but even moderation towards the Court seems to be grown matter of accusation and indifferency in religion. Then the swarms of pamphlets and the liberty of intelligence from hence [i.e. London] adds new flame ...[46]

Although traditional rhetoric about the unity and cohesion of the realm may always have represented an ideal rather than reflecting a reality, these years did further entrench divisions within local communities. This happened within parishes, towns, and counties, and in many areas led to forced political choices trumping an individual's prior loyalty to family or kin network. Many men certainly attempted to stand against the process. In Norfolk, for instance, the elderly Sir John Holland fought an increasingly unsuccessful battle to promote the values of moderation and harmony, or as he put it, the principles 'of loyalty to our king, of faithfulness to our religion, the government and ancient constitutions of our kingdom'.[47] Unfortunately for Holland an increasingly 'bi-polar' mentality developed in which each side of the Exclusion debate claimed a monopoly on loyalty, honesty, and religious sincerity. Rivals then smeared each other with accusations of lying, ambition, and hidden agendas. This battle has been best chronicled by Mark Knights, who argues that the process involved increasingly intense appeals to the public as an imagined community whose judgement was deemed more and more legitimate in political life, albeit vulnerable to systematic deception by unscrupulous politicians and writers determined to misrepresent their opponents.[48] Although this process reached a peak in the 'rage of party' during the 1690s and 1700s, fracture lines clearly did appear during the Exclusion period along the Whig/Tory divide.

This was hardly surprising. Exclusion was itself a stark choice: did James's Catholicism render him so unfit for the throne that it was a matter of vital national interest to remove him from the line of succession? Or would any such attempt be a fundamentally illegitimate intrusion into an irreversible birthright guaranteed by God? As this question was debated in parliamentary elections, it was also vigorously contested in a vibrant press, as Southwell deplored in 1679. Thanks to the accidental lapsing of the Licensing Act in that year the government temporarily lost the ability to censor written materials prior to publication. For some this recalled the collapse of censorship in the early 1640s, a period that had seen Charles I riddled with 'paper bullets' long before actual shots were fired. As the ultra-loyalist Roger L'Estrange thundered in his periodical the *Observator* in 1682,

> How can a man see So many Palpable Lyes, and Scandals Scatter'd among the Common People ... So much Plausible Poyson distill'd almost into every Sheet of Paper ... without Crying out, Look to your

selves my Masters; this way of Lying and Slandering was the Fore-runner of the Last Rebellion.[49]

A particularly telling form of poisonous paper at this time was the 'character'. These short tracts sought polemically to describe the characteristics of enemies or friends. The descriptions offered were relentlessly extreme and admitted the possibility of no good qualities in those propounding opposed political views. As might be expected, religious positions were much to the fore. According to the author of *The Character of a Thorough-Pac'd Tory, Ecclesiastical or Civil*, the 'heat' inherent in the Tory character was such 'that one would think he disgusted the Reformed Faith for nothing more, than that it doth not by some Modern dispensation consume Dissenters with fire and faggot, according to the Ancient Popish example'.[50] From the opposite perspective, a Tory author could claim that 'a Modern *Whig* is the very Spawn of *Antichrist*, the Counterpart to *Popery*, the *Jesuits* Bum-Crack, the Shame of the Reformation, and the Scandal of Christianity'.[51] This was a world in which the middle ground represented by men like Holland was under relentless assault. To offer just one local example, it is striking that in Cheshire the polarity between Whigs and Tories was so strong by the general election of 1681 that less than 3 per cent of the electorate divided their two votes between candidates on either side of the great divide. More than 97 per cent thus voted exclusively for either Whig or Tory candidates.[52]

Vigorous electoral activity and the vehement outpourings of the press were the most overt signs of the impact Exclusion had across the nation as a whole. But it also acted like a giant magnet attracting the iron filings of a myriad of pre-existing local tensions. These tended to be matters of personal rivalries, contested office-holding, and religious disputes. In many areas, long-standing conflict between local powerbrokers readily translated into opposing stances on Exclusion. Thus in Lincolnshire Sir Robert Carr and the Earl of Lindsey had jousted in the lists of county politics during the 1670s and rapidly appropriated anti- and pro-Exclusion rhetoric.[53] Similar scenarios unfolded in the far North-west and in Norfolk.[54] Such disputes were often about more than mere personal dislike – important though that could be in a world influenced by aggressive and prickly aristocratic honour codes. They could also be motivated by conflicts for office. Where men stood on the Exclusion issue increasingly served as a touchstone for their perceived reliability as local agents of the king's government. From 1680 onwards, a series of purges of local government saw many Whigs displaced and their places filled by vociferously loyal Tories.[55] Such purges effectively created a two-tier political world of 'ins' and 'outs' with the former awarded external badges of recognition, and the latter stigmatised as less worthy – in effect, Whigs were labelled as being bad subjects. However bitter they might be, personality clashes and office-holding both paled as divisive issues in comparison to religious disputes. By September 1679, one observer wrote from London that, 'The city lies now strangely divided between the mad separatists, and the Church of England men'.[56] Some evidence for this could be found in the massive petitions that were organised in 1679–80 to call on the king to allow parliaments to sit until they had transacted their business. The 'monster' petition of January 1680 featured around 18,000 Londoner's names, many of whom were open or suspected nonconformists.[57] Such activity set the scene for vigorous purges at various levels of office-holding by vengeful Anglican Tories.[58] Such clashes were evident on a much smaller scale in towns across England.[59] Individual parishes saw polarising debates about the relative need to effect further reform or defend the church as by law established that fuelled profound animosities. In November 1678, for instance, the minister of Tewkesbury, Francis Wells, preached an incendiary sermon in which he criticised Charles II for his 'adultery, whoredom, and fornication', and argued that the king's sins had brought down divine retribution on the nation: they were the reasons why 'the land mourned popish atrocities' in the form of the recently revealed Popish Plot. Once Tories gained the upper hand in Tewkesbury, Wells was rapidly eased out of his position, both for the particular sentiments he had expressed from the pulpit and the broader pro-dissenting sensibility that underlay them.[60] In many parishes, such views formed the backbone of a Whiggism that was increasingly put on the back foot by 'a popular anti-puritan Anglicanism'[61] that Charles II successfully rallied, especially after the dissolution of the Oxford Parliament in March 1681.

Cumulatively such divisions represent the emergence of Whigs and Tories as the first political parties. Although there has been dispute as to which came first – J.R. Jones arguing for the Whigs led by Shaftesbury; John Patrick Montaño for a 'court' party created by Danby – and spirited attempts to denude these groups of much in the way of organisation, relegating them to shifting points on an ideological spectrum, the Exclusion period represented a vital period of coalescence.[62] Not only did the terms 'Whig' and 'Tory' rapidly gain widespread recognition as denominating set positions, but men increasingly associated together in like-minded groups in clubs and meetings at taverns and coffeehouses. Men of each stamp increasingly avoided mingling with those who held opposed political views, to the detriment of traditional notions of sociability and hospitality.[63] This certainly built on emerging divisions during the mid 1670s when groups in particular localities pooled their financial resources to support candidates for office.[64] But the events of the Exclusion Crisis crystallised matters to an unprecedented degree. Tory supporters of James's right to succeed wore red ribbons in their hats to display their loyalty visually; Whigs who supported the rival claims of Charles II's bastard son James Scott, Duke of Monmouth, wore blue ribbons. Perceptions of an individual's Tory or Whig leanings could impact upon their trading success, or even leave them vulnerable to physical assault.

A further measure of just how divisive this new political culture was is the extent to which it survived the end of sitting parliaments in March 1681. The period up to Charles's death in February 1685 has traditionally been labelled the 'Tory Reaction', but we should be wary of seeing too great a political shift.[65] Expectations of another parliament in the future helped to maintain partisan passions, with frequent and widespread rumours leading to pre-emptive electioneering in many areas. The government did not succeed in restraining the press before the autumn of 1682, when most periodical publications were suppressed. It was also not until 1682/3 that the government achieved firm control over the administration of London. When the candidate favoured by the Court, Sir William Prichard, triumphed in the 1682 mayoral election, the Earl of Longford believed that 'now the King has master'd this greate Beast the Cittye'.[66] And when London's charter was overturned by a complex legal action in 1683, Charles was at last said to be 'King of London' again.[67] Religious issues remained to the fore. The majority of Church of England clergymen regarded James as having an indefeasible hereditary right to succeed to the throne. They had also come to perceive him as a tower of strength against disruptive Protestant dissenters whose support for exclusionists had been so prominent over the previous few years. (This view was bolstered by James's vigorous support of anti-Covenanter activity whilst in exile in Scotland for much of 1679–82.) As the Whig cleric Gilbert Burnet wrote, with the benefit of bitter hindsight in his *History of My Own Time*, between 1681 and 1685 the clergy worked 'with such zeal for the duke's succession, as if a popish king had been a special blessing of heaven, to be longed for by a protestant church'.[68] In many areas, nonconformists faced legal assault designed to debar them from supporting Whig candidates in future parliamentary elections, or otherwise to remove them from local government positions. In Great Yarmouth, for instance, an ordinance was passed 'for disfranchising about 100 whigs . . . unlesse they

prove their baptism by certificate... (which we beleive very   :m
will be able to doe).... This ordnance will we doubt not mal   all
side much the strongest'.[69] Most strikingly of all, the govern   ed
for all it was worth a failed assassination attempt against the royal brothers,
the Rye House Plot of 1683. Usefully murky in its details, this plot allowed
government polemicists to proclaim that it proved what they had been saying all along: that religious disaffection and political sedition went hand
in hand, and that Whigs were the desperate heirs of king-killing parliamentarians in the 1640s. Local Whig nobles and gentlemen had to suffer
the indignity of having their houses searched for arms, whilst pulpits and
presses rang out with Tory rhetoric.

Despite these favourable political circumstances, it is telling that when
another English Parliament was eventually called to meet in the early
summer of 1685, government ministers and local powerbrokers worked
exceptionally hard to secure the return of loyal MPs, the whole process
co-ordinated with unprecedented rigour by Robert Spencer, Earl of Sunderland. In Wales and the Marches, for instance, the Beaufort family –
from its vast seat at Badminton – exerted tremendous pressure on the
gentry who in most constituencies formed the 'magic circle' selecting the
candidates for parliamentary elections.[70] Writing to Sir Charles Kemeys,
the Marquess of Worcester sounded a warning note: 'The King being
resolved to call a Parliam[en]t we ought to bestir our selves that ill men be
not chosen'. In a scarcely veiled reference to Whigs, he went on to urge
'that we may be as quick as the other Party I think it would do very well if
you so soon as you could secured all the Interest about you' in support of
loyal candidates.[71] Worcester, Sunderland, and others may not have been
jumping at shadows. For all the impressive end results of the elections
there were still a large number of contests between rival candidates in
parliamentary seats, 72 compared to 54 in 1681 and 79 in the second general election of 1679. Fifty seven known Whigs were ultimately returned
out of a total of 513 MPs, the small but significant tip of a larger iceberg.[72]
The Exclusion Crisis did not end in March 1681: its fundamental impact
on political life was still being felt in 1685.

Conclusion

Describing proceedings in parliament on 15 May 1679, Colonel Edward
Cooke was in no doubt that 'the most remarkable was... that bill to disen-
able the Duke of York from inheriting' the throne. According to Cooke,

'possibly a more remarkable one never did happen, nor I hope ever will again'.[73] Although in the short term other Exclusion bills would render these hopes ill-founded, in the medium term Cooke's support for James was apparently vindicated. By avoiding parliament after 1681, and by recovering control of his capital in 1682–3, Charles regained the upper hand, and his brother duly reaped the benefits when he succeeded to the throne in February 1685. This stands in stark contrast to the military outcome of the major political crisis of 1640–2. The key to explaining this contrast lies in two closely interconnected issues: crown finance and differing levels of monarchical political skill. Unlike his father, Charles II was not hobbled by insolvency: he had benefitted from rapidly and substantially increasing customs revenues during the post-war trade boom that followed the Peace of Nijmegen. This allowed him greater room for political manoeuvre, something he exploited with a political adroitness alien to Charles I and which allowed him to rally critical political support behind the Crown (see Chapter 4). That support was itself a function of just how much was perceived to be at stake in the Exclusion crisis. For many there was a real risk of civil war, one that would play into the hands of political and religious radicals. This was certainly the view of the object of exclusionists' ire. Writing from exile in Brussels, James told a trusted intimate to tell Charles never to give in to the clamour against him. Things would not end with the exclusion of the next in line to the throne; they would proceed to the present government: 'they that would go so far would never thinke themselves safe so long as he [Charles] were alive, remember Edward 2, Richard 2, and the King my father'.[74] James would never forget the Exclusion crisis. Ironically the mental scar tissue it left behind would influence his whole outlook and help to pave the way for the practical achievement of Exclusion in astonishing circumstances during 1688.

Chapter 4: *Was Charles II a Successful 'Royal Politician'?*

To play the king was an exceptionally demanding role in early modern Europe. The difficulty sprang from the pressure of satisfying three distinct audiences: a monarch's own subjects; his royal peers in other states; and posterity. This was the harsh reality facing any king but the scale of the challenges facing Charles II was unusually high. For all the initial jubilation surrounding the Restoration the task of maintaining the regard of a people deeply divided by 20 years of chronic political crisis, bloody civil war, and bewildering constitutional changes would have taxed even the most brilliant ruler. Once a thousand years of monarchy had been temporarily eclipsed by a republic could its appearance of timeless invulnerability ever be rebuilt? As the Anglican cleric John Glanvill opined in 1667 with the aid of a homespun analogy:

> Though government may be fixed again upon its foundations and laws turned into their ancient channel after the violence they have suffered, yet they lose much of their reverence and strength by such disestablishment. And the people that have rebelled once and successfully will be ready to do so often. As water that hath been boiled will boil again the sooner.[1]

The situation abroad was scarcely less problematic. There the geo-political reality was that after more than a century of intense conflict between the Habsburg rulers of the Spanish kingdoms and the Valois and Bourbon kings of France, the latter was emerging as the hegemonic European power under the personal rule of Louis XIV from 1661. The Stuarts could no longer act – or pretend to act – as the balancing force between two competing powers: they would have to choose between moving within the orbit of a more powerful France or lending weight to some kind of coalition of lesser princes attempting to rein in French power and ambition. Yet arguably posterity was the toughest audience of all. Most rulers felt a need to be remembered, to take their place within the annals of their nation, and to do so in rivalry with the greatest of their predecessors. Thanks to the political developments of Charles's reign, his kingship would be subjected to severe censure from both of the rival parties that emerged and which would quickly develop their own historiographical traditions. His personality and policies did not make him an uncomplicated object of Whig celebration or Tory praise.

If these were the enormous challenges facing Charles II, how can we hope to measure the extent of his success in addressing each of them? One simple yardstick would be survival. Charles's family tree was written in blood. In 1587, his grandmother Mary Queen of Scots was executed at the hands of the English; in 1610, his maternal grandfather Henri IV of France was assassinated; and as has been discussed his father failed to die even at the hands of a foreign power or an assassin's knife – he was executed following trial in his own kingdom. By contrast, Charles died in his bed on 6 February 1685 in conditions of physical agony but political ease. But simple survival is a rather uninspiring benchmark and next to it we could attempt to gauge national prestige. The picture here is ambivalent at best. Although Charles incurred severe contemporary criticism for his apparently willing subservience to France, the close proximity and immense power of such a Catholic behemoth posed a problem of inexhaustible complexity. Finally, how does Charles's reputation now lie amongst the historians? The wittiest recent commentator on the reign has suggested that one subconscious reason for the resounding chorus of disdain for Charles amongst the 'academy' of university-based professionals is that the 'merry monarch's' indolence and pursuit of pleasure uncomfortably reminds academics of their more frustrating and feckless students.[2] It is certainly striking that the most favourable assessment of Charles as a successful 'royal politician', by J.R. Jones in 1987, has never found substantial support.[3]

In this chapter, we will explore aspects of Charles II's kingship in an effort to establish the degree of his political success. First, how did he manage the transition from titular to real power in 1660? Secondly, how successfully did he manage the most intractable problem of his reign: the religious diversity of his subjects? No previous king had ever had to face such a complex confessional situation as Charles did in the wake of rule by the saints in the 1650s. And lastly, how successfully did Charles project the restored Stuart dynasty to observers at home and abroad? Was he able to recreate a monarchical brand image sufficient to satisfy the immense expectations he encountered in 1660?

A King without a Kingdom

From the moment that Charles I's head was severed from his body, his son was, in the eyes of Royalists, the king – appointed by God.[4] This, of course, was what was enshrined in the Restoration settlement (see Chapter 1). But in 1649 it did not matter what Royalists thought. Power lay elsewhere and on 17 March 1649 the Rump Parliament passed the Act Abolishing the Office of King. Charles, never much given to introspection, did not respond to such events quiescently – waiting on Providence to return him to his throne – and having undergone a humiliating coronation ceremony in Scotland, he led 12,000 troops into England in 1651. On 3 September, he was defeated at Worcester, where his force was annihilated and Cromwell obtained what he called a 'crowning mercy'.[5] As Paul Seaward has remarked, 'Charles's escape from Worcester would become legendary, not least because of the frequency with which he retold it.'[6] Having hidden with Catholics in Shropshire and Staffordshire and up an oak tree in Boscobel, he finally made his way to Fécamp in Normandy. This began a period of exile which marked him forever: he was a king without a kingdom.

He was also a king with few really firm friends in Europe, and certainly none firm enough to risk giving him the substantial military aid he required. Moving from France to Cologne to Bruges as the political winds changed, unhappily seeking to raise pathetic plots and happily siring bastards, Charles came to learn that to be a king without a kingdom was to be nothing. This lesson was epitomised for him at the discussions which led to the treaty of the Pyrenees in 1659. These discussions between France and Spain were seen by Charles as a cause for optimism – the two major powers might be convinced to provide him with aid together. But any expectations he may have had crumbled, and it is impossible to escape the sense that Charles was seen as something of a child at an adults' party. When Charles was returned to his thrones, it was, as we saw, due to the intervention not of Royalists or foreign powers but of the army. Andrew Marvell's dictum that 'The same arts that did gain / A pow'r must it maintain' was proved to be true.[7] The humiliation that Charles had received during these years would never leave him, and it fundamentally coloured his political character. It fed two impulses which were contradictory to a degree. First, it impelled him to attempt at times to rule as king in some absolute sense, thus leading him into the arbitrary tendencies which contemporaries were so quick to criticise.[8] Secondly, it meant that in the final analysis Charles would take the route which was required to maintain immediate stability. His defining principle thus lay in a lack of principles. These two impulses may be explored effectively in relation to Charles's religious outlook and policy.

A Sacred Monarch?

On 25 May 1660, Samuel Pepys was in a boat approaching Dover as part of the armada bringing the king back to his realms:

> I went, and Mr. Mansell and one of the King's footmen, with a dog that the King loved (which shit in the boat, which made us laugh and me think that a King and all that belong to him are but just as others are) ...[9]

Charles II would not have agreed: kings were not 'just as others are', and they engaged in ceremonies which emphasised their unique status. This is most clearly seen in Charles's use of the practice of touching for the king's evil. It was held that the 'royal touch' had the magical potential to cure scrofula or the king's evil – a disfiguring skin disease.[10] Charles, who touched in exile, had a keen awareness of the significance of this display of power.[11] A statement of 27 June 1660 which appeared in *The Parliamentary Intelligencer* recorded that: 'The Kingdom having for a long time, by reason of his Majesties absence, been troubled with the Evil, great numbers have lately flock'd for cure.'[12] Charles both responded to and encouraged this popular demand, and used touching in the Restoration as a means of broadcasting his legitimacy and royal authority. In comparison to those who had gone before him Charles touched prodigiously.[13] Nor was this something he undertook lightly. The ceremony was multi-faceted and extremely time-consuming. But Charles thought it was worthwhile because the political expediency of touching was never lost on him.[14] Between 1660 and 1685, around 100,000 sufferers were the beneficiaries of his powers and in 1682, as he rallied support in the aftermath of the Exclusion Parliaments, it was recorded that he touched around 8500 of the afflicted.[15] Apart from making us wonder about just how much scrofula there was in England at this point, this demonstrates indisputably the way in which Charles was happy to manipulate his sacred role for political ends. This typifies his attitude to religion.

In his religious policy Charles's arbitrary tendencies came to the fore ironically at those moments at which he sought to increase toleration. On two separate occasions in 1662 and 1672, he sought to declare indulgence for tender consciences and thus suspend the legal strictures against dissent. On both occasions, he acted according to what he believed to be his prerogative right, and parliament soon disabused him of this notion. It made it clear that he did not have a suspending power in ecclesiastical affairs. Many have also seen in Charles's declarations a desire to provide toleration for those whose religious perspective they claim he inclined towards: Roman Catholicism. Could it be that the man who ruled over a kingdom where fears of popery were dominant was popish himself? Certainly the suspicion remains. And yet, it gives Charles too much respect for his personal morality and too little for his political acumen to see him in this way.[16]

As Ronald Hutton has brilliantly shown, the evidence for Charles's personal sympathy for Catholicism can often be read as evidence for his political machinations. Thus the Declarations of Indulgence were impelled by political circumstances. Most significantly the clause in the secret Treaty of Dover – made between Charles II and the arch-Catholic monarch Louis XIV in 1670 – in which Charles promised his future conversion to Catholicism is shown by Hutton to have been primarily brought about by political and financial considerations. Louis promised to pay £160,000 to Charles up front without insisting upon a date for the conversion, and this is what Charles focused upon. In a clinching piece of evidence, when his sister – a Catholic – wrote to him to push him to conclude the deal she only dwelt on the international political situation and not on Charles's religious interests. She realised that she could not play on her brother's religious perspective as part of her persuasive technique.[17]

Charles was political first and religious second, if at all. If maintaining and even increasing his power meant pandering to Louis XIV, then so be it. If it meant abandoning any attempts to grant dissenters toleration, as it clearly did from 1681–5, then so be it. Indeed, as Ronald Hutton writes: 'In the end, he hit upon the truth, already discovered by many other rulers, that royal power would be more easily increased if royal policy was in harmony with the prejudices of his most powerful subjects.'[18]

This does leave a striking irony, not the one that is usually claimed. It was not that a Catholic-inclined king ruled a kingdom which was terrified by popery. Rather it was that at the apex of a political system which was rent by religious fears sat a man whose own understanding of religion might be properly called Machiavellian. When necessary, religion was to be subordinated to political necessity. The problem was not that he was Machiavellian; it was that he did not hide this fact effectively. So even when he had accepted the need to follow 'his most powerful subjects', they never quite believed that his heart or – more precisely perhaps – his soul was in it.

The Image of a King

If Charles undermined the ideological foundations of his own restoration by personal immorality, and through his tolerationist agenda succeeded only in exacerbating religious tensions, the picture is no less problematic when we turn attention to the important matter of recreating a monarchical image. Partly prompted by an increasing awareness of the force of public relations, advertising, and 'spin' in modern political life, historians have been becoming more sensitive to the role played by images, rhetoric, and patronage in the early modern world. Where previous generations focused on the emergence of national representative assemblies, bureaucracies, and other institutional structures, recent historians have sought to recover the cultural dimensions of politics. Although there is considerable danger in neglecting the formal sinews of power – taxation revenues, military force, and bureaucratic expertise – those investigating the 'culture of power' can always point to the irrefutable fact that early modern politicians invested considerable time and money in aspects of display.[19] They believed such things mattered. Complex visual images, encoded literary texts, and dramatic performances that drenched audiences in political references were all part of the daily round of public life.

This chapter began by referring to the task of 'playing' the king. So pervasive was a culture of self-presentation and self-fashioning in early modern politics that some scholars have written about the emergence of 'theatre states'.[20] The magnificent royal courts epitomised by the Versailles of Louis XIV were stages on which kings could perform the rites of monarchy, and also enmesh their leading subjects in a web of obligations and expenses that bound them into an increasingly centralised state.[21]

Different words have been used to provide a shorthand description for this type of rule, 'absolute' or 'baroque' monarchy to name but two. The precise terminology used is less important than the fact that a key part of kingship lay in an individual monarch's personal style. Here instructive comparisons can be made within the Stuart dynasty. It would be difficult to imagine two more different characters than those of Charles I and Charles II. Charles I had tried to make his court the 'image of virtue' that would inspire and instruct his realm as a whole.[22] Royal portraits celebrated his personal rectitude and loving relations with his wife; a marriage that he imagined also symbolised political life within his territories. Magnificent court masques – a cultural form combining dance, theatre, and music – were intended to project complex Neoplatonic ideas of order and harmony. The king patronised Inigo Jones who introduced the benighted English to the elegance and formality of classically inspired European 'Palladian' architecture. When he was executed on 30 January 1649 on the balcony of the most striking of these buildings – the Banqueting House in Whitehall – having perhaps looked up on his way out and seen the magnificent ceiling painting of the 'Apotheosis of King James I' by Rubens, Charles learnt the harsh lesson that cultural display could inform political life, but that it was ineffective in the absence of what his subjects believed to be the norms of good government.

Part of that failure lay in the king's personality. Haughty, reserved, and afflicted with a speech impediment, Charles I lacked anything approaching the 'common touch' that could have inspired affection in subjects who would only ever see him in passing. His son could not have provided a greater contrast. Rather than being paralysed by a fear of 'popularity', of appealing to the people beyond the traditional political elite, Charles II's immense energy was effortlessly channelled into charming his subjects.[23] The contrast may be illustrated with two images. The first (Figure 5) shows a 'circle' held at St. James's Palace in honour of Marie de Medici, Charles I's mother-in-law, in 1638. The stiff formality of the court is obvious. The king is physically isolated, allowing none but members of the royal family to accompany him on the carpet of state. His courtiers stand like automata, rigid marionettes kept at a deferential distance. The whole scene in the royal drama is an eloquent expression of the exaggerated sense of regal hauteur that led Charles to the block. The second image (Figure 6) offers a profoundly different vision of kingship: Charles II walking casually around open spaces in the heart

Figure 5 'Le Cercle de Leurs Magestes dans la Chambre de Presence a S. James', from Jean Puget de la Serre, *Histoire de l'Entree de la Reyne Mere du Roy Tres-Chrestien, dans la Grande-Bretaigne* (1639). Bodleian Library, University of Oxford, F.3. 10(2) Art, plate between sign L1v and L2v.

of London. Legendarily accessible and affable, Charles was always ready with a flattering or reassuring word for any of his subjects who came near. According to the Marquess of Halifax, who wrote a brilliantly penetrating

Figure 6   Charles and his Courtiers on Horseguards' Parade with Whitehall Palace in the Background, from John Miller, *Charles II* (1991), George Weidenfeld and Nicolson, Ltd., an imprint of The Orion Publishing Group, London.

'character' of the king sometime after 1688, Charles's very love of easy exercise and walking imposed its own discipline on those seeking the royal ear:

> He grew by age into a pretty exact distribution of his hours, both for his business, pleasures and the exercise for his health, of which he took as much care as could possibly consist with some liberties he was resolved to indulge in himself. He walked by his watch, and when he pulled it out to look upon it skilful Men would make haste with what they had to say to him.[24]

In its atmosphere and public image Charles's court was far more like his grandfather's than his father's. James VI and I had been hugely accessible, partly as a political strategy designed to keep the lines of communication open to all groups and factions. Soon after his accession in 1625 Charles I had changed all this. He established strict rules about who could enter which rooms at court, based on iron principles of order and hierarchy, and inspired by the Spanish Habsburg court that had impressed him during his failed and farcical bid to woo the Spanish Infanta directly in

1623. He further guaranteed that his rules of access were followed by taking strict control of the keys that allowed passage around Whitehall Palace. Everything changed again with Charles II. Like his grandfather, he delighted in receiving information and news from all quarters in an attempt to guarantee his political independence and play off rival ministers against one another. The Marquess of Halifax was only too well aware of this, having been a prominent figure during the last years of Charles's reign. As he wrote, the king

> had back stairs to convey informations to him, as well as for other uses; and though such informations are sometimes dangerous (especially to a Prince that will not take the pains necessary to digest them), yet in the main that humour of hearing everybody against anybody kept those about him in more awe than they would have been without it.[25]

The capacity to inspire awe in their subjects was a quality that all monarchs required. Nevertheless, Halifax's coy allusion to the 'other uses' of the backstairs points towards another way in which Charles II's court resembled that of James VI and I: its moral turpitude. For all James's many intellectual qualities, his court was best known to his subjects through a series of well-publicised sex scandals that suggested a culture of vice.[26] His grandson did not share his taste for handsome young men, but a rampant royal libido was certainly a key feature of his reign. Whilst libertine poets like John Wilmot, Earl of Rochester celebrated the sheer size of the monarchical member – 'His Scepter, and's Pricke are boeth of one Length'[27] – more hostile contemporaries were appalled by the personal and financial costs that resulted from the king's open womanising. Royal mistresses were scarcely unusual in early modern Europe, yet the sheer number of Charles's amours, the brood of children he fathered by them, and his unabashed way of dealing with a group of women regarded by many as nothing more than prostitutes was wholly unusual. Despite his wife's furious attempts to prevent it, the king brutally insisted that one of his mistresses, Barbara Palmer, Countess of Castlemaine and Duchess of Cleveland should have a leading post in the queen's household. He lavished money and titles on his 14 acknowledged illegitimate children. And he conducted business with domestic politicians and foreign diplomats in his mistresses' expensively decorated apartments. Few were in any doubt that the court's 'painted ladies' possessed what the playwright Sir George Etherege viciously termed 'the powerful cunt': the sheer sexual power required to beguile and dominate the king.[28] A more balanced perspective would be that his mistresses never persuaded the king to act against his own wishes, and so may have played a less significant role in the formulation of royal policy than contemporaries feared.[29] Nevertheless, perceptions were extremely important and the care that leading ministers like the Earl of Danby took to co-opt the support of mistresses is suggestive of their significant role as mediators and patronage brokers.

It has recently been argued that Charles's relentless womanising and fathering of illegitimate offspring was a conscious strategy designed to project an air of virility and male strength as a political strategy after the dour puritanism of the previous 20 years.[30] Even if such serious purposes could be traced beneath the patina of pleasure that covered Charles's court, their value was undermined by the immense financial and political costs that they incurred. His subjects were appalled at the expense of maintaining so many living reminders of their king's immorality.[31] Hard-earned tax contributions were being frittered away satisfying the rapacious desires of the king's mistresses. But there was also a deeper worry for contemporaries. The social elite had inherited much of the intellectual tradition of ancient Rome in which personal and public virtue were regarded as inherently linked; to be unable to govern oneself reflected heavily on an individual's perceived capacity to discharge their public duties to the commonwealth.[32] Further down the social scale, crowds might exhibit a 'moral economy' of action, enforcing laws that they perceived to have been ignored by the appropriate office-holders. In 1668, mobs attacked brothels across London, incensed that a government headed by a monarch who openly consorted with prostitutes had not done more to suppress them.[33] Charles's sexual incontinence could thus be subsumed into a wider critique of his government. This was especially the case when his personal immorality clashed so obviously with his attempts to recreate the aura of divine-right monarchy through elaborate public ceremonial. Touching for the king's evil and touching his mistresses might both have seemed reasonable to Charles but for most of his subjects there was an unacceptable contradiction. The king's overt sexuality hardly made him seem like a virtuous figure instituted by God to rule over his people in their best interests. Indeed the libertine culture of Charles's court succeeded only in debasing the whole language of politics. The Marquess of Halifax's choice of metaphor to describe how the king dealt with his political advisers is telling: 'He lived with his Ministers as he did with his Mistresses; he used them, but he was not in love with them.'[34]

For many observers Charles II's court thus provided an 'image of vice' for the nation, rather than virtue, one in which a general air of sexual misconduct was matched only by the stench created by the king's beloved spaniels. As John Evelyn put it with fastidious horror in a character sketch written after Charles's death: 'He tooke delight to have a number of little spaniels follow him, and lie in his bed-Chamber, where often times he suffered the bitches to puppy and give suck, which rendred it very offensive, and indeede made the whole Court nasty and stinking.'[35] Nevertheless, amidst the squalor there were changes over time. In his last years, Charles did tighten up access to the royal person at court on political grounds, ostentatiously banishing from court Whig peers or duplicitous ministers who had angered him during the Exclusion Crisis. Those who successfully crawled back into royal favour by changing their political opinions in a Tory direction were then equally ostentatiously welcomed back to court and allowed to kiss the king's hand.[36] But even during these years of apparent political triumph the king's own most loyal supporters could still complain. Unlike his father and grandfather, Charles II was not a fanatical huntsman. But he did enjoy watching horseracing, especially at Windsor and Newmarket. When he went to Newmarket in March 1682, the Tory squire Sir John Reresby described the scene:

> The King was soe much pleased in the country, and soe great a lover of the diversions which that place did afford, that he lett himselfe down from Majesty to the very degree of a country gentleman. He mixed himselfe amongst the croud, allowed every man to speak to him that pleased, went a-hawkeing in mornings, to cock matches in afternoons (if there were noe hors races), and to plays in the evenings, acted in a barn and by very ordinary Bart[holo]mew-fair comedians.[37]

This was not an unqualified piece of praise. Accessibility could go too far: when the king preferred to play the part of an affable country gentleman, he undid much of the hard work he had undertaken to recreate an air of majesty after the republican interlude. Although he could certainly be a 'magnificent monarch' when he tried, the lack of consistency told over time.[38]

Reresby's comments on the king's low tastes in drama do not immediately tally with the bolder claims of recent scholars investigating patronage and culture in the Carolean period. Here Charles I's court has cast a very long shadow. The fabulous beauty of Anthony van Dyck's portraits and the dazzling accounts of the masques written and designed by Ben Jonson and Inigo Jones have made what followed seem decidedly inferior. Yet Charles II was not without an aesthetic agenda, and did work to recover some of his father's famous art collection that had been broken up to help finance the interregnum regimes.[39] Nor did he lack talented artists to bring such an agenda to life. Unfortunately some of the most memorable images of the Restoration period were those that encapsulated the loose morality of Charles's court (see below, Chapter 8). Nevertheless, the king did patronise a number of artistic enterprises designed to bolster his rule by advertising royal authority. An adapted form of the court masques so beloved by his father, and which the young prince would have seen in the 1630s, was given new life by Charles II especially after 1673. This coincided with the rise of Danby as the king's leading minister, and was the artistic adjunct of wider attempts to shore up the Crown by strengthening royal finances and building a body of political supporters in parliament.[40]

Party-building with the aid of money and political guile was complemented by real buildings of bricks and mortar. Charles was well-known to be mechanically minded, to prize the ingenuity of designers and inventors, and took a keen interest in building works as another aspect of the magnificence to be associated with monarchy. His success as a royal patron was, however, limited thanks to the restricted financial resources at his disposal. Ambitious building plans at the start and end of his reign either did not get off the drawing board or were only partially realised. Nevertheless, the limited amount that was achieved offers clear suggestions about the king's priorities and self-image. These are particularly valuable because of the king's legendary loquacity. Although initially charming, the torrent of disingenuous wit that the king unleashed upon his court ultimately raised deep suspicions about his sincerity and trustworthiness amongst intelligent observers. As Gilbert Burnet, the Whig cleric and future bishop, wrote in 1683, Charles

> has the greatest art of concealing himselfe of any man alive, so that those about him cannot tell, when he is ill or well pleased, and in private discourse he will hear all sorts of things in such a manner, that a man cannot know, whether he hears them or not, or whether he is well or ill pleased with them.[41]

For this reason the Marquess of Halifax recalled that 'Those who knew his face fixed their eyes there and thought it of more importance to see than to hear what he said.'[42]

Charles's architectural schemes show a consistent desire to project an air of ordered majesty in the latest European, and specifically French, style. In the 1660s, he invested considerable time in planning substantial expansion of the royal buildings at Greenwich, probably to serve as a grand staging post to London for visiting diplomats. The Stuart dynasty's pretensions would be immediately evident to representatives of foreign powers. It is striking both that Charles was sufficiently keen to secure the services of the brilliant French garden designer, André Le Nôtre, that he despatched a gift of horses, and that he nevertheless failed.[43] More progress was made on a grand palace for the ageing king at Winchester in the early 1680s. Tired of Newmarket, and mistrustful of London's political loyalties as a result of the Exclusion Crisis, Charles commissioned a new country seat that would rival Louis XIV's Versailles and assert 'a baroque and authoritarian style of rule'.[44] Although no fewer than five million bricks were contracted for by November 1684, Christopher Wren's activity as Surveyor of the King's Works was ultimately abandoned after Charles's early death.[45] By this time Wren must have been used to lost projects. In 1678, plans had been initiated for an enormous mausoleum to house the body of Charles I, the Royal Martyr. Left in a makeshift grave in St. George's Chapel Windsor, Charles's body would now be placed in a vast and opulent two-storey rotunda, 140 feet high, by 70 feet wide. As Wren himself knew, 'Architecture has its political uses', in this case royal efforts to excite loyalist pro-Stuart sentiment at the end of a tumultuous decade.[46] Although parliament initially approved the lavish spending that would be required (nearly £70,000), with the explosion of the popish plot and rapid decline into the Exclusion Crisis, the political climate became unfavourable and the project failed.

Despite this striking lack of architectural success, Charles did succeed in significantly remodelling Windsor Castle, even if the results were undone by his eighteenth- and nineteenth-century successors and have now been lost. Both the artistic schemes that Charles patronised, and the funding that allowed for this programme of works, are richly suggestive. Thirteen ceiling designs were painted by the Italian artist, Antonio Verrio, at a cost of almost £2500 out of a total expenditure of more than £50,000 between 1678 and 1684. In the Privy Chamber Verrio painted a representation of the re-establishment of the Church of England in the 1660s: 'in the Characters of England, Scotland & Ireland, attended by Faith, Hope, and Charity, Religion triumphing over Superstition & Hypocrisy'.[47] Although it is tempting to discern a high level of irony in these compositions, at the very least they indicate the kind of imagery Charles wished to have associated with his reign, and which would be inherited by his brother. The designs for the Great Bedchamber were even more extraordinary. There Verrio portrayed a suppliant figure of France and the four continents bringing their riches to Charles seated amongst clouds. At this point in his reign the king was certainly in receipt of secret French subsidies designed to encourage him not to call another Whig-dominated, anti-French parliament. Yet the triumphalist imagery points rather to an exaggerated sense of Charles's power on the European stage. Not that all the monies involved came from France: some had been siphoned off from the Irish revenues, whose farmers eagerly supplied the king with the ready cash he so delighted in. It was this kind of bizarre corruption, and self-corruption, that the Marquess of Halifax was referring to when he wrote in his 'character' of the king that:

> He was often retained in his personal against his politic capacity. He would speak upon those Occasions most dexterously against himself; Charles Stuart would be bribed against the King; and in the distinction, he leaned more to his natural self, than his character would allow.... It was not the best use he made of his backstairs to admit men to bribe him against himself, to procure a defalcation, help a lame accountant to get off, or side with the farmers against the improvement of the revenue. The King was made the instrument to defraud the Crown, which is somewhat extraordinary.[48]

Conclusion

Halifax's sardonic words would serve as a starting point for generations of criticism. Charles II's political skills were certainly insufficient to beguile posterity. Writers were able to build on two diametrically opposite traditions of commentary on the later Stuart period that testify to the depths of division within that society. According to nonconformists and Whigs, Charles's reign was 'odious', not least because it was 'profligate and Villainous'.[49] By contrast, for Tories ranging from the Kentish gentleman Sir John Heath to the Jacobite Earl of Ailesbury, Charles's reign was or had been 'golden'.[50] Yet even this golden haze wore off over time. Charles's political skills were essentially tactical rather than strategic, designed to manage crises rather than to orchestrate the kind of fundamental rethinking of English governance that his father's rule in the 1630s had briefly appeared to promise. To return to a theatrical image for the last time, the king's greatest modern biographer summed him up as being a 'monarch in a masquerade', pointing to the frequent images of masks and disguises that come up in the tortuous and mistrustful politics

of his reign.[51] Ultimately it may be better to say that he was a vaudeville
magician who misdirected his contemporaries for some of the time. Truly
successful kingship required something more effective than sleight of
hand, and Charles's subjects were always ultimately aware that they were
being tricked. As a Roffensian satire which gave the named characters the
least appropriate qualities put it:

Here's Lauderdale the pretty
And Monmouth the Witty
And Frazier the Learned Physician;
But above all the Rest
Here's the Duke for a jest
And your Majesty for a great Politician.[52]

Chapter 5: Why did James VII and II Lose his Thrones?

Chapter 3 began by analysing a print published in early 1681 illustrating dire predictions for the imminent future. This one takes as its starting point a print produced in early 1689 that reflected on the recent past. There is a clear overlap of interpretative frameworks between 'A Prospect of a Popish Successor' (Figure 4) and 'England's Memorial' (Figure 7). The first predicted 'popish villany'; the latter rejoiced in its defeat. Church buildings representing the whole Church of England are prominent in both prints. In the first 'tantivy' clergy are shown riding the church towards Rome, in the second the anthropomorphised building tells us that in clear sight of the eye of divine providence 'I breath[e] again'. Armed Catholic priests are closely associated with devils by both artists, and in both compositions the centre refers to the religious character of the state. In 1681, anxious Whigs dwelt on two closely connected monstrous figures representative of a Catholic future, the violent Irish Catholic devil 'Mack', and the deceitful clerical 'Church Papist'; in 1689, William of Orange's propagandist presented the prince – punningly depicted as an orange tree – as the guarantor of a Protestant state's security. On the left of the tree the bishop explains that he acts to 'reedify this Sion', whilst on the right representatives of the two houses of parliament – the Commons and the Lords – ask their saviour to 'heale our breaches' and to 'take from us Idolatry'. 'A Prospect of a Popish Successor' showed the burning of Protestants; 'England's Memorial' offers the mirror-image, that of Catholics fleeing to continental exile in France.

The fact that a straight line can be drawn between these two prints is both profoundly revealing and potentially misleading. James's Catholicism was the dominant political fact of the 1680s and it should hardly come as a surprise that his faith – so central to his identity, but so

75

Figure 7   *England's Memorial* (1688). © The Trustees of the British Museum.

abhorrent to his subjects – dominates the prints. Yet in order to understand why James lost his thrones we need to recognise the extent to which
a large part of the political nation disagreed with the analysis offered in
the Whig print of 1681 and felt profound unease with the consequences
of the Revolution of 1688. The linear connection between the propaganda pieces needs to be broken up. The postscript to the Exclusion Crisis
dominated the first 2 years of James's reign, during which time the king
erroneously believed that his dominant Tory allies who had secured his
succession would allow him to re-establish his faith as the core religion
within his territories. The prologue to the Revolution occupied the second 2 years of James's reign when the king turned his back on his old
friends and attempted to use a novel political alliance to secure the same
goal. If Whig ideas and personalities tend to dominate accounts of the
Exclusion period, it was the collective Tory mind that dictated James's fall.

To understand why this was so, we will disentangle for the purposes
of analysis two themes which in reality went hand in hand. The first

was a contest between different understandings of post-Reformation history: the king's belief that the period had witnessed the efflorescence of heresy, and his subjects' equally vehemently held belief that the growth of Protestantism represented the triumph of religious truth over idolatry and ignorance. The second theme followed on naturally from the first. Should the future of James's kingdoms be a Catholic one supervised by a devout king and his suitably instructed heir, James Francis Edward Stuart, Prince of Wales, or did it need to be a Protestant one dominated by the king's eldest daughter from his first marriage, Mary Stuart, Princess of Orange, and protected by her Calvinist husband William? James ultimately lost his thrones because these two issues were by 1688 fused into a present-centred concern with crucial notions of honour, interest, and conscience. The king discovered to his cost that he was more reliant on his leading subjects than he had realised, and that they no longer believed him to be the foundation of good government. Instead James was seen as a dangerous rogue elephant, one that needed either to be penned up and rendered impotent, or else driven away from the centre of affairs altogether.

Turning Back the Clock: Making England Catholic Again

The spectre of popish rule that had seemed so terrifying to many in 1679–81 proved strangely insubstantial in 1685. Whatever 'A Prospect of a Popish Successor' had predicted, James did not grow demonic horns, or start burning Protestants, the instant his brother died on 6 February. Contemporaries were pleasantly surprised by the general calm that accompanied the new king's accession to the throne, and Tories felt vindicated by their staunch defence of James's rights. On 10 February, John Dugdale informed his father, the leading herald Sir William Dugdale, that the Court was bursting at the seams with those desperate to kiss James's hands and to curry favour. Now there was 'not a Whigg to be heard of'.[1] In the nation at large a deluge of loyal sentiments greeted the new king. As one of the academics contributing to a collection of eulogies from the University of Cambridge wrote

Cease, faction, cease, and smooth thy angry brow;
No more the blasted seeds of treason sow:
Let no disloyal murmurs stain

The long, and ever-peaceful reign
Of James, the Martyr's son.[2]

Although it is tempting to hear an element of protesting too much in
these words – not least in the clumsy reminders of past problems – the
political horizons initially looked set fair. James himself achieved a rare
(positive) propaganda coup by some well-chosen words to his first Privy
Council meeting as king. He denied persistent reports that he was 'a man
for arbitrary power', instead claiming that he would 'preserve this government both in Church and state as it is now by law established'. He went on
to drive home these sentiments for the benefit of Tory Anglicans anxious
about the future of the Church of England and intellectually wedded to
due legal process:

> I know the principles of the Church of England are for monarchy, and
> the members of it have showed themselves good and loyal subjects;
> therefore I shall always take care to defend and support it. I know too
> the laws of England are sufficient to make the king as great a monarch
> as I can wish. And as I shall never depart from the just rights and
> prerogative of the Crown, so I shall never invade any mans property.[3]

If we are to understand the depth of Tory fury in the last 2 years of James's
reign, we need to remember these words and the extent to which the
king's policies would look like an utter betrayal of them. Once praised as
a man of his word, James seemed to have broken his early promises. But
in the short-term this vigorous support for the Tory church-state that had
emerged between 1681 and 1685 was intensely reassuring. It undoubtedly
helped that the reassurance went beyond mere words: James's early min-
isterial appointments were solidly Anglican. In particular, James raised his
brothers-in-law from his first marriage – Laurence and Henry Hyde, Earls
of Rochester and Clarendon – to the highest offices. They were the sons
of Charles II's first Lord Chancellor, Edward Hyde, and were widely perceived to be leaders of the Church of England interest. Rochester became
Lord Treasurer – the most senior minister of state – and Clarendon was
appointed Lord Privy Seal. Even if the king was a Catholic in his personal
devotional life he therefore seemed to be ruling publicly as a Protestant
prince.

The appearance was deceptive: James had no intention of divorcing
his religious faith from his kingship. In common with most early modern rulers, he regarded his kingly role as one requiring him to guide

the religious lives of his subjects. Possessed of a very high sense of his rights and responsibilities, James's conversion in the late 1660s had dominated British and Irish political life from the time it became publicly known in 1673. Although this is now an historical commonplace it is crucial to recognise that his conversion was also the dominant fact in James's internal life. It attained this status partly because of what his Catholicism exposed him to, notably the fury of a politically cautious brother and the opprobrium of the political nation. But more positively it also gave him a true sense of mission, a kind of vocation that drove his entire political agenda. When he tried to convert his eldest daughter and likely heir, Mary, to the Catholic faith by letter in 1687, he explained his own thinking: 'Surely it is only reasonable that this [Roman Catholic] Church, which has a constant succession from the time of the apostles to the present, should be more in the right than those private men who, under the pretext of reformation, have been the authors of new opinions'. According to James, there was no other church 'which claims, or can claim, infallibility, for there must necessarily be an infallible Church, or otherwise what Our Saviour said cannot be and the gates of Hell would prevail against her'.[4] So the Catholic Church was best because it was the oldest, and the only one with an infallible sense of the true doctrine needed to prepare Christians for the final struggle with Satan.

Fired by such sentiments, James would spend his reign attempting to reverse the English Reformation. It is worth dwelling on precisely what that entailed. We have already noted the extent to which English historical consciousness was largely shaped by anti-Catholicism. This was an intellectual landscape that was inhabited not just by an educated, literate elite. Instead it was an expansive common ground that transcended particular social groups and geographical regions. 'Popery' was derided as foreign, feared for its insidious political force, and despised for its doctrinal beliefs. Such sentiments did not necessarily translate into day-to-day hostility towards known Catholics in individual neighbourhoods where bonds of sociability tended to trump abstract fears. But at times of heightened anxiety anti-popery was an immensely powerful motivating force, driving groups and individuals to perform political acts that would not have been undertaken in quieter times. This was fully appreciated by members of older Catholic families, whose leaders would urge James not to provoke the Protestant majority for fear of a violent backlash. The king ignored such advice and preferred the less cautious counsels of English lay converts like Robert Spencer, Earl of Sunderland, priests like his Jesuit confessor, Father Edward Petre, and non-English Catholic adventurers like the bluff Irishman Richard Talbot, Earl of Tyrconnell.

The new Catholic king thus faced the challenge of fundamentally changing the mindset of the majority of his subjects. But if England was a nation of individual Protestants, it was also a Protestant nation whose collective nature was bounded by confessional legal instruments and policed by powerful interest groups. The English confessional state was structured by acts of Parliament regarded as sacrosanct by the legalistic political elite. The Acts of Supremacy and Uniformity, the Test Act, and the penal laws together comprised a statutory barrier to Catholicism that had immense psychological importance for James's subjects. As the previously impeccably loyal Earl of Abingdon told the king to his face on 18 November 1687: 'I looked upon these Acts as the bulwarks of our religion, and whilst I did so, I could not depart from them'.[5] The intransigence of the lay elite was immensely important, but so too was the degree of opposition posed by Anglican clerics. Despite James's explicit instructions to the contrary, Church of England ministers continued to preach against Catholicism. Although they could not have been unaware just how insulting James found this – both to his personal faith and his authority as Supreme Governor of the Church of England – the London clergy mounted a well-organised campaign to print collections of their anti-Catholic sermons, projecting their words well beyond the bounds of their metropolitan churches.[6]

The scale of the psychological, legal, and political obstacles in the way of a re-Catholicising policy was therefore immense. That James broke his monarchy in the pursuit of this single goal is suggestive of two things. Early in his reign, the king did not appreciate the full extent of the problems that lay ahead. And late in his reign he did not care about the immense wounds in the nation that he was opening up. Both of these points indicate that for James politics was not the art of the possible, but a barely tolerable exercise between issuing orders and securing their implementation.[7] How did James become aware of the challenges in front of him, and how ultimately did he try to overcome them?

Until the spring of 1687, James attempted to achieve his ends through his old Tory allies. Their stolid refusal to obey him astonished James, both because he was possessed of an extremely limited and autocratic mind, and because Anglican Tories had spent the previous quarter of a century emphasising their commitment to the Stuart dynasty. What James had failed to notice was that the vast majority of his Tory supporters were not unthinking royal lackeys. Whilst intensely committed to monarchical government, and deeply traumatised by the experience of the republican 1650s, most Tories had two commitments that no able monarch would have sought to test, and which even James had addressed in his opening words to the Privy Council. The first was to the rule of law. Wedded to the forms and processes of the common law, Tories consistently contrasted the rights and liberties of Englishmen with the downtrodden condition of those unlucky enough to be born the subjects of continental absolutist rulers. This chauvinistic sense of pride in English legal culture extended to a broader commitment to the English constitution. In England, unlike in France, law did not emanate from the Crown alone, but was the product of the king-in-parliament, a curious hybrid power that in practice made it very difficult for the Crown to rule against the interests of its leading subjects. Charles I had found this to his cost in the 1640s; James had evidently failed to learn the right lessons. Both kings came to be seen as dangerous innovators in the eyes of a conservative political class wedded to notions of the inherent superiority of the English 'ancient constitution'.[8]

This sense of the Stuart monarchs as innovators extended to religious affairs, and was at loggerheads with the Tories' second commitment above and beyond their loudly proclaimed royalism. Charles I had committed political suicide by backing an unpopular 'Laudian' movement within the Church of England that appeared to many of his subjects to be unacceptably tinged with 'popery'. James went one stage further and whole-heartedly backed the Church of Rome. This was of critical importance for Tories. In common with the vast majority of Englishmen, Tories fundamentally despised 'papists': their commitment to the pope – a foreign potentate – rendered them potentially disloyal to their own rulers; their doctrinal beliefs and liturgical practices – especially the prominence of images in their churches – left them open to accusations of superstitious ignorance. But Tories went further than their Whig rivals in supporting the existing rights of the Church of England 'as by law established'. Regarding Protestant dissenters as the heirs to the puritan rebels who had murdered Charles I in 1649, Tories were passionately committed to the Church of England in the narrow, persecutory, form that had emerged in 1662 (see Chapter 1). Nor was this a wholly negative stance. Tories believed the Church of England to be the best Protestant church in Europe, doctrinally pure, but untainted with any of the rebellious, anti-monarchical acts that had given shape to other Calvinist churches in Scotland, France, and the Dutch Republic.

It was James's misfortune very quickly to be regarded as a threat to both of the Tories' key commitments. He contrived to achieve this in the most provocative way possible, by promoting one institution that the English deeply feared – a standing army – and apparently threatening the integrity of another that they valued above all others – parliament. This was a remarkable achievement because the combination of an anti-Whig backlash and vigorous governmental efforts to manage the general election resulted in the return of an exceptionally loyal parliament in 1685. The contrast to the three Exclusion Parliaments of 1679–81 was extraordinary, and James was understandably delighted. But the king had not taken any chances, illegally continuing to collect customs revenues even before they were discussed by parliament during its first session in May 1685. James had also let it be known in advance of parliament's sitting that if he was not granted the same revenues for life that had been enjoyed by his brother he would dissolve parliament. This forceful agenda was neither tactful nor, in the minds of some MPs and peers, in accordance with precedent: the king's views should have been articulated in his opening speech, and without crude supplementary threats. James's approach was the product of his own disdain for representative assemblies as unnecessarily restrictive on his regal powers.[9] He continued to show his reluctance to respect older notions of what the proper relationship between king and parliament was by trespassing on the privileges of the House of Commons, his ministers intervening to lobby hard for their favoured candidate as Speaker. Although eventually accepted by MPs, this crown interference set a poor tone for the reign.

This early tension is worth stressing because historians have often been prone to create too strong a division between the first (summer) and second (winter) sessions of the 1685 English Parliament. The crucial events that are usually cited as changing the political climate in negative ways that mirrored the declining seasons are the invasions of the Earl of Argyll and the Duke of Monmouth. Each nobleman represented a strand of extreme opposition in Scotland and England, respectively, which had led them to flee into exile in Holland during the early 1680s. Each man attempted to trade on his status, Argyll as a leading noble in an 'extremely aristocratic' society;[10] Monmouth as the 'Protestant duke' who was the son of Charles II (though contemporaries passionately disagreed over whether he was legitimate or not due to murky rumours that the king had married Monmouth's mother, Lucy Walter, during his pre-1660 years of exile).[11] Both failed miserably, even if Monmouth came closer than is often credited to orchestrating a potentially lethal surprise night attack on the royal troops sent to quash his uprising at Sedgemoor in Somerset. What was significant in both cases was how little support the two rebel leaders received from the elites of Scotland and England. Dependent on poorly trained and armed members of the lower orders, they were ultimately no match for the significant numbers of regular royal troops that James had at his disposal.

Despite the superficially impressive nature of his regime's victories, the political fall-out of these events was profoundly damaging to James. The savage judicial repression which followed the military defeat of the rebels – particularly Judge Jeffreys' notorious 'Bloody Assizes' in the English West Country – tapped into pre-existing fears of popish cruelty. These were particularly acute thanks to the actions of Louis XIV across the Channel. For several years he had been increasing the pressure on his Protestant subjects, the Huguenots, by a brutal policy involving the billeting of troops on their communities, the *dragonnades*. In 'England's Memorial' Louis is shown as figure 'G', simultaneously shooting, stabbing, and trampling Huguenots. In 1685, the French king finally revoked the Edict of Nantes (1598) which had brought the French Wars of Religion to an end by guaranteeing Protestants considerable legal safeguards, and which Louis had come to see both as a threat to his sovereignty and as an unacceptable sop to heretics. No longer protected by the Edict of Nantes, Huguenots faced a stark choice: conversion to Catholicism or exile. Hundreds of thousands chose the latter in the largest forced migration of early modern European history. Although the bulk went to the Dutch Republic and some of the Northern German states, large numbers fled to English and Irish towns. They brought with them horrific tales of violence and intimidation which provided a dire backdrop to James's efforts to reassure his Protestant subjects that rule by a Catholic was safe. The Huguenot experience offered a powerful vision of the future for anxious English observers: 'The Protestants in France had free liberty, both to preach up the Protestant Religion, and to preach and write against Popery, till within eight or ten months that they began to torment and murder them'.[12]

Events within England also played a major role in exacerbating tensions since James had rapidly recruited a number of Catholic officers into his armed forces. In the king's mind there was no doubt nothing sinister about this at all: the officers were men he regarded as loyal and experienced soldiers, blooded in continental campaigns. But to a sensitive audience of Protestants the glaring fact was that their employment was illegal: the Test Act precluded Catholics holding offices of any kind. When the second session of the 1685 Parliament pointed this out to James in no uncertain terms, his efforts brusquely to say that he enjoyed the prerogative right to dispense groups of his subjects from statutory penalties aroused vehement opposition, just as Charles's Declaration of Indulgence had in 1672. The ensuing deadlock led to Parliament's abrupt prorogation in November after it had sat for less than a fortnight. Typically James argued in a letter to his son-in-law, William of Orange, that parliament had been 'deceived by some ill men who fill their ears with fears'.[13] The claim that the majority of MPs and peers had been led astray by a malevolent and sinister coterie of malcontents was not unusual in seventeenth-century England. Once again, in making this argument James was his father's son. But if there had been a number of cabals conspiring against Charles I's policies in 1640, the picture was very different in 1685. The sheet anchor of opposition came not so much from the small number of elected Whig MPs but from a general groundswell of Tory legalism, one that had been visible from the earliest part of the *first* session, not just during the ill-fated second.

Overall, the parliamentary experience of 1685 suggested that James was – at the very least – inclined to challenge traditional constitutional notions in several interconnected ways. First, the king placed great emphasis on the importance of his armed forces. In his mind this was justified by the threats posed to his regime, and by a benign desire to protect his people. James's self-image was all about strength and decisiveness, a warrior prince devoted to defending the welfare of his subjects. He had served in the forces of the king of France during exile in the 1650s, and had fought for his royal brother at sea during the second Anglo-Dutch War. Pepys described him in 1664 as 'a man naturally Martiall to the highest degree', and 21 years later medals were distributed at the time of his coronation 'with a Wreath of Bayes at the bottome as an Embleme of Conquest, and at the top an Imperiall Crown, and the Motto A Militari ad Regem ['from soldier to king']'.[14] Although the English elite often postured about their crucial role as arbiters of European affairs, and lovingly dwelt on an imperial medieval past surmounted by Henry V's great military victories, in more sober moments they infinitely preferred the security of knowing that the Crown was dependent on them for its day-to-day security in the form of a localised and gentry-dominated militia. For James the experience of Monmouth's Rebellion proved that this was a hopelessly antiquated and ineffective force. To replace or supplement it required the king to challenge constitutional tradition in two other ways: the employment of Catholic officers contrary to legislative prohibitions, and the collection of revenues even before they had been formally granted by parliament. James appeared to be trying to rule more like a king of France than the traditionally more fettered English Crown.

Despite ditching his English Parliament in November 1685, James spent the period until the spring of 1687 trying to advance his agenda through Tory political figures at both local and national levels. His catastrophic failure to make England Catholic again was the result of an unfortunate combination of his subjects' hypersensitivity to anything that looked like 'popery', and the king's intolerance of anything that looked like disobedience. This clash of perspectives naturally focused on the Church of England. James took action against some of the most prominent parts of the church: the London clergy, the bishops, and the universities. Incensed by the disobedience of the London clergy that we have already noted, the king used his authority as Supreme Governor of the Church of England to order the bishop of London, Henry Compton, to suppress controversial preaching. In particular, in May 1686, he was told to silence one of the most vehement clerical critics of Catholicism, John Sharp, Dean of Norwich, and rector of St. Giles-in-the-Fields. Compton refused. The bishop had a long history of annoying James, so much so that in 1677 he was thought to have blocked Compton's promotion to the archbishopric of Canterbury. Certainly Compton had been the most vociferous episcopal critic of the king in the House of Lords during the second session of the 1685 Parliament.

Faced with an intransigent set of clerics geographically close to the royal court in London, and unable to rely on diocesan bishops to discipline the lower clergy, James took the extraordinary step of establishing a Commission for Ecclesiastical Causes. This offshoot of the royal supremacy contained both tame clerics and laymen who could be relied upon to do as the king wished, though to general surprise the previously ultra-loyal archbishop of Canterbury, William Sancroft, persistently refused to attend the Commission's proceedings. Although not a wholly novel means of exerting discipline within the Church of England – a similar body had been established by Charles I and Laud during the 1630s, itself an unhappy precedent[15] – the Commission was intensely controversial. Not only did it demonstrate the lengths to which the king would go to dominate and control the clergy in his own interests, it also supplied a series of astonishing set-piece trials of prominent individuals and groups with which to enhance anti-Catholic fears. Compton was the uncle of the Earl of Northampton, and when he was hauled before the commissioners, his nephew and a phalanx of other peers attended the trial. Indeed 'the many hundreds' who attended in order to show support for Compton treated him with 'great honour and respect ... makeing a lane for him' towards the commissioners. As even a Presbyterian clergyman who was personally profoundly hostile to the bishop noted, 'This is certainly a very great Case, and has the whole body of the Kingdome for its defence and support'. Members of every Protestant denomination 'think themselves all Struck at by it'.[16] Although the outcome of such a kangaroo court was never in doubt, and Compton was duly suspended from his diocesan responsibilities, the case was thus a public relations disaster for James. This was compounded by the fact that when James had the opportunity to fill several other bishoprics due to the ill-timed deaths of the bishops of Chester and Oxford in 1686, he chose to appoint massively unpopular men who were reviled for their servility, and even perceived as fifth columnists for the Catholic Church. One Anglican commentator claimed that neither of the new bishops 'can well be liked of anywhere, or by any honest intelligent men', whilst another wailed 'God help the poor Church of England whose pillars fall & her foundations are undermined'.[17]

But the king pressed on. The Universities of Oxford and Cambridge together formed a third key part of the established church. Not only were they where a large proportion of the country's lay elite gained several years of their education, the universities were also the nurseries of the clergy: by the later seventeenth century, the vast majority of those in orders possessed at least one university degree. Oxford and Cambridge were thus nerve centres of the English Protestant body politic. James assumed a collision course with these prominent and powerful corporate bodies in a number of ways. He backed the rights of individual Catholic converts to retain or gain college fellowships, notably Obadiah Walker, the Master of University College, Oxford. He demanded that Cambridge grant an MA degree to a Benedictine monk. He encouraged the publication of Catholic tracts at the university presses. And most controversially of all, he tried to impose Catholic heads on a number of college's, notably Christ Church, Oxford, and Sidney Sussex, Cambridge. The former case was particularly important as, uniquely, this college also housed the cathedral for an Anglican diocese. By promoting John Massey to the deanery of Christ Church in December 1686, James was widely perceived to be sending out a wider message concerning the ecclesiastical favour that Catholics could expect. As George Hickes, Dean of Worcester, noted in a private letter to a friend in Oxford, 'I am afraid the preferment of Mr Massey will be a temptation to others to forsake our religion in hopes of preferment'.[18]

This process culminated in the ejection of a number of fellows of Magdalen College, Oxford, in November 1687 at the hands of James's Ecclesiastical Commission, after they had refused to admit a Catholic President despite direct instructions from the king. This received national attention because it was far more than a parochial matter of college governance. Above and beyond the fact that his critics felt James was blatantly trying to establish Catholic seminaries at the heart of the Anglican establishment, two other issues were hugely important. In the first place, college fellowships were in law the property of the individuals who held them. Although James at the start of his reign had promised that 'I shall never invade any man's property', he now seemed to be doing exactly that. Even more significantly, the recalcitrant Magdalen fellows argued that they had each sworn an oath to uphold the college statutes, and that those statutes directly prohibited the election of Catholics. James thus appeared to be trying to force the consciences of his subjects in the most objectionable way possible: to make them break oaths sworn before God. This was arbitrary power that seemed to be trying to bully men into damning themselves. Although James's use of the Commission was successful in a narrow sense – he removed many of his clerical critics – this was achieved at the formidable cost of playing into a number of crucial stereotypes of what a cruel and vindictive Catholic prince would be like.[19] Fears for the future thus became a supremely potent product of the campaign to turn back the confessional clock.

Fearing for the Future: Ostrich Feathers versus Orange Trees

One of James's closest Anglican associates was Francis Turner, bishop of Ely. A rising star during the last years of Charles II, Turner had been appointed Lord Almoner by the new king in 1685, a court position of considerable significance within the chapel royal. It was, therefore, unsurprising that he was chosen to preach a key thanksgiving sermon to mark the defeat of Monmouth's rebellion in the summer of 1685. What is surprising is that even such an immensely loyal man chose to lay considerable weight on his royal master's mortality. Like other apologists for the king, Turner stressed not just James's early pledges to support the rights of the Church of England, but also the fact that his daughters and heirs, Mary and Anne, had been raised within the Anglican faith and had married Protestant princes, William of Orange and George of Denmark, respectively. According to Turner, when Mary and Anne 'plighted their Troth to their two Protestant Princes by consent of their Royall Father, Then I may truly say Hee most effectually plighted His Faith to us'.[20] The emphasis on the king's daughters is highly suggestive. James was 51 when he succeeded to the throne. His brother had died aged 54. Setting aside his father and his great-grandmother – Mary Queen of Scots – who had both been executed, the new king could also have reflected that his grandfather, James VI and I, had died aged 58, and *his* grandfather, James V, had expired at just 30. The Stewarts were manifestly not a long-lived family. Comparatively speaking James must have felt like an old man in a hurry. (Ironically he would actually die in 1701 aged almost 68.) Conversely, his subjects initially felt they could afford to wait out their new king's more controversial policies: hence Turner's prompts from the pulpit.

James did not make it easy to maintain this complacent attitude. The intransigence of his Protestant subjects prompted royal irritation that in turn led to policies provoking incredulity from the political nation. James's efforts to muzzle the Church of England went hand-in-hand with attempts to reinvigorate the Catholic Church as a going concern for the future. The king established a Catholic chapel royal at court and openly attended Mass. Father Edward Petre became a leading public figure and was even appointed to the Privy Council. This came after generations of scare-stories had presented Jesuits as Catholic conspirators *par excellence*, fanatically loyal agents of a scheming papacy. Yet James re-opened full relations with that papacy, welcoming clerical diplomats – including, ultimately, a papal nuncio – as well as sending an embassy to Rome. Catholic vicars-apostolic were appointed with remits covering the whole of England in four large geographical areas, and were given magnificent consecrations in royal palaces.[21] Catholic authors – both clerical and lay – were encouraged to promote their faith through the printing presses, a striking attempt to appropriate what had been a prime means of spreading Protestant ideas in England since at least the 1540s. In 1683, just eight Catholic titles had been printed in England; 172 appeared in 1687.[22] The overall impact of James's policies profoundly unsettled his Protestant subjects. To take just one individual example, by February 1688, the Norwich clergyman, Humphrey Prideaux, had to apologise to his sister (who he did not like) for taking so long to reply to her most recent letter: 'I have been soe continually harassed in answering popish papers sent me that I have had noe time to doe any thing else for those people are now very busy'.[23] This sense of growing Catholic confidence was fed by the king's determination to provide his co-religionists with financial resources to advance their cause. We have already seen that James was actively engaged in altering the confessional complexion of several Oxbridge colleges. The king also began to leave some dioceses of the established churches of Ireland and England – notably the archdiocese of York – vacant after the deaths of bishops so that the Crown could directly collect their revenues. A Catholic mission was thus being funded out of Protestant pockets.

From James's perspective, this was only part of a still broader attempt to expand and entrench the Catholic faith in England for the foreseeable future. To do this, he needed to remove the legal penalties under which Catholics laboured. How was this to be achieved: by confrontation and subversion, or by persuasion and argument? Several recent authors have emphasised James's commitment to ideas of liberty of conscience, some stretching this into an early Enlightenment commitment to a kind of religious pluralism.[24] There is no doubt that even after his fall from power James himself placed tremendous weight on liberty of conscience, explicitly recommending it to his son and heir in a letter written whilst preparing for possible death during his Irish military campaign of 1690: 'Be not persuaded by any to depart from that; our blessed Saviour whipt people out of the Temple, but I never heard he commanded any should be forced into it'.[25] Liberty of conscience was, however, overwhelmingly conceptualised by James as a means to an end: 'many conversions will ensue'.[26] If his subjects were allowed a free choice of religious faith, unimpeded by fears of legal proscription, James believed they would inevitably make the same decision he had. This both ignored the ingrained anti-Catholicism of most of his subjects, and was undercut by the actions of his government. A particularly stark contrast to James's reference to Christ's purpose in using physical force was provided in 1686 when the de-frocked Anglican clergyman and persistent critic of the king's government, Samuel Johnson, was brutally whipped through the streets of London. He was reported as shouting 'You whip upon my back Acts of Parliament and the Church of England'.[27] It was this external appearance, rather than James's internal beliefs and published rhetoric that proved such a debilitating force against the king's core goal.

Increasingly frustrated by the intransigence of Tory Anglicans, first in parliament, and then in the English localities, James ultimately undertook a stunning political *volte-face*. In April 1687, he issued a Declaration of Indulgence in England, 2 months after introducing something similar in Scotland. This promised an end to persecution for all recusants and Protestant nonconformists, although James made clear in the declaration that 'We cannot but heartily wish ... that all the people of our dominions were members of the Catholic Church'.[28] Despite being an immense affront to Anglican Tories, James could pursue this use of crown prerogative more persistently than his brother had been able to do in 1672 because of the monarchy's improved finances. Charles had been compelled by penury to recall parliament in 1673; James was wealthy enough to avoid it. But this was still a short-term expedient: all acts of crown prerogative would lapse with James's death. Only a parliamentary repeal of anti-Catholic legislation would provide permanent protection for his co-religionists. To this end James personally interviewed leading ministers and nobles, exerting the immediate pressure of the royal presence, to try and get them to agree in advance to support the repeal of penal legislation in a future parliament. Most refused and were deprived of their offices. Those few who agreed were in turn sent out to influence the local gentlemen who would be a crucial part of the electorate, and who would also provide the majority of MPs. This became known as the 'Three Questions' campaign. Individuals were asked, first, whether if they were elected MPs, they would vote to repeal the Test Acts and penal laws; second, would they work for the election of men to parliament who would act in this way; and, third, whether they supported the king's Declaration of Indulgence. Most either refused point blank to co-operate, prevaricated, or managed to avoid placing themselves in harm's way by not going anywhere near the king and his collaborators. The Essex Tory JP, Sir John Bramston, pursued the last course: 'I would put off the evil day as longe as I can, it beinge a hard thinge to deny the Kinge any thinge; nor would I this if I could yeild obedience with a safe conscience'.[29] Like the fellows of Magdalen College, even the intensely loyal Bramston thus scrupled to obey a royal demand because he felt it would compromise his conscience. As Sir John Reresby, the Governor of York, privately recorded with palpable horror: 'This was indeed putting the thing too farr, and the wonder of all men to what purpas it was done'. He quickly answered his own query by noting that those who refused to reply positively to the questions were turned out of their local offices, especially in the boroughs – which returned four-fifths of all MPs – 'and papists or dissenters putt in their places'.[30] The king was obviously laying the groundwork to pack a future parliament with those prepared to obey him.

This was a profoundly important shift on James's part. Recognising that his old Tory friends would not co-operate in his efforts to re-Catholicise his realms, he comprehensively turned his back on them and aimed to make common cause between Catholics and Protestant dissenters. As the latter had also suffered at the hands of the established church, the king hoped that they would take advantage of his acts of clemency and go along with efforts to establish a wide-ranging liberty of conscience. The balance of evidence suggests that James was overwhelmingly motivated by a narrow desire to improve the lot of Catholics. Despite working relationships with some prominent individual dissenters – notably the Quaker leader, William Penn – James regarded most dissenters during his reign with the same disdain that he had usually displayed in the past. The observant London Presbyterian minister, Roger Morrice, was in no doubt in May 1687 that James hated Presbyterians 'with a perfect hatred, and had rather hang ten Presbyterians then a thousand of the opposite persuasion'.[31] Such suspicions were fanned by Anglican clerics who held out the possibility of some form of Protestant accommodation to keep out popery that would see an end to religious persecution. James's motives were also impugned by a number of influential pamphlets, especially the elegant and cynical *Letter to a Dissenter*. Although anonymously published, this was penned by George Savile, Marquess of Halifax, who slyly suggested that the dissenters were being 'hugged now, only that you may be the better squeezed at another time'.[32]

Even though small numbers of dissenters did co-operate with James's agenda, its whole future was thrown into doubt by wildly contrasting events in June 1688. On 10 June, Mary of Modena, James's Italian Catholic second wife, gave birth to a son, christened James Francis Edward. The queen's pregnancy had been widely known since late 1687, though many clearly doubted the veracity of the news. According to the Lincolnshire diarist Abraham de la Pryme, no one believed the story: 'They say that the Virgin Mary has appear'd to her, and declair'd to her that holy thing shall be born of her shall be a son'.[33] Such scepticism reflected the queen's tragic reproductive record: she had suffered a number of miscarriages and still-births. Small wonder that when a live Prince of Wales appeared, the French-based Commissary-General of the Irish Capuchins responded ecstatically to the news, unconsciously echoing de la Pryme's almost blasphemous account: James's son was 'the Messiah of Great Britain, whose cradle is the tomb of heresy and schism'.[34] James's ambassador at the emperor's court in Vienna, Nicholas Taaffe, Earl of Carlingford, was scarcely less pleased: 'this is so great a Providence that all Christianity is concearned in it'. In words that he must bitterly have regretted by the end of the year, Carlingford went on: 'Now I suppose people will keepe their eyes at home and not send them wandering and will consider that this, amongst the rest, is no small argument that God is with us'.[35]

For sceptical Protestants the arrival of a Prince of Wales – shown in 'England's Memorial' in his mother's arms as part of group 'I', and identified by the ostrich feathers that were his heraldic device – proved nothing of the sort. The chilling possibility that James Francis Edward embodied was of a Catholic succession in perpetuity since the heir to the throne would be surrounded with Jesuits and other priests from infancy. They could no longer confidently wait for the ageing king to die and be succeeded by his Protestant daughter. Far from occasioning joy, the Prince of Wales' birth immediately provoked hostile disbelief and mockery. Despite James's care to have a number of influential figures at the birth to prove the reality of events, a fable that the boy had actually been smuggled into the queen's bed in a warming pan by unscrupulous Catholic plotters rapidly gained credence. When prayers for the prince were read in London churches during a special day of thanksgiving, they were met with silence and then nervous laughter.[36] Even Princess Anne, the king's younger daughter by his first marriage, was scathing about the true nature of her supposed half-brother, and in correspondence with her elder sister made clear that she thought the whole affair was a Catholic plot. Indeed she was never able to bring herself to call the child the Prince of Wales, always referring simply and insultingly to 'it'.[37]

June 1688 had two other claims to be a pivotal month in James's reign. In May, he had re-issued his Declaration of Indulgence in England. This was the trigger for a decisive confrontation with the Church of England as the king also required it to be read from every pulpit in the land on consecutive Sundays. In effect, the established church was being told to broadcast the end of its privileged legal position. After a hasty series of consultations, seven bishops – including the archbishop of Canterbury, William Sancroft – endorsed a petition to the king asking to be excused from this duty, arguing that this use of the royal prerogative had been declared illegal by previous parliaments. When six bishops – Sancroft had fallen under the king's displeasure and been banned from court – presented this petition, James was incredulous. As usual when faced with opposition he chose to interpret the act in the starkest possible light, repeatedly calling the bishops' petition a 'Standard of Rebellion'.[38] Against the advice of many of his ministers, James decided to force the issue at a trial in June, having the bishops prosecuted for seditious libel on the basis that their petition had rapidly appeared in print. Throughout the legal process the bishops received support so overwhelming as to put even Compton's case 2 years earlier in the shade. Whilst awaiting trial the bishops were 'most mightily visited' and 'courted highly by the multitude'. So great were the crowds attending them and asking for their blessing 'that they could scarce get into the Tower' to be imprisoned.[39] At the end of an intensely charged trial in which even the king's secretary of state, the Earl of Sunderland, was treated with 'Great disrespect' in the crowded court room,[40] on 30 June, the bishops secured a 'not guilty' verdict after the usually vigorous judges sat back and allowed the jury free rein. London exploded with celebrations. According to one eye-witness, 'a greater ioy I have not perceived ... these many yeares, & truly I think it is because they suppose the bulk of the protestant religion was much Interrested therein'.[41]

The trial of the seven bishops was an enormously significant setback for James, but it did not alter the basic political situation created by the birth of the Prince of Wales. A Catholic king would now be succeeded by a Catholic heir. The Dutch engraver Romeyn de Hooghe brilliantly linked the two issues in his print *L'epiphane du nouveau Antichrist* (Figure 8). There could not have been a more different perspective from ecstatic Catholic references to a new 'Messiah'. The new 'antichrist' was shown in his cradle, surrounded by Catholic priests. His proud father appears pulling on a rope attached to a toy windmill positioned for the infant prince's amusement above the cradle. The blades of the windmill are clearly constructed from seven mitres, the canonical head-dress of the

Figure 8   Romeyn de Hooghe, *L'epiphane du nouveau Antichrist* (1689). © The Trustees of the British Museum.

seven bishops. Although this work was the product of a foreign propaganda campaign, James's personal popularity within his realms had
rapidly declined as a result of his Catholicising policies. Latent unpop-
ularity was transformed by the Prince of Wales' birth into active plotting.
The third great event of June 1688 occurred on the same day that the
seven bishops were acquitted. Six English lay politicians and one leading
cleric – the suspended bishop of London – sent an 'invitation' to William
of Orange to intervene directly because James had 'greatly invaded' his
subjects' 'religion, liberties and properties'. The 'immortal seven' – who
included both Tories and Whigs – claimed that 'there are nineteen parts
of twenty of the people throughout the kingdom who are desirous of
a change'. But outside military assistance was still vital: 'a protection to
countenance their rising as would secure them from being destroyed
before they could get to be in a posture to defend themselves'.[42] This
was a humiliating admission that the English – and it was very much the
English: no Scots were directly involved – could not save themselves as
James's military forces were now too great to be overcome by the king's
domestic critics alone.[43]

The invitation was an extraordinary response to an extraordinary situation. It had also been specifically solicited by William who desperately
needed to protect his wife's inheritance. Since 1672 he had led the Dutch
Republic's struggle against the military might of Louis XIV, a conflict
William felt was actually about national survival. The Stuart kingdoms
were a strategically vital piece on the European chess-board, one that until
10 June 1688 William could assume would fall, via his wife, into his control
when James died. In the wake of the Prince of Wales' birth he was forced
not only to solicit the 'invitation' from English politicians, but also to send
an embassy to the Holy Roman Emperor, Leopold I, to gain his approval
for an expedition against James. Although a militantly Catholic ruler,
Leopold was partially reliant on Protestant princes for the armed forces
that were now rapidly pushing the Ottoman Turks South-eastward from
their highpoint during the siege of Vienna in 1683. Tensions between
the Empire and France were rife thanks to Louis' aggressive efforts to
secure his eastern border by a series of forced 'reunions' with territories
such as Strasbourg and Luxembourg that he claimed a hereditary right
to inherit. Leopold therefore covertly backed William's plans. The wider
European scene was thus of vital significance for James's fall: if Louis had
not been distracted by the apparent threat posed by a resurgent Holy
Roman Emperor, and if Leopold had not for his own dynastic and strategic purposes endorsed William's invasion as an indirect assault on Louis

XIV, the Prince of Orange would never have been able to launch such a massive invasion effort. The diplomatic and military window of opportunity that opened up in the autumn of 1688 helped William persuade the leading towns of the Dutch Republic – who were normally deeply suspicious of the political agenda of the House of Orange – that it was critical for their long-term interests and safety to invade England and stop the entrenchment of a hostile Catholic regime. It was thus a bizarre combination of Imperial military success in the Balkans, strategic miscalculation by Louis XIV, and Dutch political unity that allowed William to sail a fleet four times the size of the Spanish Armada a 100 years earlier across the English Channel, landing at Torbay in Devon on 5 November 1688, a supremely auspicious day in the English Protestant calendar.[44]

James was aware from late summer that the Dutch were preparing a major military enterprise, but believed up to an astonishingly late stage that this would be directed against the French. He was also slow to realise the extent of the domestic plotting against his regime. Two weeks after William's landing James's regime was shocked to hear that the leading Whig peer in the North-west of England, Lord Delamere, was co-ordinating an armed rising against the Crown: 'this design is laid deeper than at first could be imagined'.[45] Other risings would take place in Yorkshire and in the Midlands. Although militarily far less significant than William's foreign invasion force, and treated with a degree of contempt by the prince,[46] the domestic resistance did not allow James to think that his regime enjoyed the wholesale support of his subjects. Nor would this be the only psychological trauma for James. When he travelled to Salisbury Plain to prepare to lead his troops into battle against William, the king was already weakened by persistent nose-bleeds, itself almost certainly a sign of extreme stress. Then a number of his leading military officers defected to William's army. The final, and heaviest, blow came when James received news that his daughter, Anne, had fled London in order to join rebels in the North.

Having comprehensively lost his nerve and retreated back to London, a period of confused negotiations followed. James despatched three nobles to William's camp whilst increasingly fearing for his own security. What would have been the eventual outcome of a protracted stand-off between William and James will never be known, because in the small hours of 11 December James fled his capital with the intention of going to France, where he had already despatched his wife and son. Failing even to escape properly, James was ignominiously dragged back to London, a severely traumatised man muttering that he had 'a proud city, a foolish Council & a treacherous army to deal with'.[47] Although briefly heartened by his warm reception from a metropolitan crowd anxious about anarchy, James made a more successful second attempt to flee, almost certainly with the connivance of the Prince of Orange. In the power vacuum that he left behind William rapidly gained in stature, refusing to be fobbed off by a queasy English elite with anything less than the crown. After protracted disagreements within a Convention Parliament, it was agreed on 6 February 1689 that William and Mary should be declared king and queen, 4 years to the day since James's accession to the throne.[48] 'Exclusion' had finally been achieved.

Protecting the Present: Honour, Interest, and Conscience

By December 1688, James bitterly argued that William's propaganda had made his reputation 'as black as hell to my own people'.[49] Yet as we have seen, William's intervention was only possible because of a pre-existing crisis of confidence amongst James's subjects. That crisis was the result of the king's inadvertent success in activating powerful social, political, and religious forces which combined the rational and irrational, the intellectual and emotional. In particular, he trespassed on noble and gentry honour codes; appeared to be governing against their interests; and seemed to be trying to force his Protestant subjects to act against the dictates of their consciences.

The correspondence of the Mostyn family, amongst the leading powers in North Wales, illustrates many of these concerns. One of their correspondents reacted to James's three questions campaign in October 1687 by arguing that

> The only danger in human prospect is from o[u]rselves, if we shall be so base & treacherous (any that bears the name of Protestant) to give up o[u]r walls & bulwarks & open them a passage through them – If good subjects are bound to lay down their Arms, I know n[o]t that they are to pull down their fences also . . . God keep us firm in o[u]r Religion & Loyalty.[50]

This was the writing on the wall for James's kingship as he had fashioned it since late 1685. The appeals to 'Religion & Loyalty', the equation of pro-Catholic activity with 'baseness', and the strikingly defensive military metaphor of 'walls & bulwarks' are all immensely revealing about the truculent mindset that the king's actions had fostered. By December 1687, Thomas Mostyn, advised his father to answer all three questions in the negative, 'according to the example of all the Gentlemen of the nation who have unanimously & most generously discharg'd their conscience to God & their duty to their neighbour, & at the same time most wisely done w[ha]t their own Interest & honor ableig'd them to'.[51] The picture was evidently similar elsewhere, and for the same reasons. As the Marquess of Halifax informed the Prince of Orange in September 1687: 'Besides the considerations of conscience, and the publique interest, it is grown into a point of honour, universally receaved by the nation, not to change their opinion, which will make all attempts to the contrary very ineffectuall'.[52] Most nobles and gentry did not want to be seen to sell their religion and church down the river simply to pacify an aggressive king. There is a palpable sense of an unstoppable force meeting an immovable object, or, rather, a king who – like his father – mistakenly believed himself to be an irreplaceable part of the political landscape.

To understand the nature of that clash, it is crucial to consider the extent to which English government was de-centralised, local, and amateur. The king relied on a social pyramid stretching down from leading peers acting as lords lieutenant of counties, through leading gentleman performing the functions of deputy lieutenants and justices of the peace, down to yeomen and merchants undertaking the often arduous offices located within parishes and wards. This very large number of men stood between the king and their own neighbours, and represented a Janus-faced wall of functioning administration. When looking one way, they could choose to explain and enforce the king's will; when looking another, they might represent their localities' anxieties and hopes to the king. As Charles I had discovered during the 1630s, immensely unpopular policies could only be rammed down the throats of local elites for a finite period of time before the weight of obstructionism, sometimes overt, but usually covert, proved overwhelming.

It was for this reason that by December 1687 one observer claimed that soon even those who were co-operating with the king to put the three questions to their fellow countrymen would be forced to admit that the whole campaign was 'a baffl'd fayl'd project'.[53] Men of very different persuasions shared the same descriptive language when it came to discussing James's overall policy of forging an alliance of antithetical groups for the purpose of freeing Catholics. The terms used emphasised the artificiality or foreign-ness of what the king was trying to do. Roger Morrice referred to 'this whole machin' or 'the Machine of their new policies',[54] whilst the Marquess of Halifax was sardonic about 'the great designe'. In his mocking simile,

> to men at a distance, the engine seemeth to moove fast, but by looking neerer, one may see it doth not stirre upon the whole matter, so that here is a rapid motion without advancing a step, which is the only miracle that church [i.e. the Roman Catholic] hath yet shewed to us.[55]

When in the autumn of 1688 James abruptly abandoned this policy in the face of a likely Dutch invasion, one Anglican observer was exultant. The intruded Catholic fellows at Magdalen – the 'late Vermin' – were said to have fled Oxford: 'May all the Legion that pesters the nation be swept again to the sea by the east wind'.[56] The same equation of popery with a foreign 'other' can be seen in 'England's Memorial'. At the bottom right a woman in the crowd of fleeing Catholics exclaims 'Hye for France'. Such visual arguments tapped into a rich vein of early modern iconography that presented a pure Protestant British island separate from a corrupt Catholic continent.

This bitterly hostile language and imagery is hugely important for what it tells us about noble and gentry assumptions in 1688. All office-holders ultimately executed their office for reasons of self-interest. In their different ways, and at their different levels of the governmental chain, everyone expected to derive some form of reward from administrative activity. This might be pecuniary, but was also often a matter of prestige: serving the king conferred honour and lustre on his servants. But this only worked if the king was perceived to be ruling in a politically acceptable fashion. If he was not, then to be associated with him would be seen as anything from unwise to toxic for men who rarely if ever saw the head that wore the crown, but spent their day-to-day lives interacting with their social peers and inferiors. It is certainly striking that James's royal progresses out of London into the English localities in 1686 and 1687 were apparently failures: the nobility and gentry avoided the king and the common people were said to be unimpressed by his lack of 'bounty'.[57] Any English king who was both increasingly unloved by his subjects and who did not perceive the deadweight of this 'unacknowledged republic' of office-holders was skating on very thin ice.[58]

James fell through that ice in 1688 for two reasons. Thanks to the birth of the Prince of Wales, his rule was increasingly seen not just as a temporary form of misgovernment but as a potentially permanent shift in English governance. And despite the deeply ingrained horror felt by most of the elite when it came to notions of resisting authority, James's government could be labelled unlawful and be stopped in its tracks with the aid of help from overseas. When taken together these two factors melded perceptions of the past and fears for the future in a fatally concrete way. Comparisons may be made to the 1650s. Then Oliver Cromwell had briefly experimented with direct military rule of the country through a system of Major Generals. This proved immensely unpopular not just because of English distaste for military force, but also because the nobility and gentry despised the generally low-born men who were appointed to govern them. Although not representing quite such a radical social shift, the imposition of Catholic office-holders in 1687/8 was greeted with similar disdain. In February 1688, the North-western grandee Lord Lovelace was summoned to appear before the Privy Council to explain his offer to wipe his backside with a writ served on him by a Catholic JP.[59]

Kings were titanic figures bestriding the early modern world. But when their writs were valued less for their legal authority than their absorbent qualities things were clearly going badly wrong. By late 1688, James bore some resemblance to the eponymous hero of Jonathan Swift's *Gulliver's Travels*. Shipwrecked in a strange land Gulliver woke to find himself bound helpless with hundreds of tiny cords fastened by the diminutive inhabitants of Lilliput. Although the cords were individually insignificant, they were cumulatively overwhelming. James's subjects did not need cords: thousands of individual failures to co-operate with his agenda achieved much the same end. Ultimately James was simply not up to the demanding role of a seventeenth-century king, and lacked the political skill and imagination to achieve his far-reaching goals. Foreign and domestic contemporaries were in no doubt about the obvious comparison. According to the visiting French diplomat D'Usson de Bonrepaus, James 'has all the faults of the King his father, but he has less sense and he behaves more haughtily in public', while the duke of Lauderdale – one of the canniest analysts of Restoration politics – had earlier described him as having 'all that weakness of his father w[i]thout his strength'.[60] There could be no more damning verdicts than these.

Chapter 6: How Important was the 'British' Dimension to Restoration Political Life?

In the later seventeenth century, as in other periods, the English despised the Scots, the Scots loathed the English, and nobody liked the Irish. (The Welsh were sufficiently beneath contempt that few wits even bothered to mock them.)[1] Yet these generally antipathetic peoples were all ruled by the same kings who had the unenviable task of establishing systems of government strong enough to hold them together. Their record was distinctly chequered. Scotland and Ireland played immensely important roles in the fall of the Stuart monarchy in the 1640s. Scottish armed rebellion from 1639 left Charles I looking dangerously weak, whilst the well-publicised massacres of Protestants by Ulster Catholics in October 1641 further escalated a truly 'British' crisis in which the king was deeply tarnished in many Protestants' eyes by his use of Irish troops. But the Stuarts' non-English kingdoms were also vitally important in restoring them again in 1660. Charles II was proclaimed in Dublin before London, and the military intervention of General George Monck, commander of the New Model Army in Scotland, that ultimately ensured the return of the king was possible because Monck realised the strength of royalist sentiments North of the Border in 1659/60.[2] These basic facts were not lost on Charles or his leading ministers. Nor were the 'British' aspects of the continuing complexities of government in church and state. Since they ruled three kingdoms rather than one, the Stuarts had to interact with Scottish and Irish aristocratic elites, and stood at the apex of the established Churches of Scotland and Ireland. Furthermore, if contemporaries thought historically about the dangers of renewed civil war, and wrestled with ongoing problems of coexistence, it was scarcely surprising that a

100

'British' dimension was also of considerable importance in several of the key political flashpoints and crises during the later Stuart era. A 'three kingdoms' dimension to the Restoration period is, therefore, inevitable: both government and its critics – real and imagined – spanned the two islands of Britain and Ireland.

Despite all of this, a degree of perspective needs to be maintained. 'British' interactions ebbed and flowed over the period, varying in importance as the inhabitants of each of the kingdoms became more or less aware of each other. At the highest level, Charles never deigned to visit Ireland. He was hardly unusual in this – there was no royal visit to Ireland between Richard II and James II, two strikingly unsuccessful monarchs. Charles also despised Scotland after a humiliating coronation service in 1651. On that occasion he had been strong-armed into professing Presbyterian principles he did not remotely feel, and told with great deliberation by the preacher Robert Douglas that 'There are many sinns upon our King and his Family', including 'idolatry'.[3] James's experience of his other kingdoms was greater than his brother's but scarcely happier. A period of exile in Scotland during the Exclusion Crisis had allowed him to make some useful contacts amongst the Scottish aristocratic elite, yet he was always keen to return to the centre of power at court in England where he imagined he could influence Charles. His arrival in Ireland in 1689 came only after he had lost his English throne, and was the result of considerable pressure from his French backers rather than any inherent warmth for the Irish nation. Indeed he showed his deep-seated Englishness by frequent disagreements with the 'Patriot' Parliament that he summoned to Dublin whenever its agenda seemed likely adversely to affect English political opinion.

What if we reverse the perspective and look at how the political nation in Scotland and Ireland regarded their absentee monarchs? The Stuart kings enjoyed substantial potential advantages. Crown largesse could be a significant inducement to key groups in each country. The Scottish aristocracy limped out of the revolutionary period financially poor and intellectually hostile to Presbyterian clerical pretensions that had gained ground in the 1640s. A strong monarch could offer lucrative appointments and protection from meddling Presbyterian ministers. The situation in Ireland was more complicated. Oliver Cromwell's conquest of the island had led to a massive change in landholding with the widespread dispossession of Catholics. After 1660, Catholics persistently looked to the Stuarts to break the Protestant stranglehold on land ownership; Protestants worked at least as hard to hold on to what they knew might be vulnerable to monarchical whim. Recent scholarship has thus emphasised how royalist Scottish intellectual culture was during the Restoration, and also how Irish Gaelic literature offered extravagant praise to a Stuart dynasty regarded by some as enjoying Irish descent and therefore greater legitimacy than the hated Tudors. According to the Irish poet David Ó Bruadair, Charles II was 'my Prince', 'the Prince of the three Kingdoms', and a 'prudent Prince who dearly loves his people'.[4] For their part the members of the Scottish Parliament of 1681 solemnly informed Charles that memories of the civil war period 'dispose all your majesty's subjects to higher measures of loyalty, more particularly in us, in this your ancient kingdom, being sensible as we have a more special interest in your majesty's sacred person and family'.[5] Despite this vigorous deployment of the language of lineage, there is no evidence to suggest that either Charles or James took their responsibilities as kings of Scotland and Ireland remotely as seriously as their English rule. The other kingdoms represented additional titles, potential sources of cash, and frequent headaches.

Furthermore, these rosy pictures of charmed and willingly subservient Scots and Irish can easily be exaggerated. It is hard to discern much love and deference in the Irishman Thomas Morrisey's description of Charles II as 'the old furnicator . . . who changes his wife when he pleases, and imposes soe much taxes on these three Kingedomes merely to maintain his whores and bastards'.[6] Nor was David Spence, the town clerk of Rutherglen in Scotland, much better disposed towards Charles when he failed to observe 29 May – the king's birthday and Restoration day – claiming that he did not give 'a fart' for the king or his birthday.[7] Radical Presbyterians were particularly severe critics of a king they regarded as an oath-breaker for his failure to uphold the Covenant. Some straightforwardly abused him in print as a 'tyrant' intent on reintroducing popery, while others were slightly more allusive when they lumped him together with Charles I and claimed that Scotland, following ancient Israel, 'had 2 bad Kings like Jeroboam', the noxious ruler who had introduced golden calves as objects of worship and pilgrimage.[8] Perhaps unsurprisingly James fared even less well. One perceptive observer of him during his period of Scottish exile between 1679 and 1682 mockingly described him as 'dismal Jimmy'.[9] Even more pungently his obvious English priorities and alleged cowardice in battle led to a slight shift in Ireland away from Ó Bruadair's glowing descriptions. By 1690, he was known to the Gaelic Irish as 'James the shite' ('Séamas an chaca').[10]

Between these extremes of glowing praise and scatological abuse lay a surprisingly broad middle ground of what may best be termed relieved quiescence. Ireland and Scotland had been subjected to total conquest by England during the 1640s and early 1650s. These military humiliations had been given further political shape by enforced union with the English Republic. The Irish and Scottish parliaments had been abolished and a token number of representatives for each former kingdom inserted into an expanded imperial parliament at Westminster, where they were regarded by cynical observers as little more than lobby-fodder for the governments dominated by Oliver Cromwell. After 1660, the parliaments of Ireland and Scotland were recreated, and a degree of political calm returned to the two kingdoms. Ireland in particular prospered economically with exports of goods from the island increasing in value by around 40 per cent between 1665 and 1683.[11] In Scotland the nobility quickly recovered from their temporary displacement as the overwhelmingly dominant force in Scottish political life. Although both kingdoms nevertheless continued to be adversely affected by the dominance of English trading interests, neither produced substantial sustained political problems for the Stuarts, whose occupation of the thrones of Scotland and Ireland seemed for the bulk of the period in question preferable to any likely alternative arrangement.

As this opening survey suggests, to answer the question how significant the 'British' dimension to Restoration political life was requires a degree of historical perspective beyond the immediate period under discussion. Even more than was the case in England memories of the mid-century period and its continuing consequences affected the settlements created in Scotland and Ireland during the early 1660s. They will be the subject of the next part of the chapter, before we turn to pursue their legacies for the Stuarts' triple monarchy during two periods of acute crisis: the Exclusion years at the turn of the 1670s/80s and the reign of James VII & II. In both cases, we will argue that the three kingdoms were bound together by a strong sense of their inextricably connected interests. This was a frightening sense for some; a heartening one for others. At the same time, it would be implausible to claim that the key political event of the period – the overthrow of James from December 1688 – was driven by 'British' concerns. As at other points in the seventeenth century, the Scots and Irish functioned mainly as awkward adjuncts to a ferocious English drama, albeit one given added tension by awareness of events North of the Border and across St. George's Channel.

Restoring Three Kingdoms

Ireland and Scotland were very different polities from England. Underpinning this truism were the immensely powerful forces of distance and devotion, geographical and religious landscapes that had together shaped the structures and assumptions of government. The Highlands and Islands of Scotland, and the North and West of Ireland were remote from metropolitan hubs in a way that even Cornwall and Northumberland were not cut off from London. In the summer of 1540, James V had gone on epic tours of his kingdom, reaching locations as distant as the Orkneys: no other Scottish ruler had proved similarly energetic, most preferring to stick to the Lowland central belt. Ireland remained staggeringly unknown to most English administrators whose activity was largely confined to a 'Pale' of land around Dublin. As late as 1690, William III sourly noted that when he went to re-conquer Ireland from James he would be 'as it were out of the knowledge of the world'.[12] Thanks to devolved systems of justice that English professional lawyers never tired of ridiculing, Irish and, especially, Scottish landowners enjoyed tremendous local power. Furthermore, a Gaelic world that spanned the two kingdoms was linguistically and culturally alien to English-speakers, and usually regarded as barbaric at best and often downright disobedient.

Problems of understanding distant territories and their customs were common to many of the multiple or 'composite' monarchies – *monarquia* – of early modern Europe.[13] The Stuarts were far from alone in struggling to understand the hopes and fears of local elites, the successful manipulation of which was nevertheless vital for absentee monarchs overwhelmingly based in South-east England. Another common problem facing many rulers of European *monarquia* was that of extracting the resources that were in turn necessary to maintain dominion over multiple territories. In this sphere a number of monarchs had been successful in subverting the link between national representative assemblies and taxation. Whether called diets, estates general, or another linguistic relic of the middle ages, these 'points of contact'[14] between rulers and ruled proved fragile in the early modern period when a combination of able rulers and developing state bureaucracies facing up to the increasing cost of war led to their disappearance or emasculation. Kings and princes achieved a more aggressive deployment of their prerogative rights, justifying the changes by a combination of divine right discourse and more secular appeals to 'reason of state', often under the alarmingly vague shorthand of 'necessity'. This was a trend that the Stuarts' subjects were familiar with and, particularly in England, obsessively keen to avoid.[15] The initial auguries for Scotland and Ireland seemed good: 1661 saw the return of parliaments summoned by the king in both countries. No efforts were made to continue the Cromwellian experiment of a single imperial parliament based in London. In the early 1660s, policies of intense centralisation were discredited both by association with the republican past, and seemed politically uncongenial to Charles. Given the right management, three separate assemblies might have been more biddable and less prone to shows of opposition to crown policies than one.

In Scotland something not too dissimilar to the Cavalier Parliament in England in terms of the youth and loyalty of its members was elected after careful management in the localities. Early legislative activity proved highly satisfactory to the Crown in two crucial areas: negotiating memories of the recent past, and negotiating a financial settlement for the future. A sweeping Act Rescissory (1661) annulled the proceedings of the 'pretended parliaments' of the Covenanting regime from 1640 to 1648, whilst decrying 'the madness and delusion of these times'.[16] This undid the aggressive constitutional advances of the 1640s, and signalled a distinct 'retreat from revolution'.[17] In the place of the now discredited National Covenant, the Scottish Parliament trumpeted its loyalty to the Crown via a raft of acts in early 1661 promoting the royal prerogative. This was entrenched with regard to the king's choice of officers, lawmaking, and the militia, all cemented by an act requiring the taking an oath of allegiance and assertion of the prerogative.[18] No opportunity was missed to attempt to recalibrate the nation's memory through legislative means. Acts decried the Covenant, condemned the Covenanters' decision to hand over Charles I to the English Parliament in 1647, approved the Engagement that had seen the Scots attempt to restore Charles I in 1648, and instituted a 'solemn anniversary thanksgiving' for the real Restoration that had redeemed Scotland from 'slavery and bondage' in 1660.[19] Defying national stereotypes, the Scots also bestowed what they considered to be a generous annual revenue on Charles, amounting to £40,000 sterling.[20] Small wonder that the king's chief minister in England, the Earl of Clarendon, wanted to publish the Scottish legislation South of the Border as an encouragement to the Parliament there.[21] This would not be the last time that the Stuart regime thought to use Scottish and Irish examples to influence English opinion.

The Restoration in Ireland was both more and less complicated. The Irish Parliament differed from the unicameral Scottish equivalent by having two chambers, directly mirroring the Houses of Commons and

Lords in the English Parliament. In terms of legislation and powers the Irish Parliament was encumbered less by an embarrassingly precocious Covenanting period during the 1640s than by much older legislation dating from the late fifteenth and mid sixteenth centuries which subordinated Irish constitutional arrangements to the agenda of the English Crown.[22] One consequence of this was that the Irish Parliament had a less highly developed sense of its own distinct identity and status than was the case in Scotland. If this contributed to a weaker and less complicated institution, the Irish Parliament's priorities were also shaped by different imperatives from those that existed in Scotland. Noble members of the Scottish Parliament were keen to expunge memories of the Covenanting period when their own control had been challenged. In Ireland the solidly Protestant Parliament had to take into account the fact that it was during the 1650s that a sweeping redistribution of land out of Catholic hands had taken place at the point of a sword. Before the Irish massacres of 1641, Catholics may have owned around two-thirds of the profitable land in Ireland; after the Cromwellian redistribution this may have fallen to little more than one-twentieth.[23] A simple annulment of all political activity over the previous two decades would thus have risked returning lands to their previous Catholic owners and been tantamount to economic and social suicide.

Irish affairs therefore became subsumed in attempts to create a land settlement, one that would also have to take into account Charles's well-known desire to compensate those loyal Catholics who had fought for his father. The Acts of Settlement and Explanation (1662 and 1665, respectively) became regarded by Protestants as Ireland's equivalent in importance of England's Magna Carta,[24] though as events proved this remained a vulnerable and muddled achievement. A combination of covert purchases by Catholic landowners retrieving their estates after the Cromwellian degradations and Charles's (limited) favour resulted in Catholic landholding rising by 1675 to an estimated 29 per cent of Ireland.[25] Even in the last years of Charles II's reign, 20 years after these acts, great excitement was triggered in Ireland by the creation of roving commissions for defective titles designed to adjudicate on who had the right to claim ownership of parcels of land. This process remained incomplete at the time of Charles's death in 1685. Of more immediate importance to the Crown was the fact that during its lifespan of 1661–6 the Irish Parliament also voted no fewer than 32 subsidies, equivalent to around £360,000.[26] Although initially blunted by economic depression, in the latter part of Charles's reign Ireland became a substantial net contributor to the Stuarts' coffers with annual tax revenues more than doubling between 1664/5 and 1684.[27]

By the mid 1660s, Scotland and Ireland had thus resumed their pre-Cromwellian positions as separate but linked component parts of a wider *monarquia*. Parliaments had been re-established and accommodations made with the recent past, albeit very different ones. Substantial sums of money had been voted to the Crown, and Charles's prerogative powers resoundingly endorsed. Overall the king seemed fairly successful in transcending the problems of multiple monarchy in so far as they extended to interacting with distant elites and extracting financial resources. But a third and critical problem common to rulers of *monarquia* in Europe was that of finding a peaceful means of dealing with religious differences. Here an essentially medieval mindset that emphasised the need for unity within a polity was difficult to square with the realities of post-Reformation religious division. By the later seventeenth century previous efforts to create political frameworks that would allow Protestants and Catholics to coexist within confessionally divided states were breaking down. Both the Holy Roman Emperor, Leopold I, and the French King, Louis XIV, were known to be hostile to non-Catholics, and their increasingly strong political and military positions cast a deepening pall over European Protestantism.

When they are set against such a dire backdrop, it is scarcely surprising that the later Stuarts' sternest test proved to be managing the consequences of religious divisions within and between their kingdoms. In Ireland they faced a population that was overwhelmingly Catholic, albeit divided between different factions that mapped onto European-wide divisions between those friendly or hostile to unrestrained papal (ultramontane) power. In Scotland a far more successful sixteenth-century Protestant Reformation had nevertheless failed to eradicate a stubborn Catholic world in the Highland zone. More significantly, conflicting agendas between kirk (church) and crown from the 1590s onwards had led to severe intra-Protestant conflicts over church governance. For Presbyterians there was simply no scriptural warrant for a separate and superior order of bishops, and any attempt to bring back such an order could be seen as an unacceptable return to the reviled pre-Reformation Catholic past. Both James VI and Charles I had nevertheless acted to increase their own power and influence within the kirk, particularly via the slow re-introduction of bishops dependent on royal appointment and favour. Charles's inept attempts to go further than this and use bishops as the means to introduce liturgical changes many Scots abominated as popishly tainted English-style innovations provided the spark that lit the powder-keg underneath his triple monarchy. Kings of Scotland and Ireland were also very aware of the interactions and connections between those two realms. The straits between South-western Scotland and Ulster were insufficiently daunting to deter a lively two-way traffic between both Gaelic Catholics and Presbyterians. The potential outcomes of interchanges that were so difficult to regulate haunted local governors in Dublin and Edinburgh who were only too aware that real power resided in London and that this could impede decisive or consistent action.

In both realms Charles II opted to support the return of episcopacy, not least as a means of bolstering his own hierarchical control over the established churches. In Ireland this happened exceptionally quickly, partly because of the important legislative quirk that the Church of Ireland had never been formally abolished, and partly because of the zeal of returning clerics. January 1661 saw a magnificent mass consecration of new bishops and archbishops in St. Patrick's Cathedral, Dublin. The political messages were literally sung out loud in an ecstatic anthem in which the trebles called: 'Now that the Lord hath re-advanc'd the Crown;/Which Thirst of Spoyle, and frantic zeal threw down'; and the tenors responded, 'Now that the LORD the Miter hath restor'd/Which, with the Crown, lay in the dust abhorr'd'; before a chorus of

Angels look down, and Joy to see
Like that above, a Monarchie.
Angels look down, and Joy to see
Like that above an Hierarchie.[28]

This was all very well, but the Church of Ireland continued to face a long-term opponent, as well as a formidable new one. The bulk of the Irish population remained stubbornly Catholic, as did many of the country's most influential peers. It would thus be impracticable to introduce the full gamut of anti-Catholic legislation enacted by the Cavalier Parliament in England, and a blind eye had very frequently to be turned to Catholic activity. This did not preclude a good deal of hand-wringing amongst ministers of the established Church of Ireland: as one complained to the bishop of Derry in 1682, the Catholic clergy 'are indefatigably industrious in all those methods that subtility and malice can suggest to effect the ruin of our poor afflicted Zion'.[29]

Yet more acutely troubling to the Dublin government were the activities of Protestant dissenters, particularly Presbyterians in Ulster of Scottish origin. In many parts of the North, Presbyterians outnumbered adherents of the Church of Ireland and posed formidable problems to local bishops. This was partly due to their exceptional capacity to create local, self-supporting networks that would by 1690 emerge as a general synod.[30] But it was also the result of the proximity of an aggressive and disenchanted group of Covenanting Presbyterians close by in South-west Scotland. A poisonous cocktail of Scottish legislation asserting the Crown's supremacy over the church, the re-introduction of bishops, and attacks on the Covenant led by 1663 to the deprivation of around 270 Presbyterian ministers, or between a quarter and a third of the whole clerical body in Scotland (a significantly greater proportion than were displaced in England in 1662: see Chapters 1–2). Those who were unprepared to accommodate themselves to the Restored church were especially concentrated in the South-west: 34 of the 37 ministers in Galloway, for instance, left the church.[31] Such men were often protected by a fractious local gentry. In 1666, the Pentland Rising showed the danger this powerful mix could pose. The Earl of Rothes bitterly claimed that with a few exceptions the gentry of the west would 'joayn with Turcks to feaght against the king and his guffernment'.[32] Although an exaggerated view, the fanaticism of relatively small numbers of people could nevertheless create chronic problems of governance. To an even greater extent than had proved to be the case in England, the return of bishops had signalled the theoretical triumph of the Crown's agenda, whilst exacerbating pre-existing religious tensions and divisions that would motivate men to take extreme and destabilising actions.

Scotland, Ireland, and the Exclusion Crisis

Chapter 3 analysed the extent to which England during the 1670s became riven with political divisions. These were the product of closely intertwined religious and secular issues, in particular disputes over the politics of religion and the activities and style of the king and his government. These issues were writ large in Scotland and Ireland thanks to the nature of the Restoration settlements described above which left tremendously difficult legacies centring on fears of popery and 'fanaticism'. The unfolding administration of the settlements also led to acute anxieties about the role of the government's senior representatives in Scotland and Ireland. These factors influenced English political affairs, and presented the Stuarts with problems and opportunities arising from multiple monarchy. But if ruling three kingdoms initially made the Exclusion Crisis in England more severe, ultimately it would also help Charles to extricate himself from a dire political hole.

The controversial political dominance of the Earl of Danby during the 1670s was an important factor promoting discord within England. Danby's position was, however, comparatively benign when compared to the government of his Scottish ally John Maitland, second Earl and Duke of Lauderdale. A pillar of the Covenanter governments before the Restoration, Lauderdale had demonstrated his immense abilities as a ruthless politician by sensing the way the wind was blowing in 1659–60 and jumping onto the ship of state marked 'monarchy'. Although a significant player in Scottish affairs from the earliest years of the Restoration, it was in the later 1660s that Lauderdale emerged as unquestionably the dominant voice in Scottish politics. This was achieved through monopolising the channels of access to Charles in London: the king would only hear Lauderdale's versions of events. His dominance also came through the ability to satisfy the king's demands for Scotland, which usually meant simply keeping it quiet. This he achieved through a mixture of intimidating his enemies, oppressing extreme Covenanters, and conciliating those who could help him. Lauderdale's government of Scotland became sufficiently all-encompassing for him to be criticised as 'ane deputy king'.[33] He consistently pursued policies that furthered the royal prerogative in Scotland both in church and state, and was careful to broadcast his success to his royal master. Such policies invariably involved advancing the powers of the re-established Church of Scotland, especially inserting members of a generally pliant episcopal bench into the heart of Scottish government. Even though these bishops were only a pale shadow of their English counterparts in terms of wealth and power, Lauderdale's use of them was still more controversial in Scotland than Danby's close alliance with the church hierarchy South of the Border. For hard-line Presbyterians their very existence was a dire throwback to pre-Reformation popery; for aristocratic critics of the church their employment smacked of using servile clerics to undermine the nobility's importance in government.

This was particularly the case in parliament. As this consisted of only one chamber, the readmission of bishops as the first estate in 1662 immediately substantially increased the likely number of crown supporters. Even more significantly, the following year saw an act inserting eight bishops into the powerful committee steering the legislative agenda of parliament, the lords of the articles. Lauderdale was able to write to Charles that 'nothing can come to the parliament but through the articles, and nothing can pass in articles but what is warranted by his majestie, so that the king is absolute master in parliament both of the negative and affirmative'.[34] Over time he would be able to present Charles with the same boasts in connection with church government. In 1669, the Supremacy Act ensured the untrammelled triumph of the royal prerogative within the Church of Scotland: from this time Charles could not only appoint bishops and ministers, but also deprive or move them at will. As Lauderdale told Charles, the act 'makes you Soveraigne in the Church' and 'never was [a] King so absolute as yow are in poor old Scotland'.[35] As an exceptionally learned man Lauderdale should have remembered the lessons of classical literature: hubris would always be followed by nemesis. This duly arrived both within Scotland and without: indeed Lauderdale's achievement was to drive malcontents in both kingdoms to form common cause, exactly the nightmare scenario Charles had originally sought to avoid by disentangling the three kingdoms after 1660. Within Scotland Lauderdale faced increasing parliamentary opposition to his arrogant style of rule. The culture of Scottish politics dictated that this opposition took the form of a discontented group cohering around a senior aristocrat, in this case the Duke of Hamilton, who from 1673 contrived to make governing parliament a much harder task than earlier in the reign.[36] As well as being dominated by the aristocracy, the nature of Scottish society also tended to promote religious dissatisfactions. Lauderdale's repressive policies, particularly the quartering of a 'Highland Host' of Catholics on the recalcitrant western shires in 1678, provoked armed rebellion by Covenanters. Only a substantial royal army led by Charles's eldest illegitimate son, the Duke of Monmouth, succeeded in quelling the insurrection that culminated at Bothwell Brig in 1679.

This rising had serious 'British' dimensions beyond Scotland. Lauderdale's brutality was all grist to the mill of the leading English Whig peer, the Earl of Shaftesbury. Alienated from his former ally within the Cabal ministry over the course of the 1670s by Lauderdale's high-handed interference in English government, Shaftesbury fell with relish on news of the 'Highland Host'. It reinforced all of his alarmist rhetoric about the dangers of 'popery and arbitrary government'. This was not just a distant European phenomenon; it was also a daily part of life within the island of Britain. As Shaftesbury put it in a famous speech in the House of Lords during the debates surrounding the first Exclusion Bill in March 1679:

Popery and slavery, like two little sisters, go hand in hand, and sometimes one goes first, sometimes the other; but wheresoever the one enters, the other is always following close at hand. In England, popery was to have brought in slavery; in Scotland, slavery went before, and popery was to follow.[37]

This view of Lauderdale as a kind of miniature Louis XIV with a thick accent was probably furthered by links between the Scottish chief minister's domestic critics, and 'country' critics of the court in England.[38] Its significance for the king was that his Scottish satrap was no longer able to keep the Northern realm quiet. In political terms, Monmouth's military triumph and subsequent tact in working to defuse tensions in the west of Scotland without undue brutality buffed up his credentials for government, projecting him as a plausible Protestant successor to Charles should James suffer the ultimate indignity of being excluded from the throne. James was certainly anxious enough to work successfully to prevent Monmouth's despatch to Ireland as chief governor: such a prominent position would have increased his status to dangerous levels.

Bothwell Brig also played its part in a broader trend of Ireland becoming more firmly integrated into a wider political crisis. Although this was unsurprising bearing in mind the island's frequently turbulent relations with Britain, it went against recent history. Ireland had seen a period of remarkable calm during the 1660s and 1670s, one that was partly the product of the growing economic prosperity noted above. It was also due to what could be characterised by a friendly observer as the masterly inactivity of government. The Lord Lieutenant of Ireland from 1662–9, and again from 1677–84/5, was James Butler, Duke of Ormond. Ireland's premier peer, life-long Stuart servant, and by an order of magnitude the realm's largest landowner, Ormond was an emollient figurehead for government. Pragmatically convinced of the folly of persecuting the Catholic majority, and bound by marriage alliances to many of the leading Catholic peers, Ormond sought to maintain the powers of the lord lieutenancy to ensure both his own status and the continued employment of his policies. Like so many other chief governors of Ireland, however, Ormond was removed from office in 1669 as a result of factional struggles at court in England; this time as a result of the continued fall-out from the political demise of his friend and ally Clarendon.[39] Until his reinstatement in 1677, Ireland was governed by a series of men who lacked the local status to be more effective or secure in their position than Ormond, and who increasingly found themselves subordinated to ministers and administrators in London. This was particularly the case in regard to finance, with Charles readily accepting bribes from shady farmers of the Irish revenues who were motivated by private profit rather than public accountability. It seems likely that even after his return to office in 1677 Ormond was never again the towering figure that his voluminous surviving correspondence might suggest. Ireland by the later 1670s and 1680s was bound into an administrative system in which the English treasury called the shots according to an agenda set by Charles in which a premium was placed on extracting monetary resources from Ireland to bolster his rule elsewhere.[40]

The Bothwell Brig rebellion upset this period of quiet by showing up both the potential dangers of Covenanting connections between Scotland and Ireland, and the inadequacies of government. According to the Ulster-based but Scottish-born Presbyterian minister Robert Landess, 'the noise of Bothwell in Scotland occasiond a great consternation in all Ireland'. It also led to an influx of Scottish refugees, most of whom Landess was at pains to record 'shelterd peaceablie in Ireland'. Nevertheless, even he ruefully noted that, 'alas not a few of them with tharr Imprudent Zeall wer instrumentall in sowing discord amongst bretheren and therby occasiond Many unprofitable debats to the great greiff of the presbyterian Ministers and these of the people that wer solid and Judicious'.[41] Such unwelcome migrations were difficult for the Dublin-based government to control, not least because the full panoply of anti-dissenter legislation that had been put on the statute books in England was not replicated in Ireland. Presbyterians took advantage of the absence of an English-style Corporation Act to play a significant part in town governance, even at the heart of the Pale in Dublin. In 1672, this prompted the splenetic chief governor, Lord Berkeley, to remove seven Presbyterian aldermen who allegedly opposed the regulation of the corporation in such a way that would have reduced the city 'to more monarchical principles than their present constitution allowed of'.[42] Although a biased picture, the basic thesis that Protestant dissenters were more likely to be disobedient than Catholics was one that deeply informed Ormond's world view when he returned to the Irish viceroyalty from 1677. Nevertheless, he was only too well aware of the limited resources available to the Irish government, wearily noting that without a sustained campaign to make their lives difficult, dispersing dissenters' meetings 'is no better than scattering a flock of crows that will soon assemble again, and possibly it were better to let them alone, than to let them see the impotence of the government, upon which they will presume'.[43]

Such a preoccupation with dissenters, and apparent lack of interest in Catholic activity (including that of those clergy he regarded as well-affected to the government) was bound to rouse the ire of critics in England. Having lambasted the 'slavery' that Lauderdale imposed on Scotland, Shaftesbury also bitterly described Catholic Ireland as 'the snake which we harboured in our bosom and warmed it...when it could scarcely live'.[44] English Whigs increasingly appealed to long-standing anxiety that Ireland could complete the 'Counter-Reformation encirclement'[45] of Britain by Catholic powers in order to feed fears stoked by the Popish Plot revelations. Such fears were fanned by zealous Irish Protestants like Roger Boyle, Earl of Orrery, formerly a leading Cromwellian governor of Scotland and a key member of the 'New English' interest.[46] These seventeenth-century arrivals in Ireland had perforce to rely on English dominance of the island to maintain their political position and landholding against both the Gaelic Irish and the 'Old English', those who had arrived between the first medieval Anglo-Norman incursions into Ireland and the sixteenth century. So it was with a mixture of self-interest and genuine anxiety that Orrery claimed that if Louis XIV invaded Ireland, he would rapidly be able to attract willing recruits to the tune of 20,000 men annually to the French armies. This manpower could then be combined with the island's strategic importance and excellent ports to allow him to 'distroy the traffick of the westerne world'. Worse still, if Louis took a hand in fomenting trouble in Scotland, he could use an Irish base 'and the English would then have but too much work cut out for them at home'.[47]

Such fears for the future found support in the atrocious past of Ireland. Accounts of the massacres of October 1641 were reprinted during the Exclusion Crisis, their obscene, almost pornographic, accounts of extreme violence perpetrated by Catholics on Protestants intended as a dire reminder of what could recur under a Catholic monarch. The author of one such tract in 1678 informed his readers that at Kilkenny in 1641 a Scottish Protestant man was 'stript and hewed to pieces' whilst the Catholics responsible then 'ript up his Wifes Belly, so that her Child drop out; many other Women they hung up with child, ript their Bellies and let their Infants fall out; some of the children they gave to Dogs'. In Sligo 'these Hell-hounds laid the dead naked bodies of the Men upon the naked bodies of the Women, in a most immodest posture; where they left them till the next day to be looked upon by the Irish, who beheld it with great delight'. At Portadown Bridge 'one fat man they murthered and made Candles of his grease'.[48] This kind of lurid commentary provided a promising backdrop to Shaftesbury's industrious efforts to solicit 'evidence' of a popish plot in Ireland to restore flagging interest in this crucial underpinning of the Exclusion era in England during 1680–1. He was helped by Ormond's Catholic connections and obvious indolence when it came to suppressing Catholic activity in the island. To those so inclined to make the effort, Lauderdale's use of Catholic Highlanders to crush the Covenanters and Ormond's loose hold on the reins of government in Ireland could be stitched together and made to look like part of a wider pro-popish patchwork. By 1681, the English government propagandist Edmund Warcup argued that it would be prudent to organise prosecutions for conspiracy over the allegations of an Irish plot. In his view this would 'ease the minds of Loyall People from feares and Jealousies fomented by Phanaticks'.[49]

As Warcup's words suggest, both the government and its critics were alive to the sense in which events within the three kingdoms interacted and served at a time of crisis to exacerbate fears and tensions. But they also show how an enterprising government could seek to use Scotland and Ireland to assist its efforts within England to defeat the Whig exclusionist threat. As early as 1679, tracts sought to bolster Ormond's image as a vigilant and loyal supporter of the Stuart interest in Ireland, partly as a means of lessening English fears. According to one author, all had to confess that the duke 'hath been . . . firm in all turns to the Protestant Cause'. Adopting the guise of a financially disgruntled speculator in Irish lands who had belatedly come to realise the error of his ways, the author was unequivocal that in Ireland 'Things are . . . in full Peace and Plenty', going on to make his case with the aid of government documents to which he conveniently had access.[50] The message was clear: Englishmen should not jump at shadows, or phantoms created for cynical purposes by ambitious Whigs. In more concrete terms, Irish revenues were increasingly valuable to the Crown, which was by 1681 able to play another trump card, that of a loyal Scottish Parliament specifically designed to emphasise the selfish disloyalty of some English peers and MPs. After three Exclusion Bills had been debated South of the Border, Charles was careful to appoint James as High Commissioner to the Scottish Parliament that sat during the summer of 1681. No longer irked by a powerful Lauderdale, whose influence had been broken after Bothwell Brig, this very loyal assembly passed on 28 July 'An Act acknowledging and asserting the right of succession to the imperial crown of Scotland' that clearly showed the Scots' horror at Exclusionist activity in England. In words that could scarcely have been a more pointed criticism of their Southern counterparts, members of the Scottish Parliament proclaimed that 'the kings of this realm deriving their royal power from God Almighty alone, do succeed lineally thereto, according to the known degrees of proximity in blood, which cannot be interrupted, suspended or diverted by any act of statute whatsoever'. Driving the point home further, they starkly noted that 'no difference in religion' was remotely relevant to the question of the succession.[51] The very same day Parliament made 'An Act for a voluntary offer of a new supply to the king's majesty' that gave a minor but still welcome fillip to crown finances.[52] Even more aggressively, members attacked Covenanters head-on with 'An Act anent religion and the Test' which forced all office-holders to acknowledge that the king was 'the only supreme governor of this realm' – harking back to the controversial 1669 Supremacy Act – and to swear that 'I judge it unlawful for subjects, upon pretence of reformation or any other pretence whatsoever, to enter into covenants or leagues', before specifically disavowing the National Covenant.[53] Both the splendour of the opening of this parliament and its proceedings made an impression on the 'great many gentlemen ... from the north of England' who attended James in Scotland.[54] Members of the Stuarts' diplomatic core in Europe carefully distributed news of it, with the envoy in Amsterdam going so far as to have the Acts translated into Dutch and French to influence local opinion, while his counterpart in Berlin piously hoped that news of 'the Compliance of the Parliament in Scotland' would 'alter the ill opinion' that the courts of Germany had previously had of Charles's affairs: 'I hope so good and dutifull an example will contribute very much towards procuring the same success in England'. Writing from Brussels, Sir Richard Bulstrode hoped that the good news from Scotland 'will break the Measures of those who flattered themselves with a Support from that Kingdom'.[55]

In some part it did. Radical Whig plotters had indeed hoped for support from discontented Scots; a theme the government carefully publicised as part of its wider revelation of the foiled Rye House Plot in the summer of 1683 to assassinate Charles and James. This plot seemed to justify an increasingly integrated approach to government and its ongoing security, not least since tendrils of the Plot apparently extended beyond England. But the scare also created renewed anxiety over the succession. Although heavily implicated in the Rye House Plot, Monmouth briefly catapulted to higher favour than ever before when he agreed – under heavy pressure from Charles – to sign a declaration affirming the reality of that plot against those Whigs who desperately attempted to rubbish it for their own purposes. This temporarily gave heart to James's critics in Scotland – particularly those who objected to the severity of his persecution of Presbyterian covenanters – whilst in Ireland one Henry Shrimpton was indicted at the 1683 assizes in Clonmel 'for sayeing that the Duke of Monmouth should succeede after his Ma[jes]ties and Reigne as King, or else noe King at all', while John Pryor was bound over 'for sayeing that he hoped his Royall Highn[e]ss should never be King whilst his Ma[jes]tie and the Duke of Monmouth Live'.[56] Political realities were, however, soon reversed with Monmouth's ultimate disgrace following inevitably on from his final denials of any role in the plot, and James's consequent unchallenged status as heir apparent.

Charles II's success in seeing off the Exclusionist threat has often been seen as a sign of the submerged political cunning that he rarely raised above the waterline. This had required his government to overcome hostile forces in Scotland and also to defuse fears about Catholic activity in Ireland. But most importantly of all, Charles's success had shown how Scotland and Ireland could ultimately be used like stabilisers on the bicycle of Stuart government when English politics wobbled dangerously. Yet this proved to be a temporary achievement. Failing to understand that these additional supports were based on the self-interest of his leading Scottish and Irish subjects, James would succeed only in creating punctures which he lacked the necessary skill to repair.

The Reign of James VII and II

James ultimately lost his thrones because of a fatal combination of widespread English disaffection and a Dutch invasion (see Chapter 5). Ireland and Scotland's role in that breakdown of authority was not crucially significant. Nevertheless, James's Northern and Western kingdoms played their parts in the fatal alienation of the English from their monarch, and in the extended fall-out from 1688. James's government in Scotland ripped away the diaphanous veil of loyalty that members of the parliament of 1681 had drawn over their affairs, pretending that religious impediments would never sully their attachment to the lineal successor. In reality most Scots, far more even than the English, hated Catholics; the whole dynamic of their history since the violent Reformation of 1559–60 that overthrew Mary Queen of Scots pointed towards a vehement Protestantism. And although the Catholic majority in Ireland could be expected to welcome a co-religionist to the throne, this would only make the king's task harder when it came to reassuring his Protestant subjects, both those within the Church of Ireland, and those worshipping in other denominations. The Protestant sinews of government in both kingdoms suffered extraordinary strains under James, only to snap back into place with renewed force in 1689.

James was proclaimed King of Ireland in the borough of Trim on 19 February 1685, 'with Loyall hearts and Cheerefull Voyces'.[57] The optimism of this formal account in the official assembly book was mirrored – tinged with surprise – in private correspondence. According to a member of the New English Boyle family, 'Everybody is planting, improving and trading as much as at any time in the last 7 years which is a disappointment to some who did not expect to see the King proclaimed with such genuine joy and conformity'.[58] As in England, James sought to reassure anxious observers through his early appointments, with Protestant Lords Justices given the task of governing Ireland. No parliament was called, but as none had sat since 1666 this did not appear a glaring change of direction. Nevertheless, James's policies for Ireland were rapidly to excite tremendous fears amongst Protestants there, and a widespread dread throughout the three kingdoms that the Catholic majority of the western island would soon be used to overawe Britain. This owed a great deal to James's disastrous friendship with Richard Talbot, a scion of one of the powerful Old English Catholic families, whose bluff manner and military exploits brought him to the attention of a prince rarely interested in refined subtlety. Created Earl of Tyrconnell, Talbot pursued a vigorous and highly contentious policy of Catholicising Ireland's government. Although it will remain forever open to question whether he intended this as a precursor to an independent Irish kingdom should James die without a Catholic successor, the impact of his drive to transform the civil and, especially, military government of Ireland was profound.[59] Despite occasional bursts of alarmist rhetoric, Irish Protestants had generally been complacent about their ability to suppress any Catholic insurrection since they occupied a dominant presence in town governments across the kingdom, and a near monopoly of armed force. Tyrconnell shattered such cosy assumptions. After a period of acting as the real power behind the viceregal throne occupied by the hapless Henry Hyde, second Earl of Clarendon, Tyrconnell, arrived to govern Ireland in person without further pretence in February 1687, his landfall greeted by massive crowds of people and coaches full of the politically prominent who were eager to ingratiate themselves with James's favourite.[60]

Labelled 'Turk-conel' by hostile Protestant observers, Tyrconnell's dictatorial government rapidly raised acute fears.[61] In Ireland these centred on the land settlement. Would the Acts of Settlement and Explanation finally be broken and land returned *en bloc* to Catholics? Despite intensive lobbying, even James realised that this would be a supremely controversial measure and one liable to create panic in England. Real anxieties were, however, already growing beyond Ireland, not least as a result of the 'exodus' of frightened Irish Protestants to Britain.[62] According to the English Presbyterian minister Roger Morrice, 'great multitudes' left Ireland under Tyrconnell, indeed by May 1687 'Very many, even the most Protestants that have or can raise any personall Estate are come [to England from] thence'.[63] What the leading statistician and projector Sir William Petty had once called 'the Internal and Mystical Government of Ireland' – the concealed bulk of Catholics, not least priests – was now opened up for all to see: 'the Vale [i.e. veil] is almost of[f] and now we see what is aimed at'. Increasingly doom-laden providentialist rhetoric saturated Protestant discourse in Ireland: 'God Help us to bear all things patiently'; 'God direct us'; 'Gods will be done'. By summer 1688, one Cork resident told a friend in England that 'all we can doe is to pray and drink your health and all thos that will remember the poor English of Ireland'.[64] Total Protestant oblivion seemed to be the end goal of Tyrconnell's policies, with the rapid return of Catholics to all levels of government – including the judiciary – and the wholesale change of town corporations. Having been extensively used in England to break the local power of Whigs within town governments after 1681, Tyrconnell readily utilised the writ of *quo warranto*, a legal device asking 'by what right' a corporate body enjoyed its privileges. In Ireland no fewer than 109 such writs were issued in short order from the Exchequer in the spring of 1687. As one unfriendly Anglo-Irish Protestant observer, the Earl of Burlington, argued, 'it is resolved to overthrow all the charters'.[65] New charters allowed the central government to insert large numbers of men from outside the old charmed circle of Church of Ireland Protestants. It was assumed that this wave of interference was directed towards ensuring the return of a pliant parliament that would do Tyrconnell's bidding.

Nothing on quite this scale happened in Scotland. But the political nation was both aware of developments in Ireland and exposed to the brunt of the new king's Catholicising agenda. Misled by the extravagant loyalism of the 1681 parliament, James issued an unprecedentedly extensive set of 41 instructions for those managing the first parliament of his reign in 1685, confident that his Northern subjects would willingly obey him.[66] To some extent this view had received support from the striking lack of backing that the Earl of Argyll found for his cause when he invaded the west of Scotland in May 1685. Indeed his failure proved even greater than that of Monmouth's near parallel invasion of England since Argyll's regional power in the western shires had been proverbial before his political disgrace and escape into exile in 1681 after failing to take without reservations the Test enacted by parliament. Nevertheless, the politics of religion would quickly come to upset the king's complacent plans in Scotland, largely as a result of three closely interconnected issues. First, the phrasing of the 1681 Test had been convoluted to the point of inconsistency. Argyll proved only the most socially significant of a large swathe of Scots who felt they could not take the Test without compromising their Presbyterian principles and commitment to the kirk as it had emerged since the 1560s. The government's rigorous attempts to enforce compliance with regional commissions to investigate the recalcitrant succeeded mainly in maintaining a high political temperature in the localities, even if it did exclude a number of potential trouble-makers from the 1685 parliament.

The second issue undermining the king's government in Scotland was that of the men to whom James entrusted its management. Having followed his practice in England and Ireland and initially retained the services of leading Protestant nobles like the Duke of Queensberry, he quickly turned to his co-religionists to oversee government. Like Robert Spencer, Earl of Sunderland, in England this was done in the most unfortunate way possible: the appointment of converts who were hated by Protestants and distrusted by the older Catholic nobility. John and James Drummond, Earls of Melfort and Perth, respectively, were both exceptionally loyal to the Crown but proved unable to mobilise enough support for the king's policies. Indeed they became part of the problem rather than its managerial solution. Perth's conversion in particular provoked widespread revulsion, expressed violently through anti-Catholic riots in January and February 1686.[67] This was an unpromising backdrop for the third – and greatest – issue that succeeded in turning a nation that had been in the vanguard of high-flying loyalism in the latter part of Charles's reign to the standard-bearer of opposition to James. Believing that a combination of the lords of the articles and the closely managed elections of 1685 would secure him an assembly bound to enact his will, James attempted to secure a toleration for Catholics through legislative means. To widespread astonishment outside Scotland this was soundly rejected. Writing in England, Roger Morrice – who had expected the Scottish Parliament to do exactly as the king wished through a mix of fear and self-interest – believed that 'this surprizing and Conspicuous Miscarriage ... in Scotlan[d] has clogged all theire [i.e. Catholics'] affaires elsewhere'.[68] Scottish resistance to Catholicising policies gave heart to the king's critics South of the Border, and turned on its head Charles II's success in using Scottish loyalty to influence English politics. At least

as damagingly it forced James to proceed via use of his prerogative –
in the form of toleration via royal proclamation – rather than through
traditional parliamentary means. This increased perceptions of incipient
Catholic absolutism.[69]

By the summer of 1688, James's policies and dictatorial style had
increased political and religious divisions within both Scotland and Ireland. As a result, he had also raised anxieties about his likely end goals
within England, whilst simultaneously provoking the kind of opposition
that could serve as an encouragement to the discontented in other kingdoms. Underpinning everything lay the fear of physical violence. In
Ireland Tyrconnell rapidly and overwhelmingly Catholicised the army,
opening up the twin spectre of renewed massacres of Protestants within
the island, and the use of Irish troops within Britain. When orders were
given for the insertion of Irish soldiers into companies garrisoned at
Portsmouth, the Protestant officers refused to comply and were cashiered
in a significant *cause célèbre*.[70] This ability to move armed force between
kingdoms had long been a possibility with regard to Scotland, where the
1663 Militia Act had 'cheerfully' stipulated the raising of a force consisting
of 20,000 foot and 2000 horse:

> Which forces are to be in readiness, as they shall be called for by his
> Majesty, to march to any part of his dominions of Scotland, England,
> or Ireland for suppressing of any foreign invasion, intestine trouble
> or insurrection, or for any other service wherein his Majesty's honour,
> authority or greatness may be concerned ... [71]

By the mid 1680s, this kind of ultra-loyal blank cheque to the monarchy
looked thoroughly dangerous, not least as James had rapidly expanded
the armed forces within England and maintained an annual camp on
the outskirts of London during the summer. Soldiers had not been so
prominent in the three kingdoms since the Cromwellian 1650s.

Yet from the government's perspective they were crucial for security
in an increasingly tense environment. If many Scots participated in anti-
Catholic riots after Perth's conversion, the prompt in Ireland was the
annual commemoration of the Ulster massacres on 23 October. In 1687,
'the Bustles w[hi]ch the bonefires caused in most Townes' led to a proclamation forbidding a repeat of such activity to mark the anniversary of
the Gunpowder Plot on 5 November.[72] In England when pressure was
exerted to ban bonfires the populace of London and other cities switched
their commemorative activity to displaying lit candles in windows.[73] The

Protestant calendar had become a clear threat to the Catholic government of three kingdoms. This melding of past and present reached its
apogee in mid December 1688 when in the febrile atmosphere that
accompanied the implosion of James's regime panic swept England that
rampaging Irish troops were about to massacre Protestants. This 'Irish
fright' demonstrated both the depth of contemporary fears and the
vividness of confessional memory.[74] James's pro-Catholic policies had succeeded in temporarily uniting Protestants of many different hues in their
conviction that the monarch of three kingdoms was fit to wear the crown
of none.

Conclusion

When seeking to brace his brother to face down the Exclusionist threat in
1679, James had argued that possession of Scotland and Ireland 'will make
men of estates consider well before they engage against the King'.[75] Such
claims were already being pointedly offered in the English Parliament
by those speaking against Exclusion. Should the bill pass, it would only
'exasperate the Duke and put him to try experiments upon Ireland; how
that nothing we did could oblige Scotland, and that they would be glad
when he came to the Crown to call him in'.[76] After Charles's triumph over
Exclusion, the reporter of these words – Sir Robert Southwell – was in no
doubt that had it not been for 'the menace and steddy aspect' of Scotland
and Ireland under James and Ormond, the Whigs would have got their
way in England.[77] This slightly sinister image of England's neighbours
pointing like pistols at the cockpit of politics in London was one that
Shaftesbury had tried to emphasise when he argued that Exclusion was
a crucial safeguard to prevent England descending into the tyranny that
prevailed North of the Border, and which might be unleashed in Ireland
at any moment by plotting Catholics. As another Whig peer, Lord Herbert
of Cherbury, argued in 1683, the effect of James's recent government of
Scotland had been that 'the old Laws ar[e] quite ruind . . . insomuch that
Arbitrary goverm[en]t is got thither already'.[78]

The key significance of the 'British' dimension to Restoration political
life was thus the way that it put royal powers into stark relief; something
which could appear comforting for those friendly to the monarchy at
the time of the Exclusion Crisis, but that ultimately looked dire in the
reign of an open and determined Catholic. Preaching before the Scottish Parliament in 1661 Matthias Symson, minister of Stirling, had urged

the necessity of strengthening the royal prerogative: 'if the Kingdom be headlesse, the Subjects will be brainless'. But what if the king used his grey matter in ways obnoxious to the Protestant religion? James's reign in Scotland proved to long-standing Covenanter critics that 'that Monster of Prerogative' surpassed 'all the lust, impudence & insolence of the Roman, Sicilian, Turkish, or Indian Tyrants, that ever trampled upon the Liberties of Mankind'.[79] The practical effects of what was widely seen as Catholic despotism appeared even more starkly in Ireland. When William III landed at Carrickfergus on 14 June 1689 to reclaim Ireland for Protestant rule, a laconic contemporary chronicler noted that only one of the town's aldermen was there to greet him, 'the rest eyther dead or absent by the Ruggednesse of the times'.[80] Massive social and economic dislocation stoked renewed memories of the massacres of 1641. A compendium of those events printed in 1689 noted that despite the plethora of previous accounts, 'it must not be accounted a Work improper at this time' to remind readers of Irish Catholics' proven track record of brutality. Despite the efforts of the English to civilise them, 'they have not fail'd at all times to Rise up and imbrue their hands in the Blood of their English Neighbours; so that Ireland hath for a long time been a true Aceldama, or Field of Blood, and a devouring Sepulchre of the English Nation'.[81] The final and fatal irony for James was that it was in Ireland that his personal bid to reclaim his thrones would be foiled between 1689 and 1691, even as his supporters were beaten into submission in Scotland. On the back of military triumphs in the Northern and Western parts of the British Isles, William III consolidated his hold on the English Crown.[82] In so doing he ensured a Protestant ascendancy in three kingdoms that would endure into modern times.

Chapter 7: What was the Importance of Politics Out-of-Doors in this Period?

Political activity, as we have shown in previous chapters, was not confined to the enclosed spaces of the King's court, Council chamber, and Houses of Parliament. In fact, politics out-of-doors was widespread and vibrant in this period. It took place in a variety of different locations and was manifested in a wide range of actions. Three initial examples demonstrate this variety.

On Easter Monday 1668, violent crowds dominated by young working men started to assail the brothels of London. Their attacks continued for another two days. In many ways, this is unsurprising. Apprentices had a strong and long-standing tradition of rioting against bawdy houses. To an extent this is just what apprentices did. However, it is clear that a number of those who took action in 1668 were using their violent protest to encode a political message. For these rioters the authorities were engaged in activities which smacked of rank hypocrisy: they enforced laws against dissenters (see Chapters 1–2) but failed to impose the legal strictures on bawdy houses. The rioters called for liberty of conscience and they saw themselves as entering into a negotiation. Their attack on bawdy houses was intended to send a message to the government about the iniquities of the persecution of dissent. Such a strategy was made more pointed by the comparisons that were drawn between the court and a brothel – the crowds claimed that 'ere long they would come and pull White-hall down' and in published and manuscript satire the king's mistress, Lady Castlemaine, was depicted as the greatest whore in the land.[1]

In the politically tumultuous winter of 1679/80, a 'Monster' petition circulated in London (see Chapter 3). Its request was phrased in mellifluous, suasive language:

> ... in such a time when your Majesty's person as also the protestant religion, and the government of this nation are thus in most imminent danger,
>
> We your Majesty's most humble, dutiful and obedient subjects, in the deepest sense of our duty and allegiance to your Majesty, do most humbly and earnestly pray, that the Parliament which is prorogued until the 26th day of January next, may then sit, to try the offenders, and to redress all other our most important grievances, no otherways to be redressed.[2]

The request may have been couched in the traditional language of obedience and humility, but this was a long way from being an act of straightforward deference. Underneath the rhetoric was a demand for a parliament and a critique of Charles's arbitrary tendencies in keeping it from sitting. Close to 18,000 Londoners signed it.[3]

When the Duke of York returned to London in April 1682, Tory crowds turned out in force. Various symbolic gestures were carried out. Effigies of Jack Presbyter were set alight, and in Drury Lane a reproduction of the Earl of Shaftesbury, a leading Whig politician, went up in flames. It was not just London crowds which participated in these purging rituals. In 1682, following the discovery of the Rye House Plot and Charles's 'miraculous' escape Portsmouth, Plymouth, and Wells witnessed the same kind of politically motivated celebration.[4]

These three very different examples illuminate the world of politics out-of-doors. As we saw in the first chapter, this was a world that was considerably widened, and had grown in importance, as a result of the mid-century Revolution. It is important to state at the outset that popular politics did not exist separately from high politics. Indeed, for those lower down the social scale to have had a political effect they must have been able to influence those in traditional positions of authority. Conversely, as the period progressed, it became more and more important for those in positions of authority to appeal for popular support. This can be seen from the above examples in that both the organisation of the 'Monster' petition, and much Tory crowd action was instigated and facilitated from above. It is most effective then to think of high politics and popular politics not as distinct categories but as symbiotically linked. In this chapter, we will explore the dynamics of this relationship, first by interrogating the conceptual frameworks which might be employed to discuss it; secondly through an examination of the spaces in which popular political understanding grew; and thirdly by analysing (both here and in the succeeding chapter) the media which fed, challenged, and, in some sense, educated the increasingly critical, engaged, and politically aware public. It was the discourses produced by this public, through reading, writing, and in discussion which underlay the overt manifestations of political sentiment detailed above.

Concepts

Discussions concerning politics out-of-doors in the Restoration are now almost inevitably haunted by the work of the German critical theorist Jürgen Habermas. Since its translation into English in 1989 Habermas's early study (published in German in 1962) *The Structural Transformation of the Public Sphere* has become a touchstone for historians investigating late seventeenth-century popular politics. To write of the emergence, or at least the increased importance, of the public sphere in this period has become almost axiomatic. And yet as many of those historians have recognised a number of late seventeenth-century developments actually fit uneasily within the conceptual and empirical framework laid out by Habermas. It is therefore worth engaging critically and analytically with Habermas's theory here, first as a way of clarifying what the actual nature of politics out-of-doors was in this period and secondly as a way of questioning the use of the terminology of the public sphere itself.

An immediate problem for the historian of the late seventeenth century is provided by Habermas's argument that 'A public sphere that functioned in the political realm' did not originate in England until the early eighteenth century.[5] For Habermas it was a series of key developments in 1694–5 – the establishment of the Bank of England; the 'elimination of the institution of censorship'; and the appearance of the first cabinet government – that produced the circumstances in which the public sphere could function in a politically effective way.[6] However, historians have notably ignored Habermas's own trenchant insistence that the concept of the public sphere could not 'be transferred, idealtypically generalized, to any number of historical situations that represent formally similar constellations'.[7] Claims have been made, for example, for the fifteenth-century public sphere, the Elizabethan public sphere, and, most importantly for the present purpose, the later Stuart public sphere.[8] Tim Harris, Steve Pincus, and Mark Knights in particular have demonstrated that during the period 1660–88, it became necessary for central political actors not simply to appeal at a popular level but to engage in a genuine dialogue with those outside the court and parliament. There is nothing ostensibly wrong with this: Habermas may have usefully defined a significant development, but failed to date its emergence correctly. But it is also clear that when historians have written about these earlier public spheres they have also – implicitly or explicitly – rejected Habermas's definition of the public sphere.[9]

There are, in fact, a number of problems with Habermas's delineation of the public sphere, and those detailed here are only representative of more extensive critiques. One of the most damaging attacks was launched in a penetrating article by Joad Raymond. For Habermas the public sphere first emerged as a space for reasoned and critical consideration of cultural material, and reason remained an essential characteristic when it started to function in the political realm. Raymond, drawing on his work on newsprint, showed that far from being rational the debates pursued in Restoration England were fuelled by religious and political discourses which did not deal in careful 'weighed and measured' arguments of 'experimental science'. The newspapers which catalysed much discussion (and which are analysed in the latter section of this chapter) dealt in satirical mudslinging and caricature.[10] Appeals may have been made to reason as the ultimate arbiter, and disputants might have been quick to claim that their positions were founded on Reason, but such special pleading only serves to highlight the emptiness of the claims.[11] Furthermore, Tim Blanning has criticised Habermas on three grounds – that his identification of the public sphere as bourgeois is misleading; that he sees the public sphere as being formed first in response to culture and then acting politically, when in England it was fostered by the political turmoil of the civil war and interregnum; and that his argument that the public sphere was necessarily oppositional is unfounded.[12] And yet Blanning writes that 'once the Marxist residue has been cleared away . . . what remains provides an illuminating perspective'.[13] It is unclear that 'what remains' without 'the Marxist residue' owes much to Habermas, and others have more straightforwardly sought to continue the use of the idea of the public sphere without much in the way of genuflection to Habermas at all: Peter Lake, rather brutally, writes of using the phrase in a 'de-Habermased' sense.[14] But, if when we use the phrase 'public sphere' we do not intend to invoke Habermas, it seems worth asking if the phrase itself has any particular redeeming feature? A sphere is an object with clearly defined boundaries, but is this a helpful way of conceptualising later Stuart politics out-of-doors? Politics out-of-doors was mutable. The general trend was for a greater number of people to become involved as the period progressed, but clearly this trend was not linear and there were moments of exponential and seismic growth in this number (the crucial example being the Exclusion Crisis) and also moments of regression. The fluidity of politics out-of-doors is not well characterised by a sphere. Both the terminology and the Habermasian concept of the public sphere thus appear redundant. However, rather than arbitrarily imposing another phrase in its place, throughout this chapter we will employ a variety of terms (public forum, arena, and so on) which seem both clearer than 'public sphere', and do not carry its conceptual baggage, to discuss the central phenomenon.

Spaces

Broad political engagement is to an extent dependent on interaction, and in a time before telephonic and electronic communication this meant that people required spaces in which to meet and engage with political issues. This could, of course, quite simply take place in the streets, but gradually certain spaces became recognised as the loci of political discussion and debate. The alehouse retained some significance in this context (after all much of the Levellerism of the late 1640s had been cooked up in the Nag's Head).[15] In London the major commercial centre of the Royal Exchange formed a hub for discussion, with merchants stopping to probe the issues of the day. Pepys recorded the variety of subjects which he heard debated in this context, while Dryden gave some sense of how printed works could provide material for these debates when one of his character's declared of a particular poem: 'I have seen them reading it in the midst of Change-time. Nay, so vehement they were at it, that they lost their bargain by the candles' ends.'[16] But the most important of these 'political' spaces in Restoration England were the coffeehouses.[17] Oxford saw England's first coffeehouse in 1650 and thereafter the fashion for both the drink and the place in which it was consumed grew.[18] Numerous coffeehouses sprang up in the capital, but they were not confined to London and the university cities. Indeed, in a British context, Lionel Newman launched a coffeehouse in Dublin by 1664, while John Row and Colonel Walter Whiteford started up coffeehouses in 1673 in Edinburgh and Glasgow, respectively.[19]

The initial association of coffeehouses with Oxford should not lead to the assumption that they only provided space for abstruse academic discussion. At first the coffeehouses may have been relatively socially exclusive, but even at the beginning the university authorities showed a concern for the nature of the conversations that took place within them. Cambridge's vice chancellor gave licenses to coffeehouses on the proviso that they 'suffer no scholars of this University, under the degree of Masters of Arts, to drinke coffee, chocolate, sherbett, or tea . . . except their tutors be with them'.[20] Clearly the coffeehouse was not a place in which students could be expected to discuss scholarly matters alone. As time progressed the social exclusivity of the coffeehouse diminished, and they attracted a wide range of clients including women and religious dissenters.

The coffeehouse thus achieved central importance as a place for relatively open and inclusive political discussion. In manuscript correspondence we hear of 'The politicians of the coffee-houses' while government informers remained convinced that the coffeehouses were hotbeds of sedition. Much partisan and satirical literature was produced concerning coffeehouses which, although it provides only a distorted reflection of the social reality, in order to fulfil the requirements of its genre cannot have been completely removed from the actual circumstances which prevailed in them.[21] The religious controversialist Edmund Hickeringill painted a picture of the way in which religious and political conversations could be instigated:

> at the *Rainbow-Coffee house* the other day, taking my place at due distance, not far from me, at another Table sat a whole *Cabal* of wits; made up of Virtuoso's, Ingenioso's, young Students of the Law, two Citizens, and to make the Jury full, *vous avez*, one old Gentleman . . . they all laughing heartily and gaping . . . I was tickled to know the cause of all this mirth, and presently found, it was a *Book* made all this sport; the Title of it, *The Rehearsal transpros'd*. Look you here, says one of them, do not you see, p. 309. how smartly he *ferrets* the old *Foxes*, the Fathers of the Church? (as in biting *Irony*, he calls the old Bishops:).[22]

Hickeringill referred to the satirical, tolerationist work produced by the MP, poet, and polemicist Andrew Marvell, *The Rehearsal Transpros'd*. The precise scenario may be imagined, but the Rainbow coffeehouse on Fleet Street was real enough. Through Hickeringill's prose, a world in which people read controversial religious and political material together, and laughed at their political foes together, is brought sharply into focus.[23] As partisan political culture grew so did the tales of Whig and Tory confrontations taking place in coffeehouses. The *Protestant Oxford Intelligence*, for example, regaled its Whig audience with an account of the beating taken by uncouth Tories. Disgusted by the MPs elected to the Oxford Parliament of March 1681, they had drawn their swords in a coffeehouse only to be 'handsomely' pummelled by one 'Gentleman' with nothing but a cane and his love of parliament to draw on.[24]

The significance of coffeehouses as arenas for political debate did not go unnoticed by the monarch, and indeed Charles II's reaction to coffeehouses provides compelling evidence of their potential to play a role as centres for unrest and opposition. On 29 December 1675, Charles II made a proclamation declaring the closure of coffeehouses. Ten days later, when it became clear that this was not realistic, he back-peddled, although he did try to retain some control over them. Charles recognised that conversations in coffeehouses could lead to problems. But as with so much of politics out-of-doors, he also eventually had to accept that it was impossible to return to a world where such arenas had not existed. Instead he had to accept that, while it was true that oppositional discourses could be spread abroad from coffeehouses, coffeehouse conversation could also be harnessed for the loyalist cause. This itself is revealing. Rather than closing it down, it was necessary for the king to draw on politics out-of-doors to maintain his rule.[25]

Media

Throughout the previous discussion reference was made to the ways in which actors in politics out-of-doors drew on and debated a wide range of material. In this section we examine the nature of this media: the fuel to the fire of popular politics. We might start with an observation similar to the one just made concerning coffeehouses. Although it is of central importance that all had to engage with politics out-of-doors, this was clearly more welcome for some than others. Some retained the fantasy of simply shutting down oppositional voices. One index of the subversive potential of written material is thus the attempt made to turn these fantasies into legislative reality. At the very pinnacle of the laws that could be brought to bear on the producers of seditious works was the Treason Act, in which the printing of treasonous words was explicitly condemned. It was very rare for a printer to be tried under this legislation but there were a few cases. In October 1663, the printer John Twyn was hard at work at four o'clock in the morning. He was producing a tract called *A Treatise of the Execution of Justice*, which justified rebellion. The Surveyor of the Press, Roger L'Estrange caught him in the act. Twyn's desperate attempts to destroy the evidence, in part by throwing the already printed pages out of a window, failed. He was tried for treason and executed. The full force of the most powerful law could therefore be enacted against those who printed seditious words. The ghost of John Twyn must have continued to haunt some writers' and printers' imaginations, serving as an awful reminder of what could happen to those who overstepped the mark.[26]

But it did not take the writing of treasonous material to fall foul of the law. As we saw in the first chapter, a Licensing Act was given the Royal assent on 19 May 1662. The Act disallowed the printing of books which included any doctrine or opinion contrary to the Christian faith or doctrine or discipline of the Church of England, and anything seditious. The Act was to be policed largely by the Stationers' Company, whose master printers would enjoy a virtual monopoly. The numbers of these printers was to be allowed to fall to 20 and it was then to be limited to that level. All printed works, with few exceptions, were to be entered into the Stationers' register and to undergo pre-publication review which if passed would mean that they could be licensed. Powers of search and seizure were given by the Act to certain government agents and the Stationers. On paper this Act would restrain the presses to a huge degree.[27]

Coupled with the legislation was the fervour of that hammer of the nonconformists Roger L'Estrange, the man who in a desperate desire to smash the seditious press had launched the dawn raid on John Twyn. L'Estrange was made Surveyor of the Press by a warrant of 15 August 1663. He was tireless in his work. As N.H. Keeble has argued, it was L'Estrange's 'animus and zeal which made censorship and press control during the Restoration period so much more vindictive and so much more partisan than anything experienced before'.[28]

If the measures taken had functioned in the ways which their framers and policers had hoped, then this chapter would look very different, and the vigorous political debate at the heart of politics out-of-doors would have remained stillborn. And yet, while these measures demonstrate the ways in which some sought to impede political discourse, many continued to circumvent both the legislation and L'Estrange. A network that supported clandestine printing activities was quickly established. For example, John Jekyll, a city merchant, and strident activist on behalf of dissenters was revealed in 1685 to have been secretly printing pamphlets for years.[29] Presses could be well concealed. An informer managed to narrow the location of a press down to five houses in Blue Anchor Alley, but he could not with 'so many back doors, bye-holes and passages, and sectarians so swarming thereabouts' get any closer.[30] In conjunction with this concealment of printing presses, individual works could also be safeguarded. They might not be entered into the Stationers' register and the name of the printer might be omitted from the frontispiece.[31] False imprints were also sometimes used. One group which was particularly tenacious in the publication of unlicensed material was the Quakers.[32] Of c. 34,225 titles published between 1652 and 1684, Quakers produced 3030 – 8 per cent.[33] This was a huge proportion given that they were such a small group, that the majority of what they produced was unlicensed, and that their very existence was an affront to legislation like the Licensing Act. This points not just to the inefficiency of the mechanism for censorship but also the vitality of underground print culture and the determination of those with marginalised voices to be heard.[34]

Having considered the nature and mixed effectiveness of the censorship regime, we now turn to consider the political effect of widely disseminated information and opinion. As will become clear, this was a matter of far more than just printed materials, important though those were. To take a crucial example, we have already seen how vibrant and influential the press was during the Exclusion Crisis (Chapter 3). The lapsing of the Licensing Act in 1679 allowed a torrent of literature to be published on a range of political and religious issues surrounding the central question of James's right to succeed to the throne. This was one of a series of moments in the Tudor and Stuart period in which press and people interacted to further the development of a news culture (Figure 1). This had an immense impact on political life as a whole, increasing both the geographical breadth and social depth of public debate. Before examining the nature and consequences of that trend in the Restoration period, it is necessary to trace something of its origins before 1660.

The 'rise of news' in the early modern period was the result of bursts of short-term consciousness-raising events and long-term cultural changes. Warfare and threats to national survival naturally provoked widespread anxiety and a climate suited to gossip, rumour-mongering, and an increasing appetite for written news. These conditions were particularly pervasive in the 1580s and 1620s. The Spanish Armada of 1588 and other less well-remembered invasion efforts sharpened a sense of Protestant national identity against a looming Catholic 'other'. The 1620s saw frequent parliaments called to deal with the effects of major European warfare, in particular Charles I's bungled efforts to intervene in several peripheral theatres of the 30 Years War. Proclamations against licentious speech, and proposals to the government to establish a regulated monopoly of printed news testify to the general awareness that news was increasingly important.[35] That sense can also be seen in the rapid drive to satirise news, not least for its highly unstable and variable nature: critics could claim unregulated news resembled the confusion of languages that beset the builders of the Tower of Babel.[36] A character in Ben Jonson's play *News from the New World*, for instance, referred to 'my puritan news, my protestant news and my pontifical news'.[37] All of this prefigured the explosion of printed titles in the early 1640s that signalled the collapse of Charles I's government and which was noted in Chapter 1.

Important as the stimulus provided by foreign and domestic warfare was for the circulation of news, wider cultural changes were also crucial. Over the long term several closely inter-connected factors fuelled an increasing thirst for news: in particular, education, religion, and social mobility. The sixteenth and seventeenth centuries saw an increasing emphasis on the value of educational achievements. This reflected European-wide intellectual trends, not least the humanist-inspired celebration of learning as a necessary attribute for those taking part in public life. Noble blood ought to be supplemented with knowledge and cultural skills as part of a wider 'virtue' that reflected the best practices of classical Rome.[38] Furthermore, Protestantism placed a premium on direct access to the Scriptures in vernacular languages. This was not necessarily as elitist as once believed: a popular religious culture increasingly became built around cheap print.[39] Nevertheless, religious concerns and social pretensions melded together in the emergence of a Protestant lay magistracy and highly educated clerical profession dedicated to the creation of a Christian commonwealth.[40]

Neither of these trends was restricted to England. If London enjoyed a massive predominance as a centre for printing within the British Isles, the Scots were nevertheless proud of their four universities – compared to England's two – and some Irish Protestant scholars looked back with pride on their island's medieval heritage as a great centre of European Christian learning.[41] Overall, the widespread diffusion of intellectual aspirations and religious pretensions both fuelled and fed off increased social mobility, which was itself the inevitable result of considerable economic change. Growing urbanisation, improved communications, and new agricultural and manufacturing techniques greatly increased the size and complexity of the national economy. The rise of the 'middling sorts', men and women who were part of neither the social and economic elite, nor the mass of mere labourers and servants, nuanced older social models that had been sharply divided between the few haves and the many have nots.[42]

These three trends together left contemporaries reeling in the face of day-to-day realities that no longer reflected traditional thinking. In particular, in a world of rapid change, how should the social standing of particular individuals be calculated? Increasingly information became a key commodity in an environment requiring a wider range of social capital than ever before. Educated men were expected to know the latest news, and to be able to discuss it. Manuals detailing the accomplishments expected of a gentleman included the capacity to write good letters of news. For those without a distinguished lineage, but possessing some degree of education, being a 'man of information' was a means of gaining government employment, wealth, and social status. Indeed there was a 'decorum' of news: knowledge became a means of social differentiation that had previously only been visible in dress-codes designed to mark out different strata of society.[43]

Happily, the greatest example of these trends in the Restoration period is the most immediately engaging and accessible of all early modern diarists, Samuel Pepys. He was the son of a tailor who rose to prominence through a combination of good education and good luck, tempered with a ferocious work ethic directed towards cementing his financial and social status. As he rapidly ascended the greasy pole over the 1660s, he discarded whole tiers of friends who no longer met his social aspirations.[44] And an important part of that rise was his place at the heart of a vibrant news culture: he was a true 'man of information' who needed to be so in order to succeed as a 'man of business' within government and administration in competition with colleagues who enjoyed better lineages. Pepys collected his news from a variety of different sources. On the ninth day of the diary, 9 January 1660, he visited a coffeehouse to join a political debating group, the Rota Club. In future he would also meet the celebrated poet John Dryden in such an establishment, along with 'all the wits of the town'. Nor was he only addicted to the novelty of coffee: he also frequented more than a hundred taverns, inns, and eating-houses in London where he read pamphlets, listened to rumours, and was in turn subject to the inquisitiveness of others. His contacts were impeccable. When he joined the Rota Club, he was accompanied by the celebrated journalist Henry Muddiman; when he visited the Royal Exchange on 17 December 1664, he met Roger L'Estrange, 'who hath endeavoured several times to speak with me – it is to get now and then some news of me, which I shall as

I see cause give him'. At that time, L'Estrange was busy producing the two official newspapers, *The Intelligencer* and *The Newes*, although Pepys soon contrasted these unfavourably with the more detailed and serious *Oxford Gazette*, a news-sheet emanating directly from the secretary of state's office that he was careful to collect and have bound into volumes as part of his growing library.[45]

As L'Estrange's efforts to solicit news from Pepys indicate, he was already recognised as someone appraised of the latest events, both from his gadding about town socially, and his political and administrative contacts in his capacity as a leading naval official. He personally informed Charles II of the extent of the Great Fire of London in 1666 based on his eye-witness knowledge, and became a key conduit between the court and the city government fighting the blaze. He received letters from his patron, the Earl of Sandwich, telling him of military and mercantile affairs in the Mediterranean. He heard by word of mouth that Louis XIV 'hath declared in print that he doth intend this next summer to forbid his commanders to strike to us, but that both we and the Dutch shall strike to him'. His professional involvement with the navy naturally excited his interest in news of a victory over the Dutch during the Second Anglo-Dutch War in June 1666. Although this subsequently proved to be untrue, he was initially quick to spread the news that he had originally heard at court into the Royal Exchange and then to the congregation at his parish church. Small wonder that he 'took great delight to tell them': if the battle was thought to be a victory for Stuart forces, the retelling of it was a personal social triumph for Pepys, cementing his reputation as a man at the centre of events.[46] His diary is thus an unparalleled 'narrative of social accounting by a middling man on the make'.[47]

It is also a window onto a metropolitan world that was suffused with political awareness far below the level of the elite. Although, as we have seen, this can most often be observed at times of crisis, especially when large crowds took to the streets to voice popular fears, Pepys's diary displays the way in which political news could be rapidly diffused from its traditionally legitimate sphere within the doors of parliament's two chambers to the world out-of-doors without overt fuss or violence. On 8 December 1666, he dined at home with James Pearse, the Duke of York's surgeon, and learned about the previous day's parliamentary activity, 'which makes the King and Court mad'. Despite sending messengers to London's theatres and bawdy houses in search of Court-supporting MPs to block the move, the king found himself subject to the indignity of a parliamentary committee being appointed to investigate all the accounts for monies spent in the disastrous Second Anglo-Dutch War. This committee of accounts was in effect holding the executive liable for suspected mismanagement and corruption, an extraordinary step into the Crown's prerogative right to prosecute foreign wars.[48] Pearse went further and related court gossip to Pepys as well. He claimed that the Groom of the Bedchamber would publicly tell Charles how to remedy his parlous position: he should employ ' "one Charles Stuart – who now spends his time in imploying his lips and his prick about the Court, and hath no other employment" '. The awareness of how intertwined moral decadence and public defeats were is palpable. As Pepys noted, 'the King doth not profit by any of this, but lays all aside and remembers nothing, but to his pleasures again – which is a sorrowful consideration'.[49]

Pepys's diary is a source of unparalleled detail, but the kinds of networks for the diffusion of news that he allows us to see were being replicated in many other households, coffeehouses, and taverns across London and, to a less prominent, but no less important, degree in towns and villages across the later Stuarts' territories. Two specific incidents can be used to illustrate this, and also the extent to which the Carolean government was far more willing to engage with this growing news culture than its Caroline predecessor had been during the 1630s. The first incident centres on Charles II's decision to dissolve the English Parliament in March 1681. After three Exclusion Parliaments characterised by ferocious debates and divisive electioneering in the localities (see Chapter 3), Charles can have been in no doubt as to the scale of the risk he was taking. Parliaments enjoyed totemic status as a crucial part of the constitution; they acted as the king's 'great counsel' in which he could hear the legitimate grievances of his people. Their absence between 1629 and 1640 was believed to have been a key aspect of the run-up to civil war: as John Vaughan, an MP in numerous parliaments between 1628 and 1668, and subsequently a judge, put it in 1664, 'that gave the people the greatest dissatisfaction that they had'.[50] Vaughan was too tactful to recall that the absence of parliaments had from the dissolution of 1629 been cast in the worst possible light by Charles I's truculent *Declaration Showing the Causes of the Late Dissolution*. Blaming a few 'turbulent and ill-affected' critics for all recent problems, Charles struck a consistently authoritarian note, briskly telling his subjects that he expected them to 'yield as much submission and duty to our royal prerogatives, and as ready obedience to our authority and commandments, as hath been promised to the greatest of our predecessors'.[51] Such words were not calculated to sway opinion, but rather to tell the nation what it ought to think.

Contrast that with Charles II's masterly *Declaration to all His Loving Subjects, Touching the Causes and Reasons that Moved Him to Dissolve the Two Last Parliaments* (8 April 1681). In this fundamentally persuasive document, the king declared that

> no irregularities in Parliaments shall ever make us out of love with Parliaments, which we look upon as the best method for healing the distempers of the kingdom, and the only means to preserve the monarchy in that due credit and respect which it ought to have both at home and abroad. And for this cause we are resolved, by the blessing of God, to have frequent Parliaments, and both in and out of Parliament to use our utmost endeavours to extirpate popery, and to redress all the grievances of our good subjects, and in all things to govern according to the laws of the kingdom.[52]

This *Declaration* was part of a very different political culture than Charles I's 52 years earlier. Now the king sought to influence public opinion to persuade his subjects at large to rally behind him over the heads of misguided or ambitious MPs who had illegitimately sought to interfere in the royal succession. Charles II aimed to elicit support and he succeeded: more than 200 loyal petitions flooded in from across the country. They were then carefully published in the government-controlled *London Gazette*, and subsequent pamphlet collections, in order further to sway opinion at large with a show of overwhelming backing for the Crown. Yet even these printed declarations strongly hint at the continuing divisions within political opinion 'out-of-doors'. Loyal petitioners from the Buckinghamshire corporation of Chipping Wycombe, for instance, opened their address with the bitter comment that:

> Most of our late Defeated Politicians, disappointed of their dark Designments by your Majesties profound Wisdom, and Divine Provision, have endeavoured to disparage all Loyal Addressers, either as Useless and insignificant, or as Discountenanc'd and Unregarded, and that the Glut of them doth Cloy, and Surfeit, rather than satisfy Your Majesty.[53]

Whigs in the localities attempted to undermine the show of Tory loyalist support either by saying that petitions were not weighty expressions of opinion within towns and shires, or else that the king did not really value them. Politics out-of-doors in our period was thus important not just because it was an entrenched fact of life that the royal government had to deal with, but also because it reflected a deeply divided political world. Partisanship had become the norm, criticised and deplored to be sure, but impossible to eradicate.[54]

The second incident illustrative of the supple and shifting power of news in the Restoration political world is the reaction to the Rye House Plot of 1683.[55] Between the end of the Oxford Parliament in 1681 and 1683, the royal government had sought to exert discipline on the press. In the autumn of 1682, a clampdown on periodicals – regularly published newspapers that generally espoused consistent partisan views (often Whig) – led to the suppression of all but two titles. Of these one was the *London Gazette*, which tended to focus on bland foreign news or the republication of loyal addresses. Another was Roger L'Estrange's *Observator*. Couched in the form of a dialogue between various characters, this was a formidable exercise in partisan journalism. In his first edition L'Estrange offered a clear mission statement: ''Tis the Press that has made 'um Mad, and the Press must set 'um Right again'.[56] Although in theory L'Estrange might have wished for a world in which the lower orders knew their place, and were not led astray by the outpourings of the popular press, in practice he recognised that the government needed to engage with opinion at large. This he was formidably well-equipped to do, possessing an extraordinarily vivid and accessible prose style that eschewed self-consciously learned references and Latin tags in favour of direct invective and *ad hominem* attacks. Writer's block was clearly unknown to him: he published around three million words between 1677 and 1691.[57] Small wonder that he became the most (in)famous journalist of his time, and was subjected to numerous libels and even pictorial caricatures in hostile prints. In these he was often portrayed as the restless dog, Towzer, or else demeaned as 'Crack-Fart', surrounded with imagery designed to insinuate that he was a closet Catholic.

Yet even L'Estrange's journalistic prowess could not single-handedly convince all of Charles II's subjects that his government was fundamentally beneficent. This failure reflected both the depth of Tory/Whig partisan division in the wake of the Exclusion Crisis and the variety of media available to convey news. The government could crackdown on periodicals by threatening printers, and to a lesser extent could seek to restrain other kinds of occasional literature. But it faced formidable difficulties when it came to manuscript materials and the spoken word. The seventeenth century had witnessed a growing number of professional newsletter writers catering to an elite audience, and justifying their high prices by evoking a sense of inducting their readers into a secret or semi-secret world of privileged information.[58] An atypical but prolific example of this type of intelligencer is Roger Morrice, a Presbyterian clergyman whose ejection from the Church of England in 1662 pushed him towards acting as a domestic chaplain and all round man-of-business for various leading nonconformist politicians. It seems likely that his recently published *Entring Book* – which runs to 925,000 words – was an office fair copy of a regularly produced newsletter sent out to 'puritan Whig' nobles and gentleman in the English counties.[59] Morrice continued to provide a resolutely critical vision of Carolean government long after printed periodicals were suppressed, one that was deeply inflected with fears of popery and anger at the persecution of nonconformists. When the news broke of an alleged plot by republicans and nonconformists in the summer of 1683 to assassinate the royal brothers as they travelled from Newmarket to London, Morrice was immediately sceptical. He recorded that some of those said to be involved were reported to have been 'decoys from the beginning to draw others in'.[60]

In the months that followed he continued to provide his readers with accounts that undermined the veracity of what other, less cautious, individuals were to deride in public as 'a shamm Plott...the one and twentyeth sham plott that had been putt on foot to take away [belief in] the Popish Plott'.[61] When the government proclaimed a day of thanksgiving for the royal brothers' deliverance, Morrice reproduced the text of a manuscript libel that had been dispersed in London churches:

You Hipocrates forbeare your pranks
First Murther men and then give thanks
Forbeare your tricks proceed no farther
for God accepts no thanks for murther.

He repeated a story that Charles II himself refused to accept a written narrative of the Rye House Plot whilst walking in a London park, testily exclaiming, 'I have had too much trouble about Plotts already, I will be concerned no more about any Plotts'. When discussing the trials and executions of those prosecuted for the plot, Morrice regularly spiced his account with the words of witnesses who denied the existence of any such conspiracy, and even the queen's alleged remark in Charles's presence that 'in some Places it was not the Guilty but unfortunate that suffered'. He also points to the extent to which the government tried to control public perception of the plot by influencing a number of different media. A newsletter writer was bound over for good behaviour as a result of his unpublished words; a leading Whig printer, John Darby, was convicted for printing one of the Rye House Plotter's scaffold speeches; and a Suffolk gentleman, Sir Samuel Barnardiston, was prosecuted for writing in a private letter that it was all just a 'Sham Plott'. It was no coincidence that Barnardiston was a leading Whig and supporter of Exclusion Bills in recent parliaments.[62]

The significant fact, of course, is that these government efforts were nevertheless still being reported by those whose political and religious views rendered them impervious to propaganda and threats. Although the cumulative effect of such reports is impossible to gauge with precision, it is telling that the king's declaration setting out the official version of the plot failed to quiet all minds. Whilst the Duke of Ormond hoped that this declaration, which was read from every pulpit in the land on 9 September 1683, would be 'in effect... a declaration to every parish', the following month reports were still being received of efforts to distract from the plot in a number of localities. In the Cotswolds, for instance, a rumour had been spread that played on fears of arbitrary government: farmers were told that the king planned to seize all unmarked pigs and cattle, prompting many to spend the whole Sabbath day chasing their livestock across the hills.[63] However farcical the imagery, such reports testify to the continuing political divisions and nervousness of the king's subjects. Even a determined government could not fully control news, still less how it was received by individuals already possessed of very definite points of view.

Conclusion

Politics out-of-doors was a very powerful part of the Restoration world. It was important enough to attract the condemnation of many amongst the traditional ruling elite who were troubled by popular involvement in public life. Unruly crowds, a volatile press, uncontrollable rumours, and widely dispersed manuscript correspondence combined to make those at the top of the political ladder all too aware of the precariousness of their position. The ladder had been kicked away during the 1640s, what was to stop it happening again? Such thinking must have underpinned Charles II's ill-fated attempt to shut down all coffeehouses in 1675: they provided too much space for unregulated discourse. It should certainly come as no surprise to find similar expressions of horror from across the seventeenth century. In 1642, the MP John Rous prayed 'God in mercy put an end' to the 'multitudes of bookes and papers' giving reports of political affairs.[64] In the 1680s, George Savile, Marquess of Halifax, one of Charles II's leading ministers and himself a tremendous writer, tetchily complained that he lived 'in an Age overrun with Scriblers, as *Egypt* was with flyes and Locusts. . . . That worse Vermine of small Authors hath given the world Such a Surfett that instead of desiring to write, a man would be more inclined to wish for his own ease, that he could not read'.[65] For all Halifax's patrician disdain, the market for cheap print remained buoyant, a significant part of the wider phenomenon of politics out-of-doors. When William of Orange invaded England in 1688 he brought with him a printing press and continued the trend for paper bullets to be deployed alongside lead ones. He would have appreciated the argument of the great philosopher Thomas Hobbes as it appeared in the posthumously published *Behemoth* (1682): 'the power of the mighty hath no foundation but in the opinion and belief of the people'.[66]

Recent scholarship has emphasised the degree to which the later seventeenth century saw an increasing 'struggle to represent the will of the nation'.[67] This was deeply problematic at a number of levels. Was it really safe to involve the reading public in political life? How was the public to discern truth from falsehood? If public opinion was to be courted, and even celebrated by some as a repository of common sense and native values above and beyond corrupt politicians, how should its views be solicited and fed into the political system?[68] In this sphere, as in so many others, it had proved impossible to wipe away the mid century revolution and its legacy of widened involvement in political life. But the developments of the 1670s and 1680s would ensure that the later Stuarts had to rule over subjects increasingly divided into rival partisan groups on a more or less permanent basis. Politics out-of-doors became the natural milieu of Whigs and Tories, a trend that would last well into the eighteenth century.

Chapter 8: Why Study Restoration Culture?

On 23 November 1658, three writers – John Dryden, Andrew Marvell, and John Milton – walked together in Oliver Cromwell's funeral procession. This is yet another reminder of how profoundly the Restoration, and in this case specifically Restoration culture, was to be affected by the experiences of the interregnum. The divergent paths these three men took in the Restoration form part of the subject matter of this chapter but this is only one aspect of a larger enterprise.[1]

The aphorism that practising history requires us 'to go on reading till you can hear people talking' is now most usually invoked to be scoffed at or, at least, critiqued.[2] And yet, like many such statements, what it lacks in subtlety it makes up for in insight. As historians have become more interested in both political culture and popular and elite mentalities, and therefore more concerned with the ways in which people conceptualised or presented their conceptualisation of events, they have turned increasingly to analysis of a wide range of media. This has been linked to a development in the sophistication of the methods used by historians examining texts. No longer seen as providing illustrative material for points gleaned from other sources the analysis of literary texts is now central to the historical enterprise. Neither is the practice of close reading in historical context only applied to written sources, visual material too is 'read' for what it can reveal about contemporary attitudes.

Such analyses, of course, always depend upon the understanding that the works under discussion were consumed by, and affected, significant audiences. Establishing the actual composition of these audiences is difficult, and given the available evidence it will only ever be partially possible. Nonetheless, before embarking on a discussion of Restoration culture, it is necessary briefly to consider this subject. When investigating the audiences for literary culture, we can initially turn to literacy rates. The most readily available statistics suggest that in England around 30 per cent of women and nearly 50 per cent of men could read by 1700.[3] Such blunt figures of course hide variation in literacy rates between social groups and across the kingdom. They also obscure variation dependent on an individual's religious identity. As might be expected, given the importance of nonconformist culture which we have highlighted (see Chapter 2), literacy was probably higher among nonconformists than the rest of the population.[4] However, for all that literacy figures conceal, they do suggest a large group which had the potential to engage with written material for themselves. It is also important to note that in order to be influenced by a written work an individual does not have to read it him or herself. In the last chapter, we stressed the significance of sociability, and of oral dissemination of ideas in public places. In such spaces, we can imagine one reader acting as a nodal point from which a large number might be influenced by a text spoken aloud.

It is also important to examine what kinds of material were available at different social levels. Were the discourses analysed in this chapter available to a wide audience? We will argue that Restoration culture of all kinds shared some thematic coherence, and that some of the obsessions which might be thought to be narrowly confined to the court found wider audiences in print, and through manuscripts which, as shown in the previous chapter, could reach large audiences. Audiences for theatres may have actually been smaller, and more socially narrow, than they were in the Elizabethan and early Stuart periods, but drama still provided another medium in which the various languages analysed in this chapter could be heard.[5] It should be stressed then that categorisations of culture which seek to place artefacts into hermetically sealed packages (high or low, elite or popular, religious or secular) fail to show how all the boundaries were permeable, and how the same basic ideas were available in a varied range of material. Finally, in terms of the impact of culture, it should also be recognised that even if a piece did have a narrow circulation sometimes the size of the audience is not the only thing that matters. Thus the question that sometimes needs answering relates not to how many eyes could see the material but to whom those eyes belonged.

Showing which people consumed this culture is not the only issue. Just as, if not more, problematic is showing *how* they consumed it. The kind of evidence that we might like to have to reconstruct audience responses is not abundant. There are, to be sure, for this period some remarkable diarists, and in the last chapter we showed how the most remarkable of these, Pepys, could be used to provide evidence of a consumer. However, evidence from diaries cannot stand alone. Much work has focused on manuscript copying of texts and marginalia. Here it is possible to glimpse the ways in which some readers responded to texts by passing some comment on their content through a variety of techniques. The act of manuscript copying itself reveals something about interest in the texts copied, and sometimes the ways in which the texts were copied can show them being used to aid the reader's thinking.

A striking example of this is the manuscript miscellany kept by the Gentleman of the Privy Chamber and MP William Haward.[6] Haward's miscellany contains a vast number of satirical verses intermingled with other political documents. Although he was no lover of nonconformists, he nonetheless copied out texts by the Presbyterian Robert Wild alongside other more formal material – including speeches to parliament – concerning the issues which Wild probed. In compiling his miscellany Haward was thus using the kind of cultural material we analyse to engage with the political issues of the day.[7] Haward's miscellany illuminates the ways in which Restoration culture formed part of a politician's mental framework. And if contemporaries thought about key issues in terms provided by this material then so, as historians, should we.

In part because we have had much to say about visual sources throughout this book, we concentrate here predominantly on literary sources. However, rather than being organised around different genres, the chapter revolves around broad themes which overlap in the work but which are made distinct here for the purposes of analysis. They are themes which, in a sense are universal, but which had specific applications in the Restoration: politics, sex, and religion.

Politics

At the beginning of his satire *Absalom and Achitophel* (1681), the Historiographer Royal and Poet Laureate John Dryden wrote of how 'he who draws his pen for one party must expect to make enemies of the other: for wit and fool are consequents of Whig and Tory, and every man is a knave or an ass to the contrary side'.[8] Indeed, the development of partisan politics which was cemented by the Exclusion Crisis both bred and was driven by the production of partisan culture.[9] Dryden's own satire, for all its initial protestations to moderation, is a scathing public, printed Tory attack on Whig principles and an act of counsel to a king who has been, in the poet's eyes, too weak in the treatment of his enemies.[10] His poem maps the story of Absalom's rebellion against King David from Samuel xiii–xviii on to the Exclusion Crisis, and biblical figures represent contemporary ones. Most significantly, Absalom is Charles's bastard son James Scott, Duke of Monmouth and his wicked counsellor Achitophel, who inspires and provides the (in the poem's terms) false legitimation for rebellion, is the Earl of Shaftesbury. Whig arguments are presented as emanating from satanic origins (Achitophel is 'hell's dire agent'[11]), and throughout the Whig appeal at a popular level is held up as an example of the dangers inherent in their vision of politics:

> Deluded Absalom forsakes the court;
> Impatient of high hopes, urged with renown,
> And fired with near possession of a crown;
> Th' admiring crowd are dazzled with surprise,
> And on his goodly person feed their eyes.
> On each side bowing popularly low;
> His looks, his gestures and his words he frames,
> And with familiar ease repeats their names.
> Thus, formed by nature, furnished out with arts,
> He glides unfelt into their secret hearts.[12]

The deliberate move into the world of politics out-of-doors is seen here as inherently threatening. There is an irony, of course, in that Dryden's satire was an appeal in print to the very world which he sought to degrade, but the irony does not undermine the poem. Instead the king's re-imposition of order at the end of the poem is established in part in reaction against appeals at a popular level. David implores 'From plots and treasons heaven preserve my years,/But save me most from my petitioners./Unsatiate as the barren womb or grave,/God cannot grant so much as they can crave.'[13] The only answer to those who sought to undermine his rule is the application of strong justice. Mercy had had its day and David reluctantly turns to other means of countering his enemies:

> Why am I forced, like heaven, against my mind
> To make examples of another kind?
> Must I at length the sword of justice draw?
> O cursed effects of necessary law![14]

That one word, 'necessary', is chilling. When claims to necessity are made, the full severity of the law is not tempered. For Shaftesbury – who was at the moment of the poem's publication awaiting trial for treason – and his supporters the message would have been brutally clear. But Dryden's message was not universally accepted (indeed had it been, he would hardly have felt the need to make the kind of appeal encoded in the poem). He was met by the intransigent London jury which returned an *ignoramus* verdict (that is they found there was not enough evidence for the trial to proceed) in Shaftesbury's case, and he was also met in print.[15]

Whig authors sought to undermine Dryden both politically and poetically. Samuel Pordage – son of a civil war radical – published his *Azaria and Hushai* in 1682. Pordage reconfigured Dryden's biblical allegory and turned Shaftesbury into a loyal counsellor, Hushai, and Monmouth into a good prince, Azaria. The popularity of Monmouth, seen as insidious in Dryden's work, is ascribed positive value in Pordage's work. The *'Jews'* (the English) 'cast their Eyes on *Amazia*'s [Charles's] Son,/Who, without Arts the People's Love had won'.[16] It is the king's brother, Eliakim 'Full of tormenting Jealousies and Fears', who is the figurehead for a conspiracy – a follower of the false religion of Baal: 'The sober part of the whole *Sanhedrim* [the parliament],/Desire to keep *Judea's* Crown from him.'[17] Throughout Pordage presents the Whig counterparts to Dryden's Tory arguments, while like Dryden presenting accounts of the 'bad Counsels' provided by his opponents.[18] Dryden's insistence on the necessity for harsh justice – extensively recounted by Pordage – is ultimately demolished in Pordage's poem by the king himself who promises to call the *Sanhedrim* (Charles had promised that he would continue to call parliaments in April 1681, and Pordage sought to remind him of this, see Chapter 7). The proper constitutional situation is to be reaffirmed in an atmosphere of reconciliation:

> That Body with the Kingly Head shall join,
> That Counsel and their Wisdom mix with mine,
> All former strife betwixt us be forgot,
> And in Oblivion buried every Plot.
> We'l try to live in Love and Peace again,
> As when I first began my happy Reign.[19]

Pordage also sought to reaffirm the legitimacy of politics out-of-doors and popularity in a piece of daring re-appropriation at the end of the poem. The codas to both Dryden and Pordage's poems begin with a portentous clap of thunder as 'Th'Almighty' gives his approbation to the king's speech.[20] But Pordage's poem ends:

> The Augurie was noted by the Croud,
> Who joyful shouts return'd almost as loud:
> Then *Amazia* was once more restor'd,
> He lov'd his People, they obey'd their Lord.[21]

The 'Croud', denigrated throughout Dryden's poem, is here seen as a key part of the right political situation. Their actions are seen as giving legitimacy to the king's pronouncements. This contractual sentiment emphasised in the final lines of Pordage's poem contrasts markedly with Dryden's lines inspired by divine right: 'Once more the godlike David was restored,/And willing nations knew their lawful lord.'[22]

Partisan conflict was being fought in poetry, and the poets themselves could become targets. Thus Pordage not only sought to attack Dryden's politics, but he also included him in the poem as Shimei a man whose 'Muse . . . was for hire a very Prostitute' and who had previously written of Zabed (Oliver Cromwell).[23] (This last charge was true enough, but it was the kind of thing that Dryden did not like to be reminded of – and it did his public reputation as a loyalist poet no good.)[24] Such partisan contests were not the sole preserve of poets: playwrights too entered the fray, and sought to establish political points on the stage.

Partisanship in the theatre however did not have to lead simply to blustering and name-calling any more than it did in poetry. Aphra Behn's Tory drama, for example, was often complicated by her coterminous questioning of that central Tory ideology, patriarchalism. The parallels drawn by Tories between the micro-level of government – in which households were ruled by fathers – and the macro-level – in which the king had fatherly authority over his people – were in danger of being undermined by her representation of female agency.[25] In addition, her plays could be surprisingly explicit about the faults of some Tory figureheads. In her play *The Young King: Or, The Mistake*, the excluded Orsames is shown to share some of Charles and James's libertine habits. Furthermore, the very title of the play has a potential double meaning which expresses qualms about its central character and thus about the figures to whom he is analogous. Is the mistake the exclusion or the young king, Orsames, himself? Behn's strategy might on one level seem dangerous but it was also clearly intelligent. The anti-exclusionists could not simply deny the king and his brother's moral turpitude; they had to maintain that the succession must follow the right lines in spite of these things. Admitting the problems was thus a way of disarming their opponents.

As Susan Owen has shown, however, Behn did not always maintain a strong anti-patriarchal stance. At times, she expressed her Toryism in more conventional ways. In her play *The Roundheads* of 1681, she negatively represents the wife of a leading parliamentarian, Lady Lambert, and Oliver Cromwell's widow, Lady Cromwell as, in different ways, breaking the constraints which were believed to govern proper female behaviour. Lady Lambert is, her husband says, 'an absolute States-Woman', and she asserts that the possibility of him attaining greater power rests on the fact that her 'Politicks exceeded... [his] meaner Ambition.'[26] Parliamentarianism, and in the context of 1681, Whiggism, were in this way associated with an anti-patriarchal overturning of social mores. Their political vision was thus shown to be intrinsically related to a frightening social vision.[27] Behn re-articulated fears which had been rife during the civil war and interregnum, when Parliamentarian victory was linked by critical propagandists to social inversion and cries that the world had turned upside down were frequent.[28]

Behn's *The Round-heads* therefore also reveals another quotidian aspect of Restoration political culture: its obsession with the past. As we have argued throughout this book, and as the initial vignette concerning Dryden, Marvell, and Milton reinforced, this was a period in which the past, and the desire not to repeat it, was a present concern. Behn's play is based on John Tatham's *The Rump* (first performed in 1660) which lampooned leading figures of the interregnum.[29] The satirical treatment of these men and women remained a powerful way of attacking contemporary Whigs, and behind the satire lay a disturbing political message: any constitutional concessions made to Whigs could open up a passage that led directly back to the 1650s.

But the political language of the past was not simply a Tory one, and it was not just heard during the Exclusion Crisis. The Irish politician and writer the Earl of Orrery – a man who having been a leading figure for a time in Cromwellian Scotland knew more than most about the realities of power in the past and present[30] – reacted in verse to the disturbing political situation in 1675. In response to what many saw as the incipient tyranny being nurtured under Danby (see Chapter 3), the Commons refused the king supply.[31] Meditating upon this vote, Orrery produced 'A vision' in which 'a Ghost... without a Head' conveyed him through the air to the bedside of the sleeping Charles II. The Royal Martyr's spirit and

Orrery looked on as 'An Airy Dame' – the Genius of France – sought to attract the king with all the benefits of French baroque monarchy. French kings had escaped 'Puny Monarks Fates' when they had 'Damn'd' the Estates General; they were not dependent on a representative assembly to raise taxes. Charles II should also accept the power to be obtained from becoming a 'Papist' – the essential religion for any who sought to become 'a Boundlesse King'. In the face of this onslaught, Charles I's ghost dispensed advice to his son on correct constitutional behaviour, stressing that the laws which the Genius of France urged him to break were his 'Bullworks' and had been crucial in ensuring his return in 1660 (see Chapter 1). He also emphasised the role of the Church of England: 'Romes Church, out of Theire Throns, does Monarks fling/Our Church, brings back, a Twelve year Exild King.' Finally, Charles I's ghost turned to Orrery himself and made it clear that politicians too had a part to play in maintaining a healthy reciprocal relationship with the king, and in ensuring that they did not drive him into arbitrary rule.[32] Overhanging the whole poem, metaphorically and literally, is again the spectre of past events and the warning this time that foolish behaviour by king or parliament could easily revive the horrors of the 1640s. The ghost of Charles I was also raised, in an even more incendiary way, in Andrew Marvell's *The Last Instructions to a Painter*.

Marvell's poem was written as part of a series that responded to the second Anglo-Dutch War (1665–7). Early victory had been met by panegyric, and Edmund Waller had rejoiced in the Duke of York's victory off Lowestoft in his *Instructions to a Painter* in 1665. However, as England's prospects in the war became bleaker so did the poetry, and writers criticised not just the course of the fighting but also the government at home. In particular, the king's leading minister, the Earl of Clarendon, was the target for much of the satire. Marvell's poem was written in the aftermath of the humiliating moment in June 1667 when the Dutch Admiral de Ruyter raided the Medway, set three ships alight, and made off with another two including the hubristically named *Royal Charles*, and Clarendon's resignation at the end of August. In one of its most remarkable passages Marvell resurrects key figures from Charles's family:

> Shake then the room, and all his curtains tear,
> And with blue streaks infect the taper clear,
> While the pale ghosts his eye does fixed admire
> Of grandsire Harry and of Charles his sire.
> Harry sits down, and in his open side

> The grisly wound reveals of which he died,
> And ghastly Charles, turning his collar low,
> The purple thread about his neck does show,
> Then whispering to his son in words unheard,
> Through the locked door both of them disappeared.
> The wondrous night the pensive King revolves,
> And rising, straight on Hyde's disgrace resolves.[33]

With exceptional daring Marvell summons forth the ghosts of Charles's grandfather and father. Both had died before their time: Charles I, as Marvell had recorded, on a 'tragic scaffold';[34] Henri IV of France, Charles II's maternal grandfather, at the hands of an assassin in 1610. The advice Charles I gives his son is not revealed to the reader, but the implication is that had Charles II not followed it and resolved on Clarendon's 'disgrace', then the fate of regicide might have befallen him. In an atmosphere where any association with regicide was an irremovable stain on a person's reputation, Marvell's use of it as a warning is startling. It does show, however, that the past provided lessons that could be interpreted and presented differently according to the political position of the writer. Here Marvell's point was more intensely radical than those normally produced, but his method was unsurprising and many others too sought to explain oppositional positions with reference to the past.

Marvell's poem is not simply concerned with the meaning of the past for the present; it is also almost obsessively detailed in its recounting of present events. And a consideration of contemporary political characters, and the reigning monarch, inevitably, inescapably, meant a consideration of sex.

Sex

Marvell instructs his painter to 'Raise up a sudden shape with virgin's face'. Naked, her arms bound behind her back with her own hair, her mouth blocked and her eyes covered, she 'blushes', weeps 'silent tears', and 'Her heart throbs, and with very shame would break.'[35] In the poem Charles responds at first to the virgin with pity but then with erotic intent:

> He wondered first, then pitied, then he loved,
> And with kind hand does the coy vision press
> (Whose beauty greater seemed by her distress)[36]

Charles's impulse to act upon his sexual desires is soon sublimated:

> But soon shrunk back, chilled with her touch so cold,
> And th' airy picture vanished from his hold.
> In his deep thoughts the wonder did increase,
> And he divined 'twas England or the Peace.[37]

As the vision of the virgin fades away Charles recognises that the woman on whom he wished to press himself was England – the king in Marvell's poem was implicated in the attempted rape of his own country. Beyond this general allegory the fabric of the poem at this point is also, as Steven Zwicker has brilliantly demonstrated, woven from a series of specific referents. Charles had been chasing with a notable and unusual lack of success the court beauty Frances Stuart. In February 1667, Stuart had sat as the model for Britannia for Jan Roettier's medal the Peace of Breda which commemorated English naval achievement in the wars.[38] In March, she 'could no longer continue at court without prostituting herself to the king, whom she had long kept off' and ran away and married the Duke of Richmond.[39] Marvell recalled these facts with brutal economy: the vision escapes from Charles's clutches and Marvell punningly referred to her as 'England or the Peace'. Peace meaning 'whore', 'money', and the medal.[40] Thus the specificity of Marvell's poem emphasises the point that Charles's sexual desires and attempted whoring were to the detriment of Britannia.

The specificity of Marvell's reference points to a central reason why sexual language was so significant as a political language in this period. Charles wrote to his sister in 1668: 'If you were as well acquainted with a little fantastical gentleman called Cupide as I am, you would nether wonder nor take ill any sudden changes which do happen in the affaires of his conducting.'[41] When cupid fired shots at Charles's heart, he used not a bow but a machine gun. As we saw in Chapter 4, in contradistinction to previous lascivious courts, his revelled explicitly in its excess. The king's mistresses were publicly acknowledged, and their characters and beliefs were widely discussed and dissected. Thus, while the sense that sex and politics were linked was nothing new, the vigour in the use of this discourse, and its ubiquity, in the Restoration surpassed anything that had preceded it. The king's sexual mores were both literally taken as a sign of corruption and, as in Marvell's poem, were at the centre of a developing metaphorical language which probed Charles's political machinations through sexual discourse.

It appeared in all cultural forms. John Blow's opera 'Venus and Adonis' of c. 1683 reconfigured Ovid's myth for the circumstances of the Restoration court. Of all cultural forms it is easy to believe that opera contains an innate potential to glorify the monarchy, but this potential is undercut in Blow's work by its concentration on the dangers of love. Much ink has been spilt on trying to identify precise contemporary referents in 'Venus', working from the assumption that it has allegorical meaning. However, rather than considering it in these terms, it is more fruitful to examine the general meaning which it may have had within the context of Restoration culture.[42] In Blow's tale, in contradistinction to Ovid's, Adonis is incited to join the hunt by Venus. She justifies this in terms which are pregnant with meaning for Charles's libertine court:

> My Shepherd will you know the Art
> By which I keep a conquer'd Heart.
> I seldom vexe a Lovers ears
> With business or with jealous fears;
> I give him freely all Delights,
> With pleasant Days and easie Nights.[43]

The fact that she is impelling Adonis to leave by emphasising his freedom highlights the way in which, to its critics, libertinism paradoxically imposed a form of tyranny. The tyranny of love, which by sending Adonis forth into the hunt ultimately costs him his life, is further emphasised in Act II in darkly comic fashion. In answer to Venus's question 'how shall I make *Adonis* constant still?' Cupid replies jokingly 'Use him, use him very ill.' Venus's response is to laugh but this laugh does not share in any light-heartedness.[44] Indeed, as Curtis Price notes, 'Blow writes out Venus's *terrifying* laugh note-for-note.'[45] Whether paradoxically in allowing freedom, or in seeking to impose constancy, Venus's tyranny and domination over Adonis is inescapable, its practice only cut short by his death during the hunt which she had implored him to participate in.

In a court where the tyranny of love expressed itself both in the general ways in which Charles's head was ruled by his 'prick', and in the specific ways in which individual mistresses were seen to dominate his affairs, it is not difficult to see the ways in which this opera punctured its own propensity to act as a mode of glorification of monarchy. But unsurprisingly what this opera did not do was to deal in precise terms with particular individuals – that was left to other media.

The individuals most pertinent to the present discussion were of course the king's mistresses. Caught both in the public gaze and in the more confined world of the court they were represented in a number of forms. They were depicted in portraiture which emphasises the roles they played in witty, deliberately shocking pictures. In this picture of Charles's now most famous mistress, Nell Gwyn, the brazen sexuality leaps off the canvas. (Figure 9) She is shown as Diana with both breasts uncovered, a common visual trope to indicate a prostitute. Also outrageous, if for different reasons, is this portrait of Barbara Palmer, Countess of Castlemaine. (Figure 10) Here the seemingly pregnant Castlemaine and her illegitimate child (although the infant has been identified as Castlemaine and

Figure 9 Nell Gwyn Posing as Diana, Simon Verelst (1644–1721). Courtesy of Sotheby's Picture Library.

Figure 10   NPG 2564, Barbara Palmer (née Villiers), Duchess of Cleveland with her son, Charles Fitzroy, as Madonna and Child, after Sir Peter Lely, oil on canvas, *c.* 1664. National Portrait Gallery, London.

Charles's first offspring Charles Fitzroy, there is no seventeenth-century corroboration of this[46]) are portrayed – surely comically and with more than a hint of blasphemy – as the Virgin and child.[47]

These portraits could produce laughter and erotic frisson in some circles but they also adumbrated themes which took on sharper political edges in different forums. As we saw in the previous chapter during the attacks on brothels in 1668, manuscript and verse satire sought to draw links between the court and brothels and portrayed Castlemaine as the greatest whore in the land. These attacks were given added potency by the relation of Castlemaine's whoredom to her Catholicism. In *The Gracious Answer of the most Illustrious Lady of Pleasure*, the persona of Castlemaine writes of the reasons why Catholicism is the best religion for whores:

> ... the worthy Fathers and Confessors ... do declare, That Venerial Pleasures, accompanied with Looseness, Debauchery, and Prophaneness, are not such heinous Crimes and crying Sins, but rather ... they do mortify the Flesh, And in the general Opinion of the Holy Mother Church, is That Venerial Pleasures, in the strictest sence, are but Venial Sins, which Confessors of the meanest Order can forgive. So that the Adoring of Venus, is by the Allowance of Great Authority, Desirable, Honourable, and Profitable.[48]

The links between popery and whoredom could be drawn out in other ways too. At its heart the discourse concerning the mistresses was deeply misogynistic, but it was not simply condemnatory of their sexual behaviour. At times, comparisons were drawn between the sexual proclivities of different mistresses in order to make points about where true political danger lay. The following poetic extract examines Nell Gwyn and the mistress who as both Catholic and French was doubly threatening, Louise de Kéroualle, Duchess of Portsmouth from 1673:

> Have you not heard how our *Soveraigne* of late
> Did first make a *Whore* then a *Dutches* Create
> A notable *Wench* of the *Catholick* kinde
> A *Whore* not onely before, but a *Bugger* behinde
> Poor *Protestant Nell*, well were it for thee
> Wert thou a *Whore* of a double Capacity
> Alas the *Royall Pintle* never yet went
> Into thy *Maiden Lach* or *Fundament*
> Thou art Resolv'd, what e're on it come
> *Protestant* like to keep *Chast* thy *Bum*.[49]

Nell Gwyn's anal 'chastity' is portrayed as part of her Protestantism in contrast with Portsmouth's popish acceptance of buggery. Portsmouth's popery is thus linked to the sexual wiles she uses to impose herself on the king, and the perceived aberration of one is strengthened by its association with the other.[50]

The way in which the mistresses' bodies became sites on which the politics of the age were inscribed finds its most (in)famous expression in the poetry of John Wilmot, Earl of Rochester. Rochester's verse is robbed of erotic charge by the all pervasive self-loathing which drives his horrific desire to penetrate in order to provide his life with meaning. His consideration of female sexual power is never entirely removed from political questions – the awful power that women can obtain over men is often broached: 'A Cunt has no sence of Conscience or Law.'[51] But at times the political significance of his writing is brought more explicitly to the fore. In a poem written in the aftermath of a contest for the king's affections between Nell Gwyn, Portsmouth, and another foreign influence Hortense Mancini, Duchesse de Mazarin a personified people plead: 'Now Heav'ns preserve our *Faiths Defendor,*/From *Paris* Plotts, and Roman Cunt.'[52] Rochester brings into stark relief the disjunction between Charles's title *defensor fidei* (a title which was, in the eyes of many, as ironic for Charles as it became for its first recipient Henry VIII) and his sexual habits, which endangered both his ability to provide the moral leadership required from the holder of the office and the faith itself. Rochester was vocalising widely held concerns rather than providing a strong religious argument himself. He was more concerned with the poetic potential in the irony of the situation than the threat to Protestantism, but at other times he clearly linked the amoralism of the court with political tyranny.

In 'I'th'Isle of great Britain' Rochester probed these connections. First, Charles's sexual appetite and his (mis)rule are joined: 'His Scepter, and's Pricke are boeth of one Length,/And she may sway the one, who plays with th'other.'[53] Secondly, the English Crown is set next to the French one in Rochester's opprobrium: 'I hate all Monarchs, and the Thrones, they sitt on,/From the Hector of France to the Cully of Brittaine.'[54] Thirdly, Charles's conquest of 'Wenches' is set next to his lack of international and domestic standing: 'He Victory, and Honour refuses,/And, rather then a Crowne, a Cunt he chooses.'[55] From the links Rochester forged between the king's 'Scepter' and his 'Pricke', 'Hector' and 'Cully', and the choice of 'a Cunt' over the 'Crowne' he created the chains that threatened to hold England in bondage.

Sexual language thus was political language – the nature of Charles's court made sure of that. Sexually explicit content also hit the stage. The ban on public theatres which had been in place since 1642 was lifted in 1660 but for some contemporaries the moral qualms about theatrical practices remained. Thus it was that one of the key measures which established the potential for sexual material to be explored in a new light – the permission granted for women to perform – was rationalised in language intended to assuage these fears. The patent given to one of the two men who had a monopoly in the theatre, Thomas Killigrew, records:

> for as much as many plays formerly acted doe conteine severall pro-
> phane, obscene, and scurrulous passages, and the women's parts
> therein have byn acted by men in the habit of women, at which
> some have taken offence, for the preventing of these abuses for the
> future . . . wee doe likewise permit and give leave, that all the woemen's
> part . . . may be performed by woemen soe long as their recreacones,
> which by reason of the abuses aforesaid were scandalous and offensive,
> may by such reformation be esteemed not onely harmless delight, but
> also useful and instructive.[56]

The fears were well founded and the rationalisation proved to bear little relation to reality.[57] In the 1670s, the vogue for sex comedies took off. A series of plays put libertine exploits on the stage, and invited audiences to laugh at, be titillated by, and to some extent be complicit in the deeds of young men in thrall to this modish behaviour.[58] Inevitably at the end of such plays orthodox understanding of patriarchy was affirmed through marriage, but such moralising can hardly have effectively closed down the experience provided by the majority of the play.[59] Whilst libertinism could be criticised as part of a political discourse, it was also deeply attractive, and indeed fashionable. For some, Rochester included, this fashion was legitimised through a partial reading of the philosopher Thomas Hobbes. His view of the state of nature – in which 'notions of Right and Wrong, Justice and Injustice have . . . no place' – was seen as indicative of human behaviour, inescapable, and indeed to be embraced.[60] But it also formed a language which did not require these philosophical underpinnings, pervaded much Restoration culture, and was appropriated for some surprising purposes by some surprising people. Perhaps most surprising of all was its use in religious writing.

Religion

In the heady days of the Exclusion Crisis in 1679, the Particular Baptist Benjamin Keach published *The Glorious Lover*. In this work of epic length Keach attempts to explain the ways in which Christ, the Glorious Lover, wins his desired spouse – the Soul – in the face of the attentions of various enemies. Keach was in this poem engaged in a series of dialogues with libertine culture. On one level this engagement amounts to a rejection of this culture, and as such fits within a moralising framework (although as we argued such a framework could exist in libertine plays without negating the bawdy and subversive elements). So we hear the soul complain: 'He suits not my Conditions, doth not please/My curious fancy; I le content mine Eye./Will you the liberty of Choice deny?'[61] Christ the soul claims: 'Is not a person lovely in my sight;/He's not so modish, pleasant, Debonair,/As those brisk Gallants, whom my Fancy share.'[62] The libertine 'Gallants', the men of mode, usurp the position that should be held by Christ, and the character of the Theologue in the poem laments for the Soul's rotted state: 'Her Breath once sweeter than *Arabian* Spices,/Whose rare Perfumes make Houses Paradises,/Offensive is to all that come but near her,/Her Tongue is so unclean, God loaths to hear her.'[63] But despite this moralising the libertines are not the only lovers in the poem. As the title proclaims this is about the Glorious Lover, come to win the unchaste soul as his spouse. The irresistibility of Christ's love and of grace is produced in terms of a military victory in which the passive female soul has no choice but to succumb: 'Where he lays Siege, he'l make the Soul to yield,/By love he overcomes and wins the Field.'[64] The Soul celebrates Christ's victory over her in sexual terms:

> You Virgins who yet never felt the smart
> Of Love's soul-piercing and heart-wounding Dart.
> If all these sacred Raptures you admire,
> Know, Virgins, know that this Celestial Fire
> That's kindled in my breast, comes from above,
> And sets my Soul into this flame of Love.[65]

Keach thus continued to use certain sexual languages, even though he redefined them within his theological schema. His work took on a new edge through its engagement with a specifically libertine language concerning love. His poem titillated, and whilst it ultimately contrasted libertinism with the free love given by Christ to the elect, it still tried to arouse the reader with passion for Christ in terms which were not so far removed from the terms it had critiqued. It might also be noted that Christ as the Glorious Lover must by the very nature of his role be promiscuous and therefore he – in a radical and shocking act of re-description – becomes the greatest libertine.

The transactions between libertine and dissenting culture traced here bring sharply into focus a theme which has run throughout this chapter. From Dryden and Pordage's mock-biblical poems to the links made between popery and whoredom much of the culture explored has been underpinned by religion and expressed in religious terms. The period's culture was thus both reflective of the religious concerns which dominated the age, and also in some sense constitutive of those concerns.

As Keach's writing shows, and as we discussed in Chapter 2, religious dissenters became lively producers of Restoration culture. Our analysis of Keach further suggests that in their attempts to proselytise they were prepared to engage with some of that culture's less salubrious aspects. Clearly the written word became central to the self-expression of these groups.

Emblematic of the way in which literature became a *modus operandi* for dissenters wishing to engage with their brethren and their oppressors – although unusual in many other ways – is John Milton's *Samson Agonistes*.[66] Milton's tragedy, written according to classical conventions, retells the last day of Samson's life. Originally broken and in servitude to the Philistines he undergoes a series of trials. Seemingly, at least, by withstanding these trials through the active exercise of his virtue he is regenerated, and when the Philistines demand his presence at the theatre he exacts a bloody vengeance upon them by bringing it down upon 'Their choice nobility and flower'.[67] Much discussion has focused on whether Milton wrote 'a work in praise of terrorism', that is whether he intended his readers to condone Samson's final actions and thus to accept the uses of political violence in some circumstances.[68] Such discussions may to an extent miss the point. Milton deliberately established that his work is intended to function as a tragedy. The outcome of tragedy he wrote is 'said by Aristotle to be of power by raising pity and fear, or terror, to purge the mind of those and such-like passions, that is to temper and reduce them to just measure with a kind of delight, stirred up by reading or seeing those passions well imitated'.[69] Witnessing Samson's final action should return us to a state of equilibrium, not drive us into a replication of the action. The point is made at the end: 'His servants he with new acquist/Of true experience from this great event/With peace and consolation hath dismissed,/And calm of mind all passion spent.'[70] In the context of its publication in 1671 it is easy to imagine how dissenters might have found its fantasy of retributive violence purgative.

But if Milton did not offer any easy answers in terms of political violence, did he provide any other modes of action for those suffering under

Restoration oppression? He tells us at the start of his text that 'this work never was intended' for the stage.[71] It thus remains a curiously inactive drama, and this sense is compounded by its following of another classical convention: Samson's violent action is reported not shown. The reader encounters the intense description of Samson's action, how he came like 'an evening dragon', how 'as an eagle/His cloudless thunder bolted on their heads', but he or she does not witness it.[72] This may be what Milton leaves his reader with a demonstration of – not action but words. Words could provide a powerful means of religious and political engagement which violence could not. In his vindication of carrying on the battle through the deployment of artistic weapons Milton provides the ultimate answer to the question: why study Restoration culture?

Chapter 9: What were the Main Forces for Change and Continuity in the Post-Revolutionary World, 1688–1714?

Viewing the immensely volatile European scene of the 1830s and 1840s from the safety of London, by then the hub of a worldwide empire, Thomas Babington Macaulay – the most popular historian of the age – was unshakeable in his belief that 'It is because we had a preserving revolution in the seventeenth century that we had not a destroying revolution in the nineteenth'.[1] The British could rejoice that 1688 had seen a 'sensible revolution', one that had clipped the wings of over-ambitious rulers and established the basic framework for constitutional monarchy, representative government, and economic prosperity that led ultimately to the high noon of British imperial dominance in the Victorian era.[2] Several generations of scholars have since largely destroyed this complacent view and established beyond doubt that William II and III's position in his new kingdoms was actually vulnerable until at least 1692, when the threat of imminent French invasion was averted by the great naval victory at La Hogue. Even after that William's monarchy was beset by problems right through to his death in 1702, a year after the demise of James VII and II and the bellicose recognition by France of James Francis Edward – the 'Old Pretender' – as King James VIII and III.

Once again it was in large part the politics of religion that bedevilled the situation, albeit in new and increasingly complex ways. Three core factors shaping the post-revolutionary world may be identified. First, the power of guilty consciences to trouble early modern minds undoubtedly poisoned political life. Although, as we argued in Chapter 5, most Tories had been desperate to foil James's Catholicising policies, many subsequently found it hard to live with the consequences of William's invasion. This soured English affairs – not least as Whigs felt no such qualms and poured scorn on their lily-livered opponents – and fractured the established church. Secondly, the familiar spectre of upheavals within the British Isles left William's government vulnerable. The difficulties of ruling three kingdoms did not suddenly disappear after 1688; indeed they were further complicated by the fact that William was also the stadholder of the Dutch Republic. This leads directly to the third key theme in the post-revolutionary world: William's wars, and the extent to which they and their consequences were bequeathed to his successor, Queen Anne. Between 1689 and 1713 the Stuarts' realms were part of general European conflicts for all but 5 years. This exerted a major impact on society and marked a new stage in the process of state formation. The reverberations caused by the Revolution of 1688 thus affected the political landscape into the eighteenth century, and the last section of this chapter will focus on analysing the degree of continuity and extent of change that the Stuarts' multiple monarchy had experienced by the death of Queen Anne in 1714.

The Tory Conscience

Sir John Bramston and Sir John Reresby were deeply unhappy men in the spring of 1689. Both were sound royalists and churchmen, firm Tories from the days of the Exclusion Crisis. Both had been MPs. Both were representative of the English gentry ruling elite as a whole in the way that they combined punctilious public service with the dedicated pursuit of their families' private interests. Both had acted as justices of the peace, the workhorses of early modern local government and administration, in their respective home counties of Essex and Yorkshire. Both had found their natural instincts of loyalty to the Crown shaken during the reign of James II but were now discomforted by the political exigencies thrown up by the Revolution. In particular, they struggled to reconcile the oaths of loyalty that they had taken to James II with the new oaths that all office-holders were required to swear to William and Mary in 1689. In calmer times oaths were a thoroughly accepted part of the world inhabited by such men: as Bramston confided to paper in his private writings, there could be no assurance of general submission to a government but by 'a religious tye and obligation'. Nevertheless, swearing to do something before God, with the possibility of divine vengeance in the event of oath-breaking, was an awesome responsibility for the conscientious. Neither man viewed the prospect of taking the new oath with anything other than profound unease, even though a major effort to conciliate Tories had been made by removing the usual description of new monarchs as 'rightful and lawful' from the oath of 1689.[3] Bramston tried to comfort himself with the argument that since James had fled the kingdom and made no provision for government, all of his subjects who remained in England could not pay him allegiance under the terms of their pre-existing oath. Indeed that oath was 'abrogated, or at least during his absence is in abeiance, as lawyers call it, and suspended'. Following through this line of argument, Bramston went on to exclaim with extraordinary ingenuousness, 'Marrie, if he [i.e. James] returne, I do think our allegiance will also returne to him.'[4]

If these were unsettling thoughts for the 77-year-old Bramston, they had an even more powerful relevance for Reresby. Twenty-two years Bramston's junior, Reresby was in far greater need of royal favour in order to find the cash and offices required to secure his family's position in Yorkshire society. He had also played a much more prominent part in recent events having been the governor of the key strategic town of York. Captured by members of a pro-William rising in the North of England on 22 November 1688, Reresby's instinctive personal loyalty to James was well known and he came to be looked on as a 'disaffected' man; an accurate view in light of his truculent claim that 'I was for a Parliament and the Protestant religion as well as they, but I was also for the king'. His memoirs show him wrestling in early 1689 with the urgent necessity of deciding what to do in relation to his allegiance. When the bishop of St. David's asked Reresby 'my opinion if he should take the oaths of allegiance and supremacy' the straight-talking Yorkshireman's reply was testy: 'I tould him it was fitter for his lordship to advise me in such a case'. He heard much gloomy commentary about the state of central political affairs from his patron, the Marquess of Halifax, who was irked by William's style of governing: 'this King used noe arts' and 'was very delatory too in his resolutions, which was a great prejudice to business at a time when it soe much required dispatch'. But when Reresby started to reveal his mind in return, and to discuss the degree of discontent against the new regime, Halifax quickly stopped him with the telling argument, 'Come, Sir John, we have wives and children, and we must consider them and not venter too far.' By late April, Reresby was desperate to secure an ambassadorship overseas in order to get away from awkward questions about where his loyalties lay. 'The truth is I found it was hard for one that did not heartily and early come into the present government to live either in town or country without censure'.[5] Only an early death in May 1689 released Reresby from these agonies of conscience. For his part Bramston consulted with his family and chose to avoid all public offices so that he would not be asked to swear oaths he knew he could not in good conscience accept.[6]

The dilemmas posed by the oath of allegiance were deeply felt by Bramston and Reresby as members of the English governing class, but they were even more pressing for clergymen. They had spent the previous three decades preaching up loyalty to the Crown, in terms underpinned by doctrines of passive obedience and non-resistance. More than 300 Church of England clergy – including 9 bishops – refused to take the new oaths and thus became non-jurors. Apart from the immediate traumatic sense of a schism within the established church, the non-jurors proved to be an ongoing thorn in the side of Tories who had taken the oaths, publishing prolifically and energetically maintaining their own sense of purity, ultimately via a separate order of bishops.[7] One such author was the self-exiled dean of Durham, Denis Granville. Whilst falling into poverty in France in late 1689, Granville wrote a new preface to accompany the ultra-loyalist sermon he had preached ten days after William invaded in November 1688. Lambasting the 'new government' and 'the babell which they are building in England', Granville clung to his principles, 'valueing my innocency and quiet of conscience more than I doe the best deanery or bishoprick in Christendom'. Twisting the knife still further in the bowels of less scrupulous clergymen, Granville thanked God that 'nothing yet hath tempted me ... to complement away my religion'. Just as he had maintained his Protestant faith during the period of 'God's raising and settling over us a Prince of a different communion; soe noe consideration whatever ... shall be able to prevaile with me to prostitute it, by falling down to adore the multitude, or any image, (tho' it be of gold) which the people shall set upp'.[8] Granville and others like him were unrelenting in their view that the clergy who took the oaths to William and Mary had cashed in their consciences for their livings.

What the tortured reflections of these three individuals show is that many contemporaries felt the results of the Revolution proved that they had been conned, or else were simply the victims of foreign invasion aided and abetted by discontented Whigs within England. When William abruptly halted debates about whether he or his wife would be the acknowledged sovereign of England by harshly stating that he 'would not like to be his wife's gentleman usher', the Earl of Danby bitterly told assembled peers that 'he hoped they all knew enough now, for his part he knew too much'.[9] Danby had been one of the 'immortal seven' who had invited William to invade England to prevent Catholic tyranny, and had gone so far as to raise troops to support him in the North of England. Yet his disillusionment was clear: rather than selflessly stepping-in to save English civil and religious liberties, William had actually just been interested in securing the royal title. Such sentiments may now seem naïve or self-serving, *ex post facto* rationalisations of why Tories had not done more to safeguard the position of the king whose rights they had so vociferously defended since the Exclusion Crisis. But they do also reflect a literal reading of William's own propaganda at the time of his invasion, which portrayed the prince as selflessly intervening in English affairs to securing the Protestant religion and to trigger the calling of a parliament that had not been packed with lackeys by a Catholic king.[10]

Faced with such widespread discontent amongst a large part of the political ruling class, the most subtle and sensitive of monarchs might have struggled to engage the affections of his new subjects. Unfortunately William was neither particularly subtle, nor remotely sensitive to what he seems to have regarded largely as whinging. In an age in which power was projected through elaborate cultural forms, and in which monarchs were generally praised for the qualities of accessibility and affability (see Chapter 4), William seemed coldly practical and aloof. As the ever observant Roger Morrice noted in October 1689, 'his Majesty loves not a Croud'.[11] In part, this reflected his poor health. Severe asthma left him vulnerable to the smoky atmosphere of London and he preferred to spend time at Hampton Court, then still in the countryside beyond the metropolis. Even when he did grant audiences he could be disconcertingly brusque, not least to those who felt they had the greatest need to acknowledge his intervention in English affairs. When the dissenting minister John Howe travelled to Hampton Court in June 1689, he offered to solicit an address of thanks to William for his efforts to secure a Toleration Bill that removed the Church of England's ability to persecute those Protestants outside its ranks: the king dismissively replied that it was 'not needfull'.[12] He was simply far more interested in doing things than in sugaring the political pill or playing to the gallery, not least as he felt that the English ought to be more grateful than they were for his endeavours on their behalf. To the destabilising effects of guilty Tory consciences we can thus add the wounded pride of the new king, who was disconcerted to find that he had to go cap in hand to a frequently truculent parliament to secure the funds for his European wars. Nor were the legendarily xenophobic English prepared to accept William's largesse to his Dutch favourites with any more grace than they had reacted to James I's generosity to Scots after 1603.

Overall, as Julian Hoppit has acutely observed, William was 'easier to love as an idea than as a man'.[13]

The British Context

How did this difficult, brave, determined, clever, aloof man go about securing his realms beyond England? In Scotland he was pushing at a partly open door. There, as we have seen in Chapter 6, the majority of the population had always resented the Episcopal church structure that a narrow clique of ministers had foisted onto the country after the Restoration. The Scots were particularly proud of their sudden Reformation of 1560, which had been conducted by nobles and lairds against the authority of a Catholic crown. Long memories had ensured that James's pro-Catholic policies had been especially hated North of the Border. In March 1689, a Convention of Estates was treated to the unusual experience of a kind of political beauty contest between two rival suitors for their affection. Both James and William had sent letters setting out their respective stalls. James's was disastrous, lacking in any kind of conciliatory tone and almost calculated to offend. By contrast, William's struck a complimentary note: 'it lyes to you to enter upon such consultations as are most probably to settle you'.[14] With little ado the Scots declared that James had 'forefaulted' the Scottish Crown by virtue of his misgovernment and failure to take the coronation oath as a Protestant, as required by Scots law. William was thereafter under no illusions about the basis of his support beyond the Tweed. When the senior Scottish noble, the Duke of Hamilton, tried to intercede with his new king on behalf of the episcopalian clergy, William 'interrupted him and said He had no friends in Scotland but the Presbyterians'.[15] The price of Scottish support for his regime would prove to be acceptance of a Presbyterian settlement of the church, a result that many Scots had been working for throughout the seventeenth century.

Nevertheless, James did retain the support of many of his Scottish subjects. His time in Scotland during and immediately after the Exclusion Crisis in England had not been entirely unsuccessful, and he had gained the personal loyalty of a number of leading members of the Scottish elite.[16] Nor did the revived Presbyterian structure of the state church in Scotland endear itself to all. Episcopalian sentiment remained strong in the North-east of the country – especially around Aberdeen – and in the Highland zone Catholic clan chiefs were not natural supporters of the new regime. James's problems were, however, substantial. How could he appeal to both Lowland Protestant episcopalians and Highland Catholics at the same time? This was a problem he never really surmounted, not least because of his failure to visit Scotland personally. Lacking the totemic royal presence, his supporters – notably the very able, and widely feared, John Graham of Claverhouse, Viscount Dundee – had a difficult job in securing tangible backing for James's cause. Memories of the reality of his reign were impossible to smooth away with promises of loyalty and reward in the future. Claverhouse's correspondence features a number of letters appealing to members of the Scottish elite in which he was often forced to play the game according to a Williamite agenda, denying the propaganda which was being disseminated by the new regime. As he wrote to one potential supporter, no one ought to be alarmed by 'the danger' William's supporters 'would make the world believe the Protestant religion is in. They must make the religion the pretext as it has been in all times of rebellion'. But Claverhouse knew he could not provide direct assurance of James's future aims and so had to fall back on his own reputation: 'I am as much concerned in the protestant religion as any man, and will doe my indevors to see it secured.' Unable to provide an unequivocal and convincing sense of James's Protestant credentials, Claverhouse turned instead to traditional notions of monarchical largesse and rewards to their faithful servants: the king 'promises not only to me, but to all that will join, such marks of favour, as after ages shall see what honour and advantage there is, in being loyall. He sayes, in express terms, that his favours shall vy with our loyalty'.[17] Claverhouse's persuasive wiles and skills as a soldier were often enough to put the Williamite regime on the back foot until his death during the Battle of Killiecrankie (27 July 1689). Even after that important loss of key personnel, the Jacobite cause in Scotland could still trade on significant political and religious issues for decades to come. Superficial British Protestant solidarity was cemented by the union of parliaments in 1707. But the background to this epochal constitutional event demonstrated little in the way of Anglo-Scottish fraternity. Instead the union was preceded by years of exceptionally acrimonious debates, Scottish fears of marginalisation and lost identity vying with optimism about influence within a broader polity and the extent to which that might result in enormous economic opportunity. As one sceptical Scot, William Black, put it, the prospect of gaining access to English spheres of trade was not 'a sufficient Equivalency for our Sovereignty, Independency and Laws'.[18]

If the situation in Scotland was fraught with difficulty for William, in Ireland it was critically dangerous.[19] On 12 March 1689, James became the first Stuart to set foot in Ireland during the seventeenth century when he landed at Kinsale and tried to rally support with which to defeat William in all three kingdoms. Significant military and strategic opportunities were undoubtedly available for a king dispossessed of his English throne by alienated Protestant subjects. James's trusted henchman, Richard Talbot, Earl of Tyrconnell, was running a Jacobite state with the aid of large numbers of local troops and French support. A Jacobite Parliament met in Dublin in May and provided a constitutional carapace to the armed activity that had been developing in Ireland since the previous December.[20] This all presented a formidable threat to William, one serious enough to force him to devote massive military resources and, ultimately, his own presence to a campaign that fundamentally distracted him from the European theatres of conflict that he really cared about. If his descent on England had been a huge gamble, the later descent on Ireland was replete with risk. Only Oliver Cromwell of all the many English commanders who had tried to pacify Ireland over the previous century and a half had succeeded quickly. And William could not afford to get bogged down in Ireland: he needed to co-ordinate anti-French military affairs on the continent.

Bearing in mind the support that his Catholic co-religionists could offer to James, and the logistical difficulties facing William, James's military defeat by 1691 may initially seem surprising. Anxious English Protestant observers like Roger Morrice were certainly prone to fear the worst during the Williamite wars, and to suspect that the new king's efforts would be hamstrung by shadowy Tory plotters within England.[21] Nevertheless, James's broader 'three kingdoms' concerns held him back from ever being the ideal rival dynast to William in any of his former realms. His overwhelming desire to regain his English throne left him uncomfortable with the anti-Protestant agenda of the 'Patriot Parliament' in Dublin. Its determination to overthrow the Protestant land settlement of 1662 (see Chapter 6) and passing of an Act of Attainder against more than 2000 Irish Protestants in effect attempted to confine him to the role of a sectarian king of Ireland. James's obvious reluctance to play such a role did not enthuse his Catholic Irish subjects. Nor did his decision to return to exile in France after defeat at the Battle of the Boyne (1 July 1690), but before his forces were subdued across much of Ireland, do anything to help his cause.

Yet James's half-hearted activity in his western kingdom prevented him from appearing in person in Scotland, where he might have been better able to secure meaningful military support. As Morrice noted at the time, James's 'probablest attempt' to regain all of his thrones would have required him to go into Scotland 'and fall in with the Prelatists there' – in other words, the dispossessed episcopalians – a move which might also have rallied support amongst discontented Tories within England. But James was temperamentally unable to do that as it would have required him to 'quitt in appearance his Priests and Jesuits and the Papists'.[22] Confident in his Catholic faith, and obstinately convinced that his fate was to be a martyr for his religious beliefs just as surely as his father had been a martyr for the Church of England, James could not appeal to many Protestants. This formidable confessional barrier was reinforced by an awareness of the fact that those few Protestants who had gone into exile with him received little favour. Despite being the highest ranking Protestant cleric at the Jacobite court, Denis Granville, for instance, was sufficiently abused by Catholic priests that he withdrew into a penurious existence elsewhere in France.[23] Like the non-juring clergy, James retained a clean conscience, but at the expense of the kind of tangible support a suppler politician might have garnered within his former kingdoms, not least as the financial consequences of William's continental wars slowly dawned on his British and Irish subjects.

War and State Formation

'War made the state, and the state made war' is a phrase so often repeated that its status has almost altered from being a quotation to an aphorism.[24] Given this, it is necessary to examine the impact that the extended experience of war had on English society and state formation. Certainly the importance of war within state-formation has been carefully demonstrated, even if questions remain over when key developments took place and how precisely state power was extended into the localities and peripheries.[25] Thus it might be expected that England – following a period of Stuart rule when its military incapacity to fight anyone but itself had been shown up – embarked upon a major stage in its development as a 'modern' state in the wars of 1689–1713. To some extent this is the case, but the process was far more complex than this bald analysis allows. It was affected by the way in which England had already become a strong state by the late seventeenth century, and the forces which had driven this previous development.

Two key factors might be delineated in England's state formation prior to the reign of William: law and confessionalisation. The enactment of the common law throughout the king's lands obtained a talismanic quality by the mid seventeenth century. To a significant degree this fact points towards centralisation – it was after all the *king's* justice which was being carried out, which overrode local customs and jurisdictions, and which provided a unifying ideology that took precedence over particularist interests. However, it was centralisation that in many ways remained dependent on local unpaid officials. The influence of the centre was felt throughout the kingdom, but it was only able to function through negotiation with local agents. Thus the rising status of the common law across the realm points to the increasing sophistication of the state, but the means by which it was performed left the potential for tensions between the centre and localities to be realised.[26]

A similar set of observations might be made about confessionalisation. The English Reformation, it is clear, was a long and tempestuous process. And yet, by 1640 an engrained and popular Protestantism, which revolved to some extent around shared prejudice against popery, was in place. Like the common law, religious belief could act as an ideology which cut across local allegiance. But again, whilst the internalisation of these beliefs countered localism, the potential for tensions with the centre to develop remained.[27]

Of course, whether the tensions exploded was to a large extent dependent on who was at the centre. Under Charles I, who abrogated the trust of many of his subjects on confessional and legal grounds, the outcome was civil war. The coming of civil war and the division into two sides also highlighted the fact that the two processes of state formation contained not only the potential to conflict with the centre but also tensions within the processes themselves. Thus debate could escalate over the right interpretation of the law and where the true threat to Protestantism should be located. Where an individual stood on these issues could decide his or her civil war allegiance.

Thus the history of state formation in England up to 1689 seems rather contradictory. England was at once a centralised and sophisticated strong state and at the same time highly dependent on local co-operation with the king's agenda. Furthermore, centralising ideologies, whilst they could be harnessed by an astute monarch, could also produce both the reasons for conflict with the monarchy and the languages by which such conflict could be legitimated.

This is the context for understanding the impact that the wars of 1689–1713 had on England's state development. They represent not the crucial moment at which England became a modern state but a stage in a longer process. The ways in which the three components – law, religion, and war – interacted provided the basis for both the continued political conflicts of the period and the peculiarities of the English state.[28]

As an unimpeachably Protestant monarch William was in a strong position to harness even greater financial resources than those which England had shown itself to be capable of producing in civil war, and to deploy them militarily on the continent against the might of Louis XIV. No longer could there be any question that the monarch was involved in nefarious popish schemes, and thus fears that had previously hindered the granting of money could be assuaged.[29] Indeed, to an extent the wars could be portrayed as England finally grasping the Protestant military destiny which some believed to have been thrown off course by the advent of the Stuarts following the glorious reign of Elizabeth.[30] As one versifier put it in a poem which imagined the meeting between Elizabeth and William's joint monarch Queen Mary in heaven:

> Q. Mary II
> What *Philip* try'd to compass in your Reign,
> Lately proud *LEWIS* fancy'd to obtain,
> But Heaven indulgent still to Me and Mine,
> Ruin'd his Hope, and blasted his Design.[31]

Certainly judged in terms of hard cash William was able to gain considerable support for his ventures. During the Nine Years War (1689–97), the average raised through taxation was £3.64 million a year – around twice as much as had previously been extracted.[32] The impact of both this and then the similarly remarkable sums raised under Anne was ironically in part, as Tim Harris has suggested, to produce 'a monarchy with more real power, as a result of the creation of the fiscal military state'.[33]

But the development of the state along fiscal-military lines ran parallel with the continued importance of its legal and confessional foundations. For all their power the monarchs of 1688–1714 had to continue to contend with major political conflict which grew out of these foundations.[34] This conflict may be examined in relation to two particularly explosive moments: the standing armies debate and the Sacheverell controversy.[35]

Following the end of the Nine Years War with the Treaty of Ryswick in 1697, William intended to maintain a large army in peacetime. He was met by a storm of protest. A key writer, John Trenchard, powerfully expressed the opposition view of the dangers inherent in the standing army:

> What if they should say, Parliaments are seditious and factious assemblies, and therefore ought to be abolished; What is become of your Freedom? Or, if they should encompass the Parliament-House, and threaten if they do not surrender up their Government, they will put them to the Sword; What is to become of the old English Constitution.[36]

So virulent were these fears that some critical writers began explicitly to compare William to Oliver Cromwell.[37] The implications of this were hardly complimentary: many contemporaries remembered the 1650s as a time of military despotism in which Cromwell had often cut Gordian knots in the constitution with the point of a sword. William's desires hit the rocks of the ancient constitution – the war state met its match in the law state.[38]

The Sacheverell controversy demonstrates how confessional politics remained central to party strife, and illuminates how, even if in certain debates (not least the ones concerning standing armies) cross-party alignments could occur, partisan conflict remained the *sine qua non* of English politics. Henry Sacheverell was an angry clergyman.[39] To him dissenters were a seditious force, threatening to bring England to its knees. When he stepped into the pulpit on 5 November 1709, the modern observer might be forgiven for thinking that he had been possessed by the ghost of Roger L'Estrange. He raged for an hour and a half against pernicious nonconformists and their Whig supporters. At one point he articulated the points that had been made in the previously analysed print *The Committee* (Figure 2): 'the old leaven of their forefathers is still working in their present generation and this traditional poison still remains in this brood of vipers to sting us to death'.[40] The dissenters remained potential regicides. Sacheverell's outburst – performed on a day of national Protestant celebration for the Jacobean escape from the Gunpowder Plot – was widely publicised: around 100,000 copies of the printed sermon flew off booksellers' stalls. This publicity partly drove the Whig government's resolve to impeach Sacheverell. Impeachment in turn created a greater market for the sermon.[41] As this suggests, the Sacheverell controversy was one which, inevitably by this stage, took place in the world of politics out-of-doors. Although Sacheverell was impeached, he garnered a great deal of popular support. His conviction can hardly be seen as a triumph for the Whigs, and the pathetic sentence he was given led to nationwide Tory expressions of joy. Such expressions took traditional celebratory and violent forms. As one dissenting minister in Sherborne wrote:

> There being also some bottles of wine sent into the Church for another select company, the Doctor's health (as I am informed) was drunk by both sexes at the top of the tower, with lights in their hands to give notice of it.... the rabble, who cursed the Presbyterians to the pit of Hell, beat a drum about the town, threatened to burn or pull down our meeting-houses, and having guns with them, they made a halt at several houses and fired at them, at my own in particular ... [42]

In part because of the Sacheverell controversy, the Tories went on to win a thumping electoral victory in 1710. The issue of Church and dissent thus remained alive and divisive in parliament and in popular politics. England's reformation was proving to be very long indeed, and the nature of English Protestantism was still contentious.[43] This more than anything else continued to fuel conflict and harden divisions.

Conclusion: Continuity and Change

It has recently been argued that in 1688 William of Orange and his Whig allies 'decided to wind up the old England and invent a new one'.[44] Such clear-cut analysis rests on a preoccupation with foreign policy in the post-revolutionary world and the sense that the Dutch stadholder's takeover of Britain and Ireland fundamentally and consistently involved it in European affairs in a novel way. As we have argued, this sense of 1689 as a kind of 'Year Zero' for re-born liberties may reflect the more strident claims of some of William's propagandists and supporters, but it underestimates the continuity of many of the issues that had bedevilled political life before 1688, and indeed across much of the seventeenth century. The real difficulty for those studying the period between the Glorious Revolution and the Hanoverian succession in 1714 is how to balance the competing forces of continuity and change.

One approach is to recognise how many significant dimensions of the eighteenth-century experience became so only after – and in some instances long after – 1714. Britain may ultimately have become the hub of a maritime empire with immensely important components in coastal North America and South Asia, but in the early eighteenth century its navy was generally more preoccupied with the long-standing strategic significance of the Baltic and Mediterranean Seas than with the possibilities of the Atlantic and Indian Oceans.[45] Another approach involves explicitly de-coupling notions of progress and development from the straightforward passage of time. The 'long eighteenth century' is often 'book-ended' by the Glorious Revolution and the Great Reform Act of 1832. This can too readily lead to a false teleology based around notions of inevitable constitutional development, and, in particular, the rise of the House of Commons. Yet the percentage of the population able to vote in the reign of Queen Anne was significantly greater than in 1831, and the monarchy and the aristocracy (both within and without the House of Lords) demonstrated time and again a capacity to exercise real and perceived political influence that runs counter to any simplistic notion of a long-term 'rise' of the House of Commons.[46] A third approach is to give due attention to the crucial aspects of continuity across the 1688 divide in order the better to show what really did change. It is with this vital issue that we will conclude, focusing on the issues and media that shaped public life in the period.

By 1722, the authors of *Cato's Letters*, John Trenchard and Thomas Gordon, could complain that political parties were as variable as the English weather: 'a *Tory* under oppression and out of place is a *Whig*: a *Whig* with power to oppress is a *Tory*.... We change sides every day, yet keep the same names for ever'.[47] In doing so they pointed to the crucial fact of post-revolutionary life, namely that party politics was at once ubiquitous and immensely malleable. As Geoffrey Holmes, the greatest historian of this period, famously pronounced, 'the division of men into Whig and Tory...was an utterly basic fact: the most dominating, inescapable fact of political life at all levels from the very beginning of [Queen Anne's] reign to the very end'.[48] Furthermore, although slower to take hold, and never as all-pervasive, this bi-polar division began to be significant in Scotland and Ireland too.[49]

Small wonder that Tory and Whig politics captured the attention of contemporaries, and have continued to puzzle modern historians. In the intense melting pot of war, state-building, dynastic conflict, and religious upheavals that occurred between 1688 and 1714, contemporaries utilised many languages to explain the fundamental divisions in their public environment. Reconsiderations of the past and discussions of God's intentions for the future were two of the most important. Around the turn of the eighteenth century, a slew of published editions of texts illustrating the mid-century revolution were produced, not least an edition of John Milton's works.[50] Especially during the debates over the standing army, certain radical Whig authors had turned to the past and made it speak to the present. Most famously a version of the *Memoirs* of the mid-century republican, Edmund Ludlow, was produced. The didactic intent behind the edition was made explicit: 'Men may learn from the issue of the Cromwellian tyranny that liberty and a standing mercenary army are incompatible.'[51] What was not made explicit was the way in which the editor(s) had altered the text in order to sharpen its contemporary significance, effectively bleaching out Ludlow's fervent religiosity and re-casting him as a secular republican.[52] But Providentialism continued to bolster the hopes of many, not least the Whig judge Thomas Rokeby who wrote in his diary for 1689 that he believed 'the cause wherein King William and Queen Mary and the parliament of England are now ingaged [i.e. war with Louis XIV and his client, James VII and II] to be the cause of God and AntiChrist'.[53] The implication was clear: political positions could be mapped onto absolute rights and absolute wrongs. Yet over time, the fact that intensely divisive party politics did not result in the implosion of the British polities began to soften attitudes towards the implications of vigorously expressed disagreements. Classical notions of inherently 'bad' factions corroding public order could still be invoked, but at a day-to-day level Whig and Tory partisanship became accepted, however grudgingly, as the reality that politicians and the electorate had to work within.[54]

Until the passage of the Septennial Act in 1716, party political combat was rarely out of mind since the Triennial Act of 1694 had stipulated that general elections had to occur every 3 years. Politics out-of-doors thus remained immensely lively, with a key part of this 'rage of party' during the early eighteenth century being the continued power of religious issues to motivate attitudes and actions.[55] The Sacheverell crisis was just one, albeit very important, part of a wider ongoing crisis about the identity of the Church of England.[56] Far from drawing a line under past debates, the Toleration Act of 1689 that removed penalties from those Protestants choosing to worship outside the Church of England served only to transmit them to a new generation under a different guise. Since the Toleration Act had not superseded the Test Acts that required all office-holders to be communicating members of the Church of England, some prominent dissenters adopted the practice of 'occasional conformity', that is they took Anglican communion just frequently enough to qualify for office whilst obviously continuing the bulk of their religious lives in nonconformist meeting houses. Tories abhorred this strategy, not least as it brought a number of able and committed individuals into the ranks of their Whig opponents. Indeed Tories often adopted for themselves the label of the 'Church Party', and Sacheverell and a host of other controversialists used 'the church in danger' as a powerful rallying cry. The intensity of this re-shaped 'politics of religion' permeated society, splitting it from top to bottom, from the House of Lords to local communities within individual counties.[57]

If frequent general elections were the fields within which party politics flourished, they were irrigated by the printed outpourings of the press. Here the floodgates had opened in 1695 with the lapsing of the Licensing Act.[58] Removing the shackles from writers seemed to many hostile contemporaries merely to put the people in chains formed by lies and half-truths produced by unscrupulous hacks.[59] This was particularly true in Augustan London, where there were probably twice as many printing houses in 1710 as there had been during the Exclusion Crisis. These spewed out large numbers of titles, often in huge print runs and in increasingly sophisticated forms, notably periodicals printed on regular days of the week and maintaining a persistent partisan slant based along party lines.[60] But if the metropolitan readership was peculiarly sophisticated, and had unrivalled access to printed materials, this is not to suggest that the provinces lacked political information. Far from it: the early decades of the eighteenth century witnessed the emergence and rapid growth of provincial newspapers and periodicals catering to local audiences keen to hear national news.[61]

As this account suggests, party political life may not have been new after 1688, but its consistent intensity was. The 'rage of party' evident during the reign of Anne vitally affected politicians' relationship to power. Although William III had tried to avoid being captured by ministries composed exclusively of either Whigs or Tories, such 'mixed ministries' proved increasingly difficult to sustain as partisan feelings deepened. This was certainly in part a matter of the pursuit of power and privilege by individuals, but it was also a quest to be able to direct policy based on ideological beliefs.[62] Ultimately the period after 1688 saw profound change and manifest continuity in terms of what politicians fought about. In particular, two opposed visions of what imperilled the nation were spun from materials with long pedigrees.

Whigs feared that Louis XIV, whose omnipresent shadow darkened the first age of party, was a greater threat than ever precisely because of William's success in 1688. The exiled James VII and II, and, after 1701, his son could be used to sow internal dissension within England, Scotland, and Ireland in pursuit of a restoration of the senior Stuart line.

The years 1701–13/14 witnessed a massive war over the dynastic fate o̲ Spain, but the campaigns fought by William III and John Churchill, Duke of Marlborough, were also about the British succession. Only by defeating Louis in Europe could a Protestant settlement at home be assured in the form of the nearest Protestant claimants, the Electress of Hanover and her descendents.[63] For their part, Tories feared that foreign warfare might also disturb domestic affairs, from their perspective in the form of a rapidly expanding fiscal-military state that gave the Crown unprecedented resources and powers of patronage. Military muscle and financial clout threatened the creation of a tyranny under William, or a subtler threat under Anne if the queen listened too much to the counsels of her favourite Sarah Churchill, and the latter's husband, the same Duke of Marlborough lionised by Whigs as a new Protestant hero.[64]

For all the fiscal-military changes wrought by the Revolution, religion remained key to these rival visions of liberty and slavery. Whigs enjoyed close alliance with Protestant dissenters, and feared that their Tory opponents aimed to re-impose the penalties that the Toleration Act of 1689 had removed. Tories resented what they perceived as abuse of the sacraments of the Church of England by dissenters whose professed zeal was nothing more than a blind for their secular and material ambitions. At the elections of 1710, Surrey Tories circulated mass produced bills that proclaimed their candidates for parliament to be in opposition to 'all managers of Oliver [Cromwell]'s party and principles, that once murdered their King and thousands of the nation to rule over us'.[65] The Hanoverian succession of 1714 would see the briefly triumphant Tories of 1710 cast into the political abyss for decades by a new dynasty that saw its own interests best served by Whig ministers. But the forces that had shaped Restoration politics, religion, and culture would continue to provide the fuel that stoked the fires of partisanship long into the eighteenth century.[66]

Notes

Introduction: Why Study Restoration History?

1. Quoted in Paul Seaward, 'Charles II', *ODNB*; L.G. Mitchell, 'Charles James Fox', *ODNB*.
2. C.R.L. Fletcher, *An Introductory History of England* (5 vols, 1904–23), III, p. 57. For Fletcher, see Michael Bentley, *Modernizing England's Past: English Historiography in the Age of Modernism 1870–1970* (Cambridge, 2005), p. 183.
3. For telling examples from another nation in a slightly earlier period, see J.H. Elliott, 'Self-Perception and Decline in Early Seventeenth-Century Spain', *P&P*, 74 (1977), 41–61, esp. 46–7.
4. 'The Dutch in the Medway (1664–1672)', in *Rudyard Kipling's Verse: Inclusive Edition 1885–1918* (1918), p. 760.
5. Three examples of continuing importance are as follows: Andrew Browning, *Thomas Osborne, Earl of Danby and Duke of Leeds* (3 vols, Glasgow, 1944–51); J.P. Kenyon, *Robert Spencer, Earl of Sunderland 1641–1702* (Cambridge, 1958); and K.H.D. Haley, *The First Earl of Shaftesbury* (Oxford, 1968).
6. A.M. Starkey, 'Robert Wodrow and the History of the Sufferings of the Church of Scotland', *Church History*, 43 (1974), 488–98.
7. S.J. Connolly, *Religion, Law and Power: The Making of Protestant Ireland 1660–1760* (Oxford, 1992).
8. J.C.D. Clark, *English Society 1660–1832: Religion, Ideology and Politics During the Ancien Regime* (Cambridge, 2000). The first edition (1985) began in 1688. For a vigorous response to Clark's arguments, see Joanna Innes, 'Jonathan Clark, Social History and England's "Ancien Regime"', *P&P*, 115 (1987), 165–200.

NOTES 179

9. Jonathan Scott, *England's Troubles: Seventeenth-Century English Political Instability in European Context* (Cambridge, 2000). Scott has gone on to sketch the history of English republicanism across the seventeenth century as a whole: *Commonwealth Principles: Republican Writing of the English Revolution* (Cambridge, 2004).
10. See Chapter 6.
11. Peter Gay, *The Enlightenment: An Interpretation, the Rise of Modern Paganism* (1967); Theodore K. Hoppen, 'The Nature of the Early Royal Society', *British Journal for the History of Science*, 9 (1976), 1–24, 243–73; Christopher Hill, *Intellectual Origins of the English Revolution* (Oxford, 1965).
12. A.S.P. Woodhouse (ed.), *Puritanism and Liberty: Being the Army Debates from the Clarke Manuscripts, with Supplementary Documents* (1950); Christopher Hill, *The World Turned Upside Down: Radical Ideas During the English Revolution* (1972).
13. Fundamentally important in establishing this position was Tim Harris, Paul Seaward, and Mark Goldie (eds), *The Politics of Religion in Restoration England* (Oxford, 1990).
14. The classic study remains Conrad Russell, *The Fall of the British Monarchies, 1637–1642* (Oxford, 1991).
15. See most notably Tim Harris, *Restoration: Charles II and His Kingdoms, 1681–1685* (2005); Tim Harris, *Revolution: The Great Crisis of the British Monarchy, 1685–1720* (2006).
16. For a useful overall introduction, see Tim Harris, 'The Parties and the People: The Press, the Crowd and Politics "Out-of Doors" in Restoration England', in Lionel K.J. Glassey (ed.), *The Reigns of Charles II and James VII & II, 1660–1689* (Basingstoke, 1997), pp. 125–51.
17. Joad Raymond, *Pamphlets and Pamphleteering in Early Modern Britain* (Cambridge, 2003); Harold Love, 'The Look of News: Popish Narratives 1678–80', in John Barnard and D.F. McKenzie (eds), *The Cambridge History of the Book in Britain, vol. 4: 1557–1695*; with the assistance of Maureen Bell (Cambridge, 2002), pp. 652–6; Mark Knights, *Representation and Misrepresentation in Later Stuart Britain: Partisanship and Political Culture* (Oxford, 2004).

Chapter 1: What was Restored in 1660?

1. John Milton, *Areopagitica*, in D.M. Wolfe (ed.), *Complete Prose Works of John Milton* (8 vols, New Haven, 1952–82), II, p. 558.

2. John Milton, *The Readie and Easie Way to Establish a Free Commonwealth*, in *ibid.*, VII, p. 463.
3. Quoted in Tim Harris, *London Crowds in the Reign of Charles II: Propaganda and Politics from the Restoration to the Exclusion Crisis* (Cambridge, 1987), p. 51.
4. Esmond S. De Beer (ed.), *Diary of John Evelyn* (6 vols, Oxford, 1955), III, p. 246.
5. N. H. Keeble, *The Restoration: England in the 1660s* (Oxford, 2002), pp. 52–3.
6. Quoted in *ibid.*, p. 53.
7. De Beer (ed.), *Diary*, III, p. 246; Gary S. De Krey provides the best account of the Restoration in the capital: *London and the Restoration, 1659–1683* (Cambridge, 2005), pp. 3–66.
8. An excellent general survey, which we have drawn on here, and in addition to the specific works noted below, is David L. Smith, *A History of the Modern British Isles 1603–1707: The Double Crown* (Oxford, 1998).
9. Clive Holmes, *Why was Charles I Executed?* (2006), ch. 1; Conrad Russell, *The Fall of the British Monarchies, 1637–1642* (Oxford, 1991). For an opposing view of Charles I's personal rule, see Kevin Sharpe, *The Personal Rule of Charles I* (New Haven and London, 1992). Richard Cust has provided a judicious account of Charles I: Richard Cust, *Charles I: A Political Life* (Harlow and New York, 2005).
10. D.L. Smith, *Constitutional Royalism and the Search for Settlement, c. 1640–1649* (Cambridge, 1994).
11. Joyce Lee Malcolm, 'Charles II and the Reconstruction of Royal Power', *HJ*, 35 (1992), 317.
12. *Ibid.*, 316.
13. Ronald Hutton, *The Restoration: A Political and Religious History of England and Wales, 1658–1667* (Oxford, 1985), pp. 148–9, 157–8; C.D. Chandaman, *The English Public Revenue 1660–1688* (Oxford, 1975). Chandaman sees the court interest as key in deciding upon the excise, but it does not seem unreasonable to hear the collective sigh of relief breathed by the gentry MPs when this was agreed: *ibid.*, pp. 37–9.
14. *EHD*, pp. 164–5, quotation at p. 164.
15. David Norbrook, *Writing the English Republic: Poetry, Rhetoric and Politics, 1627–1660* (pbk edn, Cambridge, 2000), p. 1.
16. *His Majesties most Gracious Speech together with the Lord Chancellors, to the Two Houses of Parliament; on Thursday the 13 September, 1660* (1660), pp. 11–12; partially quoted in Jonathan Scott, *England's Troubles: Seventeenth-Century English Political Instability in European Context*

(Cambridge, 2000), p. 394. See more generally Scott's analysis of the importance of public memory which runs throughout his book.

17. Matthew Jenkinson, 'The Politics of Court Culture in the Reign of Charles II' (University of Oxford DPhil thesis, 2007), pp. 67–8; Keeble, *Restoration*, pp. 55–7, 71–6.

18. De Beer (ed.), *Diary*, III, 259; *Fifth Report of the Royal Commission on Historical Manuscripts* (1876), p. 174.

19. John Adams to Thomas Jefferson, 1815, quoted in Bernard Bailyn, *The Ideological Origins of the American Revolution* (Cambridge, 1967), p. 1.

20. For the Clubmen see John Morrill, *Revolt in the Provinces: The People of England and the Tragedies of War, 1630–48* (1999), pp. 132–51.

21. Joad Raymond, *Pamphlets and Pamphleteering in Early Modern Britain* (Cambridge, 2003), p. 163. These figures include all surviving books published in Britain and English works produced abroad.

22. John Morrill, 'The Causes and Course of the British Civil Wars', in N.H. Keeble (ed.), *The Cambridge Companion to Writing of the English Revolution* (Cambridge, 2001), pp. 13–31, statistics at pp. 21–2.

23. 'Charles II, 1662: An Act for preventing the frequent Abuses in printing seditious treasonable and unlicensed Bookes and Pamphlets and for regulating of Printing and Printing Presses', *Statutes of the Realm: volume 5: 1628–80* (1819), pp. 428–35. http://www.british-history.ac.uk/report.aspx?compid=47336. See also Keeble's comments: N.H. Keeble, *The Literary Culture of Nonconformity in Later Seventeenth-Century England* (Leicester, 1987), p. 96.

24. *Journals of the House of Commons, 1547–1714* (17 vols, 1803–52), VIII, 425.

25. This section on the constitutional legacy is indebted to the analysis of Tim Harris: Tim Harris, *Politics Under the Later Stuarts: Party Conflict in a Divided Society 1660–1715* (1993), pp. 33–9.

26. The best account of this year remains Austin Woolrych, 'Historical Introduction', in Wolfe (ed.), *Complete Prose*, VII, pp. 1–228.

27. Accounts of tactical alliances and the forces which brought about Restoration may be found in De Krey, *London and the Restoration*, introduction and ch. 1; Barry Reay, 'The Quakers, 1659, and the Restoration of the Monarchy', *History*, 63 (1978), 193–213; Holmes, *Why was Charles I Executed?*, ch. 8.

28. Ronald Hutton, 'George Monck', *ODNB*.

29. Hutton, *Restoration*, p. 105.

30. *A Remonstrance of his Excellency Thomas Lord Fairfax* (1648), p. 62.

31. Andrew Lacey, *The Cult of King Charles the Martyr* (Woodbridge, 2003).
32. Junius Brutus (pseud.), *An Appeal from the Country to the City* (1679), p. 5, quoted in Raymond, *Pamphlets and Pamphleteering*, p. 323.
33. Paul Seaward, *The Cavalier Parliament and the Reconstruction of the Old Regime, 1661–1667* (Cambridge, 1989), pp. 17–25.
34. J.G.A. Pocock, *The Ancient Constitution and the Feudal Law: A Study of English Historical Thought in the Seventeenth Century* (Cambridge, 1957).
35. Holmes, *Why was Charles I Executed?*, ch. 7.
36. Quoted in Harris, *Politics Under the Later Stuarts*, p. 37.
37. Quoted in Seaward, *Cavalier Parliament*, p. 19.
38. George Morley, *A Sermon Preached at the Magnificent Coronation of the Most High and Mighty King Charles IId* (1661), p. 36, partially quoted in Harris, *Politics Under the Later Stuarts*, p. 36.
39. Charles Cotton, *A Panegyrick to the Kings most Excellent Majesty* (1660), p. 9.
40. Thomas Fuller, *A Panegyrick to his Majesty on his Happy Return* (1660), p. 11.
41. John Morrill, 'The Church in England, 1642–9', in John Morrill (ed.), *Reactions to the English Civil War, 1642–1649* (1982), pp. 89–114; Judith Maltby, 'Suffering and Surviving: The Civil Wars, the Commonwealth and the Formation of "Anglicanism", 1642–60', in Christopher Durston and Judith Maltby (eds), *Religion in Revolutionary England* (Manchester, 2006), pp. 158–80.
42. On these attempts, see Claire Cross, 'The Church in England 1646–1660', in G. E. Aylmer (ed.), *The Interregnum: The Quest for Settlement, 1646–1660* (rev. edn, 1974), pp. 99–120.
43. The classic account of radical thought remains Christopher Hill, *The World Turned Upside Down: Radical Ideas in the English Revolution* (Harmondsworth, 1972).
44. J.C. Davis, *Fear, Myth and History: The Ranters and the Historians* (Cambridge, 1986).
45. M.R. Watts, *The Dissenters: From the Reformation to the French Revolution* (Oxford, 1985), p. 509.
46. Christopher Durston and Judith Maltby, 'Introduction: Religion and Revolution in Seventeenth-Century England', in Durston and Maltby (eds), *Religion in Revolutionary England*, p. 1.
47. 'The Declaration of Breda', in S.R. Gardiner (ed.), *The Constitutional Documents of the Puritan Revolution 1625–1660* (3rd edn, Oxford, 1906), p. 466.

48. Some had been ejected before the Act came into force. These figures, and other issues examined in this section, are discussed in far more detail in Chapter 2.
49. Jonathan Scott, *Algernon Sidney and the Restoration Crisis, 1677–83* (Cambridge, 1991), p. 8.
50. For a useful introduction to debates concerning change and continuity, see Alan Houston and Steve Pincus, 'Introduction. Modernity and Later Seventeenth-Century England', in Alan Houston and Steve Pincus (eds), *A Nation Transformed: England After the Restoration* (Cambridge, 2001), pp. 1–19. Scott's work is briefly discussed on pp. 4–5. Houston and Pincus point to the critique of Scott provided in Tim Harris, 'What's New about the Restoration?', *Albion* 29 (1997), 187–222, which has also informed our thinking.
51. Andrew Marvell, *An Account of the Growth of Popery and Arbitrary Government in England*, in Martin Dzelzainis, N.H. Keeble, Annabel Patterson, and Nicholas von Maltzahn (eds), *The Complete Prose Works of Andrew Marvell* (2 vols, New Haven and London, 2003), II, p. 225.

Chapter 2: Why were Dissenters a Problem?

1. Pepys, *Diary*, II, p. 9. The best account of Venner's rising is Richard L. Greaves, *Deliver us from Evil: The Radical Underground in Britain, 1660–1663* (Oxford, 1986), pp. 50–7.
2. B.S. Capp, *The Fifth Monarchy Men: A Study in Seventeenth-Century English Millenarianism* (1972), p. 14 and *passim*. On the debate within Fifth Monarchism of the role that Christ himself would play during the millennium, see *ibid.*, p. 137.
3. *A Door of Hope* (1661), p. 4. This manifesto is analysed in Bernard Capp, '*A Door of Hope* Re-Opened: The Fifth Monarchy, King Charles and King Jesus', *Journal of Religious History*, 32 (2008), 16–30.
4. Pepys, *Diary*, II, pp. 10–11, quotation at p. 11.
5. Richard L. Greaves, 'Thomas Venner', *ODNB*.
6. Pepys, *Diary*, II, p. 10.
7. *Ibid.*; Greaves, 'Thomas Venner'.
8. Greaves, *Deliver*, p. 52.
9. *Ibid.*; Richard L. Greaves, *Enemies under his Feet: Radicals and Nonconformists in Britain, 1664–1677* (Stanford, 1990); Richard L. Greaves, *Secrets of the Kingdom: British Radicals from the Popish Plot to the Revolution of 1688–89* (Stanford, 1992).

184 NOTES

10. Greaves, *Deliver*, p. 121; William Hill, *A Brief Narrative of that Stupendious Tragedie* (1662), p. 34.
11. The best account of the Tong plot, to which this section is indebted, is Greaves, *Deliver*, ch. 4.
12. Robin Clifton, *The Last Popular Rebellion: The Western Rising of 1685* (1984); Peter Earle, *Monmouth's Rebel's: The Road to Sedgemoor, 1685* (1977).
13. The National Archives, SP 29/109, f. 56.
14. See for example Mark Goldie, 'The Hilton Gang and the Purge of London in the 1680s', in Howard Nenner (ed.), *Politics and the Political Imagination in Later Stuart Britain* (Woodbridge, 1998), pp. 43–73.
15. N.H. Keeble, *The Restoration: England in the 1660s* (Oxford, 2002), pp. 154–6.
16. 'The Declaration of Breda', in S.R. Gardiner (ed.), *The Constitutional Documents of the Puritan Revolution 1625–1660* (3rd edn, Oxford, 1906), p. 466.
17. Quoted in John Spurr, *The Restoration Church of England* (New Haven and London, 1991), p. 31.
18. The surplice was still enforced in the chapel royal, cathedrals, collegiate churches, and in the universities.
19. *Journal of the House of Lords* (22 vols, 1846), XI, 179–82, quotations at 180, 181, 182.
20. N.H. Keeble, 'Richard Baxter', *ODNB*; Spurr, *Restoration Church*, pp. 40–1. As Spurr notes, it is perhaps surprising that the small revisions that were made do not reflect the 'Laudian' hue of some of the revisers (Cosin and Wren, for example), but seem to have been influenced by puritan suggestions. This was perhaps due to the intervention of Robert Sanderson and Edward Reynolds. See *ibid.*, p. 40.
21. 'Charles II, 1662: An Act for the Uniformity of Publique Prayers and Administrac[i]on of Sacraments & other Rites & Ceremonies and for establishing the Form of making ordaining and consecrating Bishops Preists and Deacons in the Church of England', *Statutes of the Realm: volume 5: 1628–80* (1819), pp. 364–70. http://www.british-history.ac.uk/report.aspx?compid=47307.
22. N.H. Keeble, *The Literary Culture of Nonconformity in Later Seventeenth-Century England* (Leicester, 1987), p. 31.
23. John Oliver, vicar of Montacute, Somerset to John Thornton, chaplain to William Russell, Earl of Bedford, London, September 1662, quoted in R.A. Beddard, 'Nonconformist Responses to the Onset

of Anglican Uniformity, 1661–1664: Letters to John Thornton, The Earl of Bedford's Presbyterian Chaplain', *Bodleian Library Record*, 17 (2000), 138.

24. Joseph Baker to Richard Baxter, 30 December 1662: letter 706, in N.H. Keeble and Geoffrey F. Nuttall (eds), *Calendar of the Correspondence of Richard Baxter* (2 vols, Oxford, 1991), II, p. 33. The allusion is to Jer. 13: 16.
25. Quoted in David J. Appleby, *Black Bartholomew's Day: Preaching, Polemic and Restoration Nonconformity* (Manchester, 2007), p. 99.
26. Keeble, *Literary Culture*, p. 32.
27. *Ibid.* On the Cromwellian Church, see Jeffrey R. Collins, 'The Church Settlement of Oliver Cromwell', *History*, 87 (2002), 18–40.
28. 'Charles II, 1662: An Act for preventing the Mischeifs and Dangers that may arise by certaine Persons called Quakers and others refusing to take lawfull Oaths', *Statutes of the Realm: volume 5: 1628–80* (1819), pp. 350–1. http://www.british-history.ac.uk/report.aspx?compid=47304.
29. 'Charles II, 1664: An Act to prevent and suppresse seditious Conventicles', *Statutes of the Realm: volume 5: 1628–80* (1819), pp. 516–20. http://www.british-history.ac.uk/report.aspx?compid=47357.
30. 'Charles II, 1665: An Act for restraining Non-Conformists from inhabiting in Corporations', *Statutes of the Realm: volume 5: 1628–80* (1819), p. 575. http://www.british-history.ac.uk/report.aspx?compid=47375.
31. See for example Clive Holmes, *Seventeenth-Century Lincolnshire* (Lincoln, 1980), pp. 228–34; Grant Tapsell, *The Personal Rule of Charles II* (Woodbridge, 2007), ch. 3.
32. Vavasor Powell, *Tsofer Bepah or The Bird in the Cage* (1661), pt 2, pp. 1–26.
33. Tim Harris, *Politics Under the Later Stuarts: Party Conflict in a Divided Society 1660–1715* (1993), pp. 65–73. Harris's analysis informs and complements the one offered here.
34. Harris, *Politics Under the Later Stuarts*, p. 67. Harris gives the figure as 322. This figure, drawn from Basil Duke Henning (ed.), *The House of Commons, 1660–1690* (3 vols, 1983), I, p. 52, may underestimate the total. See Morrice, *Entring Book*, I, App. 41, pp. 507–10, which provides a list of MPs from 1661–95 with some sympathy for dissent, and suggests that previous figures for such MPs have been too low.
35. Seaward, *Cavalier Parliament*, pp. 162–95.
36. Gary S. De Krey, 'The First Restoration Crisis: Conscience and Coercion in London, 1667–1673', *Albion*, 25 (1993), 565–80; Gary S. De

Krey, 'Rethinking the Restoration: Dissenting Cases for Conscience, 1667–1672', *HJ*, 38 (1995), 53–83.

37. This account of the trial of William Mead and William Penn is based on: De Krey, 'The First Restoration Crisis', 527–4; Craig W. Horle, *The Quakers and the English Legal System, 1660–1688* (Philadelphia, 1988), pp. 116–17; Gil Skidmore, 'William Mead', *ODNB*; Mary K. Geiter, 'William Penn', *ODNB*. The analysis is particularly indebted to Gary S. De Krey.

38. Quoted in De Krey, 'The First Restoration Crisis', 573.

39. John Miller, *Popery and Politics in England, 1660–1688* (Cambridge, 1973), ch. 4.

40. On claims that Quakers were Roman Catholics see Horle, *The Quakers and the English Legal System*, pp. 11, 220–1. The accusations had a long pedigree going back to the early days of the movement, see Rosemary Moore, *The Light in their Consciences: Early Quakers in Britain, 1646–1666* (University Park, 2000), p. 92.

41. See also the analysis offered of this print in Tim Harris, *Restoration* (2005), pp. 249–50.

42. Geoff Kemp, 'The Works of Roger L'Estrange: An Annotated Bibliography', in Anne Dunan-Page and Beth Lynch (eds), *Roger L'Estrange and the Making of Restoration Culture* (Aldershot, 2008), p. 202.

43. John Marshall, *John Locke, Toleration and Early Enlightenment Culture* (Cambridge, 2006), pp. 455–8.

44. Mark Goldie, 'Sir Peter Pett, Sceptical Toryism and the Science of Toleration in the 1680s', *SCH*, 21 (1984), 247–73; Mark Goldie, 'The Theory of Religious Intolerance in Restoration England', in O.P. Grell, Jonathan Israel, and Nicholas Tyacke (eds), *From Persecution to Toleration: The Glorious Revolution and Religion in England* (Oxford, 1991), pp. 331–68.

45. Both Keeble, *Literary Culture* and Christopher Hill, *The Experience of Defeat: Milton and Some Contemporaries* (1984) ultimately perhaps overemphasise the internalist aesthetic. However, the subtlety of their arguments cannot be overlooked and they certainly cannot be set up simply as straw men.

46. *This to the King and his Councel . . . in Answer to an Order . . . for the Breaking Up of the Meetings of . . . Quakers* (1660), p. 3. The underlined text is in black letter in the original.

47. 'Declaration of Breda', in Gardiner (ed.), *Constitutional Documents*, p. 466.

48. Robert Wild, *On the Death of Mr Calamy* (1667).

49. Robert Wild, *The Recantation of a Penitent Proteus* (1663).
50. Robert Wild, *Dr Wild's Humble Thanks...for Liberty of Conscience* (1672). For more on Wild, see George Southcombe, 'The Responses of Nonconformists to the Restoration in England' (University of Oxford DPhil. thesis, 2005), ch. 1.
51. *An Expostulation with the Bishops, So Called, in England* (1674?), p. 7. This is our dating of the pamphlet, see Southcombe, 'Responses', pp. 115–16.
52. Mary Mollineux, *Fruits of Retirement* (1702), p. 22. This is partially quoted in Sharon Achinstein, *Literature and Dissent in Milton's England* (Cambridge, 2003), p. 82. Achinstein also provides a valuable analysis of these lines and of Mollineux in general, *ibid.*, pp. 80–2.
53. William Shakespeare, *Hamlet*, ed. Ann Thompson and Neil Taylor (2006), pp. 284–5 (III.i.56–9).

Chapter 3: What was at Stake in the Exclusion Crisis?

1. Anchitell Grey, *Debates of the House of Commons, from the Year 1667 to the Year 1694...* (7 vols, 1763), VII, pp. 396, 399, 400–1, 404, 408.
2. Reresby, *Memoirs*, p. 223.
3. [Charles Blount], *An Appeal from the Country to the City...* (1679), pp. 2–3.
4. Ronald Hutton, *Charles II, King of England, Scotland and Ireland* (Oxford, 1989), chs 13–14.
5. Jonathan Scott, *England's Troubles: Seventeenth-Century English Political Instability in European Context* (Cambridge, 2000), chs 8, 19.
6. Conrad Russell, *The Crisis of Parliaments: English History, 1509–1660* (Oxford, 1971). Russell took the phrase from a parliamentary speech by the MP Sir Benjamin Rudyerd.
7. Andrew Marvell, *An Account of the Growth of Popery and Arbitrary Government*, in Martin Dzelzainis, N.H. Keeble, Annabel Patterson, and Nicholas von Maltzahn (eds), *The Complete Prose Works of Andrew Marvell* (2 vols, New Haven and London, 2003), II, pp. 223–377.
8. Mark Knights, *Politics and Opinion in Crisis, 1678–81* (Cambridge, 1994).
9. The most influential text here was J.H. Plumb, *The Growth of Political Stability in England, 1675–1725* (Cambridge, 1967). For a series of commentaries on this work to mark its 25th 'birthday', see *Albion* 25 (1993).

188   NOTES

10. Gary S. De Krey, 'The First Restoration Crisis: Conscience and Coercion in London, 1667–73', *Albion*, 25 (1993), 565–80; Lois G. Schwoerer, *No Standing Armies! The Anti-army Ideology in Seventeenth-Century England* (1974). Richard L. Greaves pointed to an even earlier crisis that polarised political opinion at the birth of the Restoration itself: 'Great Scott! The Restoration in Turmoil, or, Restoration Crises and the Emergence of Party', *Albion*, 25 (1993), 605–18.

11. Quoted in Knights, *Politics and Opinion*, p. 18.

12. The exchanges between the king and parliament can conveniently be followed in *EHD*, pp. 77–81.

13. Quoted in John Spurr, *England in the 1670s: 'This Masquerading Age'* (Oxford, 2000), p. 41.

14. Maurice F. Bond (ed.), *The Diaries and Papers of Sir Edward Dering Second Baronet 1644 to 1684* (House of Lords RO Occasional Publications, 1, 1976), p. 125.

15. Quoted in Mark Knights, 'Thomas Osborne', *ODNB*.

16. Printed in Andrew Browning, *Thomas Osborne, Earl of Danby and Duke of Leeds, 1632–1712* (3 vols, 1944–51), II, pp. 66–7.

17. A major theme of John Patrick Montaño, *Courting the Moderates: Ideology, Propaganda, and the Emergence of Party, 1660–1678* (Newark, 2002).

18. A particularly important example is Denzil Lord Holles, a leading MP and peer in parliaments from 1624–1679: Basil Duke Henning (ed.), *The House of Commons 1660–1690* (3 vols, 1983), II, pp. 560–3; Morrice, *Entring Book*, I, pp. 177–85.

19. Browning, *Thomas Osborne*, II, p. 75.

20. Mark Goldie, 'Danby, the bishops, and the Whigs', in Tim Harris, Paul Seaward, and Mark Goldie (eds), *The Politics of Religion in Restoration England* (Oxford, 1990), pp. 75–105.

21. W.D. Cooper (ed.), *Savile Correspondence. Letters to and from Henry Savile...* (Camden Soc., 71, 1858), p. 76: Viscount Halifax to Henry Savile, 20/30 March 1678/9.

22. R.C. Munden, 'James I and the "Growth of Mutual Distrust": King, Commons and Reform, 1603–1604', in Kevin Sharpe (ed.), *Faction and Parliament: Essays on Early Stuart History* (Oxford, 1978), pp. 43–72; J.W. Daly, 'Could Charles I be Trusted? The Royalist Case, 1642–6', *JBS*, 6 (1966), 23–44.

23. HMC, *Ormonde*, new series, IV, pp. 470–1: Sir Robert Southwell to Duke of Ormond, 12 November 1678.

24. Montagu's career provides a good example of the close connections between sex and Restoration politics stressed in ch. 8: he was

recalled from France when Charles learned that he had slept with both the king's mistress – the Duchess of Cleveland – and her illegitimate daughter, Lady Sussex. Henning (ed.), *House of Commons*, III, p. 87.

25. HMC, *Egmont*, II, p. 77: John Perceval to Sir Robert Southwell, [Oxford], 20 October 1678.
26. HMC, *Kenyon*, p. 105: [account of the popish plot], 31 October 1678.
27. Quoted in David Smith, *A History of the Modern British Isles, 1603–1707: The Double Crown* (Oxford, 1998), p. 251.
28. HMC, *Egmont*, II, pp. 78–9: John Perceval to Sir Robert Southwell, Oxford, 28 January 1678/9.
29. HMC, *Finch*, II, pp. 53–4: Daniel Finch to Sir John Finch, 2 June 1679.
30. Quoted in Knights, *Politics and Opinion*, p. 4.
31. Cooper (ed.), *Savile Correspondence*, p. 134: Earl of Halifax to Henry Savile, [London], 8/18 January 1679/80.
32. Quoted in Knights, *Politics and Opinion*, p. 4.
33. *EHD*, pp. 113–14 (the text is that of the 1680 bill).
34. HMC, *Ormonde*, new series, IV, p. 514: Sir Robert Southwell to Duke of Ormond, 17 May 1679.
35. Quoted in Howard Nenner, *The Right to be King: The Succession to the Crown of England, 1603–1714* (Basingstoke, 1995), p. 100. For the concept of 'throneworthiness', see *ibid.*, pp. 105–6.
36. [True Patriot], *Great and Weighty Considerations Relating to the D[uke], or Successor of the Crown...* (1679), p. 2.
37. HMC, *Ormonde*, new series, IV, p. 512: Sir Robert Southwell to Duke of Ormond, 13 May 1679.
38. *Ibid.*, p. 511.
39. E.g., HMC, *Egmont*, II, p. 99: Rev. Robert Altham to Sir John Perceval, Oxford, 21 September 1680.
40. Anthony Fletcher, *The Outbreak of the English Civil War* (1981), ch. 3.
41. *The Character of a Modern Whig...* (1681), p. 1.
42. HMC, *Montagu*, pp. 174–5: Thomas Carew to Duke of Albemarle, Barly, 5 March 1678/9. (For a modern account, see Henning (ed.), *House of Commons*, I, p. 199.)
43. Henry Horwitz, 'Protestant Reconciliation in the Exclusion Crisis', *JEH*, 15 (1964), 201–17.
44. Gary S. De Krey, 'Reformation in the Restoration Crisis 1679–1682', in Donna B. Hamilton and Richard Strier (eds), *Religion, Literature, and Politics in Post-Reformation England, 1540–1688* (Cambridge, 1996), pp. 231, 243.
45. *The Character of a Fanatick...* (1681), p. 1.

46. HMC, *Ormonde*, new series, IV, pp. 535–6: Sir Robert Southwell to Duke of Ormond, London, 20 September 1679.
47. Quoted in John Miller, 'A Moderate in the First Age of Party: The Dilemmas of Sir John Holland, 1675–85', *EHR*, 114 (1999), 868.
48. Mark Knights, *Representation and Misrepresentation in later Stuart Britain: Partisanship and Political Culture* (Oxford, 2004), helpfully summarised in his 'Public Politics in England' *c.*1675–1715, in Nicholas Tyacke (ed.), *The English Revolution, c.1590–1720: Politics, Religion and Communities* (Manchester, 2007), pp. 169–84.
49. Roger L'Estrange, *The Observator...*, 223 (14 October 1682).
50. *The Character of a Thorough-Pac'd Tory, Ecclesiastical or Civil* (1682), p. 1.
51. *The Character of a Modern Whig, or An Alamode True Loyal Protestant* (1681), p. 2.
52. P.J. Challinor, 'Restoration and Exclusion in the County of Cheshire', *Bulletin of the John Rylands University Library*, 64 (1982), 379.
53. Clive Holmes, *Seventeenth-Century Lincolnshire* (Lincoln, 1980), ch. 14.
54. H.S. Reinmuth, jr., 'A Mysterious Dispute Demystified: Sir George Fletcher vs. The Howards', *HJ*, 27 (1984), 289–307; Victor L. Stater, 'Continuity & Change in English Provincial Politics: Robert Paston in Norfolk, 1675–1683', *Albion*, 25 (1993), 193–216.
55. Lionel K.J. Glassey, *Politics and the Appointment of Justices of the Peace 1675–1720* (Oxford, 1979), ch. 2, esp. pp. 39–54.
56. HMC, *Seventh Report*, appendix, part I, p. 475: John Verney to Sir Ralph Verney, London, 29 September 1679.
57. Mark Knights, 'London's "Monster" Petition of 1680', *HJ*, 36 (1993), 39–67.
58. The most detailed account of conflicts in London at this time is now Gary S. De Krey, *London and the Restoration 1659–1683* (Cambridge, 2005), chs 4–7.
59. John Miller, *Cities Divided: Politics and Religion in English Provincial Towns 1660–1722* (Oxford, 2007), chs 7–9.
60. Dan Beaver, 'Behemoth, or Civil War and Revolution, in English Parish Communities 1641–82', in Tyacke (ed.), *The English Revolution*, p. 145.
61. For a detailed example of this in practice, see Newton E. Key and Joseph P. Ward, ' "Divided into Parties": Exclusion Crisis Origins in Monmouth', *EHR*, 115 (2000), 1159–83, quotation at p. 1183.
62. J.R. Jones, *The First Whigs: The Politics of the Exclusion Crisis, 1678–1683* (Oxford, 1961); Montaño, *Courting the Moderates*; Jonathan Scott, 'Restoration Process. Or, if This Isn't a Party, We're Not Having a Good Time', *Albion*, 25 (1993), 619–37.

63. Newton E. Key, 'The Political Culture and Political Rhetoric of County Feasts and Feast Sermons, 1654–1714', *JBS*, 33 (1994), 223–56; Peter Clark, *British Clubs and Societies 1580–1800: The Origins of an Associational World* (Oxford, 2000), pp. 280–6.
64. James M. Rosenheim, 'Party Organization at the Local Level: The Norfolk Sheriff's Subscription of 1676', *HJ*, 29 (1986), 713–22; P.R. Seddon, 'The Origins of the Nottinghamshire Whigs: An Analysis of the Subscribers to the Election Expenses of Sir Scrope Howe and John White', *Historical Research*, 69 (1996), 218–31.
65. For a much more detailed discussion of this period, see Grant Tapsell, *The Personal Rule of Charles II, 1681–85* (Woodbridge, 2007).
66. Bodl., MS Carte 216, f. 222: Earl of Longford to Earl of Arran, London, 24 October 1682.
67. HMC, *Twelfth Report*, appendix, part V, p. 55: Thomas White to Earl of Rutland, 21 June 1683 [miscalendared as 1681]; Bodl., MS Smith 48, f. 97: Edward Chamberlayne to [?Dr Thomas Smith], London, 4 October 1683.
68. Osmund Airy (ed.), *Bishop Burnet's History of My Own Time* (2 vols, Oxford, 1897–1900), II, p. 290.
69. BL, Add. MS 27448, f. 279: Bailiffs of Yarmouth to Earl of Yarmouth, Yarmouth, 25 February 1683/4.
70. For this theme, see Mark A. Kishlansky, *Parliamentary Selection: Social and Political Choice in Early Modern England* (Cambridge, 1986), esp. ch. 8.
71. National Library of Wales, Kemeys-Tynte Papers, C64: Marquess of Worcester to Sir Charles Kemeys, 13 February 1684/5.
72. Tim Harris, *Revolution: The Great Crisis of the British Monarchy, 1685–1720* (2006), pp. 57, 55.
73. HMC, *Ormonde*, new series, V, p. 102: Col. Edward Cooke to Duke of Ormond, 16 May 1679.
74. HMC, *Dartmouth*, 34: Duke of York to Col. George Legge, Brussels, 28 May [1679].

Chapter 4: Was Charles II a Successful 'Royal Politician'?

1. Quoted in Andrew Lacey, *The Cult of King Charles the Martyr* (Woodbridge, 2003), p. 147.
2. Ronald Hutton, *Debates in Stuart History* (Basingstoke, 2004), ch. 5.
3. J.R. Jones, *Charles II: Royal Politician* (1987).

4. The clearest and most succinct account of the years of Charles's life recounted here is Paul Seaward, 'Charles II', *ODNB*. The factual information that follows in this section is drawn from this unless otherwise stated.

5. Quoted in John Morrill, 'Oliver Cromwell', *ODNB*.

6. Seaward, 'Charles II', *ODNB*; Brian Weiser, 'Owning the King's Story: The Escape from Worcester', *Seventeenth Century*, 14 (1999), 43–62.

7. Andrew Marvell, 'An Horatian Ode upon Cromwell's Return from Ireland', in Nigel Smith (ed.), *The Poems of Andrew Marvell* (2003), p. 279 (ll. 119–20).

8. John Miller, 'The Potential for "Absolutism" in Later Stuart England', *History*, 69 (1984), 187–207.

9. Pepys, *Diary*, I, 158.

10. Marc Bloch, *The Royal Touch: Sacred Monarchy and Scrofula in England and France* (1973). Our account of Charles's touching is indebted to Harold Weber, *Paper Bullets: Print and Kingship under Charles II* (Lexington, 1996), pp. 50–87; and (the most detailed account) Anna Keay, *The Magnificent Monarch: Charles II and the Ceremonies of Power* (2008), pp. 112–19.

11. On Charles's touching during exile see Keay, *The Magnificent Monarch*, pp. 70–1.

12. Quoted in Weber, *Paper Bullets*, p. 61.

13. Weber, *Paper Bullets*, pp. 61–3.

14. Keay, *The Magnificent Monarch*, pp. 115–18.

15. Figures from *ibid.*, pp. 118, 211.

16. On the first Declaration of Indulgence (including a reminder that the label is spurious), see N.H. Keeble, *The Restoration: England in the 1660s* (Oxford, 2002), pp. 122–3. On the second Declaration of Indulgence, its context, and the reaction it provoked, see John Spurr, *England in the 1670s: 'This Masquerading Age'* (Oxford, 2000), pp. 28–39.

17. Ronald Hutton, 'The Religion of Charles II', in R. Malcolm Smuts (ed.), *The Stuart Court and Europe: Essays in Politics and Political Culture* (Cambridge, 1996), pp. 228–46.

18. *Ibid.*, p. 246.

19. For the most accomplished example of this style of culturally enriched political history, see T.C.W. Blanning, *The Culture of Power and the Power of Culture: Old Regime Europe 1660–1789* (Oxford, 2002). This may be complemented by John Brewer, *The Sinews of Power: War, Money and the English State, 1688–1783* (1989).

20. A term particularly associated with the sociologist Norbert Elias, *The Civilizing Process* (2000) and the anthropologist Clifford Geertz, *Negara: The Theatre State in Nineteenth-Century Bali* (Princeton, 1981).

21. For an excellent collection of essays, see John Adamson (ed.), *The Princely Courts of Europe 1500–1750* (1999). A detailed account of Louis XIV's concern with his image can be found in Peter Burke, *The Fabrication of Louis XIV* (New Haven and London, 1992).

22. Kevin Sharpe, 'The Image of Virtue: The Court and Household of Charles I, 1625–1642', in David Starkey (ed.), *The English Court: From the Wars of the Roses to the Civil War* (1987), pp. 226–60.

23. Richard Cust, 'Charles I and Popularity', in Thomas Cogswell, Richard Cust, and Peter Lake (eds), *Politics, Religion and Popularity in Early Stuart Britain: Essays in Honour of Conrad Russell* (Cambridge, 2002), pp. 235–58.

24. J.P. Kenyon (ed.), *Halifax: Complete Works* (Harmondsworth, 1969), p. 261.

25. *Ibid.*, p. 256.

26. Alastair Bellany, *The Politics of Court Scandal in Early Modern England: News Culture and the Overbury Affair, 1603–1660* (Cambridge, 2002).

27. John Wilmot, Earl of Rochester, 'A Satyr', in Harold Love (ed.), *The Works of John Wilmot, Earl of Rochester* (Oxford, 1999), p. 87 (l. 11).

28. Catharine MacLeod and Julia Marciari Alexander (eds), *Painted Ladies: Women at the Court of Charles II* (2001); Kevin Sharpe, ' "Thy Longing Country's Darling and Desire": Aesthetics, Sex, and Politics in the England of Charles II', in Julia Marciari Alexander and Catherine MacLeod (eds), *Politics, Transgressions, and Representation at the Court of Charles II* (New Haven and London, 2007), p. 16.

29. Sonya Wynne, 'The Mistresses of Charles II and Restoration Court Politics', in Eveline Cruickshanks (ed.), *The Stuart Courts* (Stroud, 2000), pp. 171–90.

30. Sharpe, ' "Thy Longing Country's Darling and Desire" ', pp. 1–32.

31. Tim Harris, ' "There Is None That Loves Him but Drunk Whores and Whoremongers": Popular Criticisms of the Restoration Court', in Marciari Alexander and MacLeod (eds), *Politics, Transgressions, and Representation*, pp. 35–60.

32. Jonathan Scott, 'What were Commonwealth Principles?', *HJ*, 47 (2004), 591–613.

33. Tim Harris, 'The Bawdy House Riots of 1668', *HJ*, 29 (1986), 537–56.

34. Kenyon (ed.), *Halifax*, p. 255.

35. Esmond S. De Beer (ed.), *Diary of John Evelyn* (6 vols, Oxford, 1955), IV, p. 410.
36. For the overall theme, see Brian Weiser, *Charles II and the Politics of Access* (Woodbridge, 2003).
37. Reresby, *Memoirs*, p. 259.
38. Keay, *The Magnificent Monarch*.
39. Jerry Brotton, 'The Art of Restoration: King Charles II and the Restitution of the English Royal Art Collection', *Court Historian*, 10 (2005), 115–35.
40. An argument particularly associated with Andrew Walkling, 'Court, Culture and Politics in Restoration England: Charles II, James II, and the Performance of Baroque Monarchy' (Cornell University PhD thesis, 2 vols, 1997). Some of this thesis has been made more widely accessible, notably in 'Court Culture and "Absolutism" in Restoration England', *Court Historian*, 6 (2001), 225–33; 'Politics and Theatrical Culture in Restoration England', *History Compass*, 5:5 (2007), 1500–20 [http://www3.interscience.wiley.com/cgi-bin/fulltext/118491930/PDFSTART].
41. Richard Ollard, *The Image of the King: Charles I and Charles II* (1979), p. 173.
42. Kenyon (ed.), *Halifax*, p. 252.
43. Simon Thurley, 'A Country Seat Fit for a King: Charles II, Greenwich and Winchester', in Cruickshanks (ed.), *Stuart Courts*, pp. 219–22.
44. *Ibid.*, pp. 226–33; Weiser, *Charles II and the Politics of Access*, p. 48.
45. Howard Colvin (ed.), *The History of the King's Works, 5: 1660–1782* (1976), p. 309.
46. Quoted in R.A. Beddard, 'Wren's Mausoleum for Charles I and the Cult of the Royal Martyr', *Architectural History*, 27 (1984), 36.
47. A description from c.1800 quoted in Colvin, *King's Works*, V, p. 322.
48. Kenyon (ed.), *Halifax*, p. 261.
49. W.H.D. Longstaffe (ed.), *Memoirs of the Life of Mr. Ambrose Barnes...* (Publs of the Surtees Soc., L, 1867), p. 225; John Toland, quoted in Craig Rose, *England in the 1690s: Revolution, Religion and War* (Oxford, 1999), p. 65.
50. BL, Egerton MS 2985, f. 240: loyal address to the Crown, 1681; William E. Buckley (ed.), *Memoirs of Thomas, Earl of Ailesbury* (The Roxburghe Club, 2 vols, 1890), I, p. 10.
51. Hutton, *Charles II*, conc.
52. Rochester, '[Impromptu on Court Personages]', in Love (ed.), *Works*, p. 295.

Chapter 5. Why did James VII and II Lose his Thrones?

1. William Hamper (ed.), *The Life, Diary and Correspondence of Sir William Dugdale...* (1827), p. 450.
2. Quoted in Mark Goldie, 'Joshua Basset, Popery and Revolution', in D.E.D. Beales and H.B. Nisbet (eds), *Sidney Sussex College Cambridge: Historical Essays in Commemoration of the Quatercentenary* (Woodbridge, 1996), p. 118.
3. *An Account of what His Majesty Said at his First Coming to Council...* (1685).
4. Quoted in John Miller, *The Glorious Revolution* (Harlow, 1983), p. 100.
5. HMC, *Lindsey*, p. 272: 'James Earl of Abingdon's Discourse with King James the Second, November 18th, 1687, from his own Memorandum of it'.
6. The future archbishop of Canterbury, William Wake, was a key figure in this campaign: Norman Sykes, *William Wake, Archbishop of Canterbury* (2 vols, Cambridge, 1957), I, ch. I.
7. For a similar view of Charles I, see Conrad Russell, *The Causes of the English Civil War* (Oxford, 1990), p. 198. I am grateful to James Smith for reminding me of this link.
8. J.G.A. Pocock, *The Ancient Constitution and the Feudal Law* (rev. edn, Cambridge, 1987).
9. F.C. Turner, *James II* (1948), pp. 266–75.
10. Bruce P. Lenman, 'The Scottish Nobility and the Revolution of 1688–1690', in Robert Beddard (ed.), *The Revolutions of 1688* (Oxford, 1991), p. 139.
11. Mark Goldie, 'Contextualizing Dryden's Absalom: William Lawrence, the Laws of Marriage, and the Case for King Monmouth', in Donna B. Hamilton and Richard Strier (eds), *Religion, Literature, and Politics in Post-Reformation England, 1540–1688* (Cambridge, 1996), pp. 208–30.
12. Morrice, *Entring Book*, III, p. 212.
13. Quoted in Turner, *James II*, p. 296.
14. Pepys, *Diary*, 4 June 1664; Morrice, *Entring Book*, II, pp. 513–14.
15. J.P. Kenyon, 'The Commission of Ecclesiastical Causes, 1686–1688: A Reconsideration', *HJ*, 34 (1991), 727–36.
16. Morrice, *Entring Book*, III, p. 237.
17. HMC, *Seventh Report*, appendix, part I, p. 500: Dr William Denton to Sir Ralph Verney, 8 September 1686; UWB (Bangor) Mostyn correspondence, vol. IV (1684/5–1686), no. 58: Ph[ilip] Fowke to Thomas Mostyn, Salop, 3 August 1686 (transcribed in NRA 22953, p. 93).

18. Quoted in R.A. Beddard, 'James II and the Catholic Challenge', in Nicholas Tyacke (ed.), *The History of the University of Oxford, Volume IV: Seventeenth-Century Oxford* (Oxford, 1997), p. 934, n. 181.

19. L.W.B. Brockliss, G.L. Harriss, and Angus MacIntyre (ed.), *Magdalen College and the Crown: Essays for the Tercentenary of the Restoration of the College, 1688* (Oxford, 1988); J.R. Bloxam (ed.), *Magdalen College and King James II, 1686–1688: A Series of Documents* (Oxford Hist. Soc., 6, Oxford, 1886).

20. Bodl., MS Rawlinson E.8, f. 141: sermon on I Cor. 10: 13 ('Thanksgiving Day for the Victory over the Duke of Monmouth's Rebells 1685').

21. Dom Basil Hemphill, *The Early Vicars Apostolic of England 1685–1750* (1954), pp. 16–18.

22. T.H. Clancy, SJ, *English Catholic Books 1641–1700: A Bibliography* (Aldershot, 1996), p. 199. These represent the most striking years. In 1684 24 Catholic titles had been printed, in 1685 the figure was 41, in 1686 121, and in 1688 100.

23. Devon RO, Z19/40/7: H[umphrey] P[rideaux] to Mrs [Anne] Coffin, Norwich, 23 February 1688.

24. John Miller, *James II* (New Haven and London, rev. edn, 2000); Evelyn Cruickshanks, *The Glorious Revolution* (2000), esp. ch. 4; Scott Sowerby, 'Of Different Complexions: Religious Diversity and National Identity in James II's Toleration Campaign', *EHR*, 124 (2009), 29–52.

25. Printed in J.S. Clarke, *The Life of James the Second*... (2 vols, 1816), II, p. 621.

26. *Ibid.*, p. 622.

27. *The Autobiography of Sir John Bramston, K.B., of Skreens, in the Hundred of Chelmsford* (Camden Soc., 32, 1845), p. 249.

28. Quoted in *EHD*, p. 395.

29. *Autobiography of Sir John Bramston*, p. 267.

30. Reresby, *Memoirs*, pp. 478–9.

31. Morrice, *Entring Book*, IV, p. 60.

32. [George Savile, Marquess of Halifax], *A Letter to a Dissenter Upon Occasion of His Majesties late Gracious Declaration of Indulgence*, in J.P. Kenyon (ed.), *Halifax: Complete Works* (Harmondsworth, 1969), p. 106.

33. Charles Jackson (ed.), *The Diary of Abraham de la Pryme* (Publications of the Surtees Soc., 54, 1869), p. 12.

34. Quoted in Steve Pincus, 'The European Catholic Context of the Revolution of 1688–89: Gallicanism, Innocent XI, and Catholic Opposition', in Allan I. Macinnes and Arthur H. Williamson (eds), *Shaping*

the Stuart World 1603–1714: The Atlantic Connection (Leiden, 2006), p. 100, n. 109.

35. David Worthington, 'The 1688 Correspondence of Nicholas Taaffe, Second Earl of Carlingford (?–1690), from the Imperial Court in Vienna', *Archivium Hibernicum*, 58 (2004), 189–90: Carlingford to the Earl of Middleton, Vienna, 8 July 1688.

36. Morrice, *Entring Book*, IV, p. 285.

37. Edward Gregg, *Queen Anne* (New Haven and London, 1980), p. 58.

38. John Gutch, *Collectanea Curiosa; Or Miscellaneous Tracts Relating to the History and Antiquities of England and Ireland...* (2 vols, Oxford, 1781), I, p. 340.

39. HMC, *Seventh Report*, appendix, part I, p. 502: Dr William Denton to Sir Ralph Verney, 13 June 1688.

40. Morrice, *Entring Book*, IV, p. 293.

41. Devon RO, Z/19/3: Richard Lapthorne to Richard Coffin, London, 30 June 1688.

42. *EHD*, p. 120.

43. Grant Tapsell, 'The Immortal Seven', *ODNB* [online group entry].

44. Jonathan I. Israel and Geoffrey Parker, 'Of Providence and Protestant Winds: The Spanish Armada of 1588 and the Dutch Armada of 1688', in Jonathan I. Israel (ed.), *The Anglo-Dutch Moment: Essays on the Glorious Revolution and its World Impact* (Cambridge, 1991), pp. 335–63.

45. HMC, *Seventh Report*, appendix, part I, p. 349: Lord Preston to the Earl of Middleton, London, 19 November 1688.

46. J.P. Kenyon, *The Nobility and the Revolution of 1688* (Hull, 1963).

47. UWB (Bangor) Mostyn correspondence, vol. V (1686/7–1688), no. 25: Hum[phrey] Humphreys to Thomas Mostyn, 2 December [1688] (transcribed in NRA 22953, p. 113).

48. Robert Beddard, 'The Unexpected Whig Revolution of 1688', in *idem* (ed.), *The Revolutions of 1688*, p. 91.

49. Ted Rowlands, ' "As Black as Hell to My Own People": James II's Reputation in Herefordshire', *Midland History*, 14 (1989), 43–52.

50. UWB (Bangor) Mostyn correspondence, vol. V (1686/7–1688), no. 21: Ph[ilip] Fowke to Thomas Mostyn, Salop, 22 October [1687] (transcribed in NRA 22953, p. 104).

51. *Ibid.*, no. 25: Thomas Mostyn's appended answer to Sir R[oger] Mostyn's letter of 15 December [1687] (transcribed in NRA 22953, p. 105).

52. Quoted in H.C. Foxcroft, *The Life and Letters of Sir George Savile, Bart: First Marquis of Halifax* (2 vols, 1898), I, p. 486.
53. UWB (Bangor) Mostyn correspondence, vol. V (1686/7–1688), no. 25: Thomas Mostyn's appended answer to Sir R[oger] Mostyn's letter of 15 December [1687] (transcribed in NRA 22953, p. 105).
54. Morrice, *Entring Book*, IV, pp. 113, 368.
55. Foxcroft (ed.), *Life and Letters*, I, pp. 482, 509, 495.
56. UWB (Bangor) Mostyn correspondence, vol. V (1686/7–1688), no. 43: Ph[ilip] Fowke to Thomas Mostyn, Beaumaris, 11 October [1688] (transcribed in NRA 22953, p. 112).
57. Morrice, *Entring Book*, III, p. 243; HMC, *Seventh Report*, appendix, part I, p. 501.
58. Mark Goldie, 'The Unacknowledged Republic: Officeholding in Early Modern England', in Tim Harris (ed.), *The Politics of the Excluded, c. 1500–1850* (Basingstoke, 2001), pp. 153–94.
59. Robin Eagles, 'Unnatural Allies? The Oxfordshire *Élite*, from the Exclusion Crisis to the Overthrow of James II', *Parliamentary History*, 26 (2007), 358.
60. Quoted in Turner, *James II*, p. 235; William Bradford Gardner, 'The Later Years of John Maitland, Second Earl and First Duke of Lauderdale', *Journal of Modern History*, 20 (1948), 121–2.

Chapter 6: How Important was the 'British' Dimension to Restoration Political Life?

1. David Hayton, 'From Barbarian to Burlesque: English Images of the Irish c.1660–1750', *Irish Economic and Social History*, 15 (1988), 5–31.
2. Aidan Clark, *Prelude to Restoration in Ireland: The End of the Commonwealth, 1659–60* (Cambridge, 1999); Frances Dow, *Cromwellian Scotland 1651–1660* (Edinburgh, 1979), ch. 12.
3. Robert Douglas, *The Form and O[rder] of the Coronation of Charles the Second... 1651* (1700), pp. 12, 27–8.
4. Quotes from Breandán Ó Buachalla, 'James Our True King: The Ideology of Irish Royalism in the Seventeenth Century', in D. George Boyce, Robert Eccleshall, and Vincent Geoghehan (eds), *Political Thought in Ireland Since the Seventeenth Century* (1993), p. 28.
5. National Archives of Scotland, PA2/31, f. 4v: letter to Charles II, 28 July 1681, reproduced at www.rps.ac.uk [*The Records of the Parliaments of Scotland to 1707*, K.M. Brown et al. eds (St Andrews, 2007) [hereafter *RPS*], date accessed: 3 September 2008].

6. NLI, MS 4909, ff. 59v, 61v: Clonmel assize records, 1684.

7. *Register of the Privy Council of Scotland, 1681–1682*, p. 274: 6 December 1681.

8. W. Croft Dickinson and Gordon Donaldson (eds), *A Source Book of Scottish History. Volume Three: 1567–1707* (1954), pp. 178–9 (the Sanquhar Declaration, 22 June 1680); Sir John Lauder, *Historical Observes of Memorable Occurents in Church and State, From October 1680 to April 1686*, ed. Adam Urquhart and David Laing (Bannatyne Club, Edinburgh, 1840), p. 141.

9. Quoted in Gary S. De Krey, *Restoration and Revolution in Britain: A Political History of the Era of Charles II and the Glorious Revolution* (Basingstoke, 2007), p. 60.

10. Quoted in Éamonn Ó Ciardha, *Ireland and the Jacobite Cause, 1685–1766: A Fatal Attachment* (Dublin, 2004), pp. 82–3.

11. S.J. Connolly, *Divided Kingdom: Ireland 1630–1800* (Oxford, 2008), p. 155.

12. Quoted in *ibid.*, p. 119.

13. The classic account remains J.H. Elliott, 'A Europe of Composite Monarchies', *P&P*, 137 (1992), 48–71.

14. The phrase was made famous by G.R. Elton in his Royal Historical Society Presidential addresses, published in the *TRHS* between 1974 and 1976.

15. For a brilliant account of such intellectual struggles in early Stuart England, see Clive Holmes, 'Parliament, Liberty, Taxation, and Property', in J.H. Hexter (ed.), *Parliament and Liberty from the Reign of Elizabeth to the English Civil War* (Stanford, 1992), pp. 122–54.

16. *RPS*, 1661/1/158. Date accessed: 9 September 2008.

17. Ronnie Lee, 'Retreat from Revolution: the Scottish Parliament and the Restored Monarchy, 1661–1663', in John R. Young (ed.), *Celtic Dimensions of the British Civil Wars* (Edinburgh, 1997), pp. 185–204.

18. *RPS*, 1661/1/16, 17, 24, 88. Date accessed: 9 September 2008.

19. *Ibid.*, 1661/1/36, 74, 67, 255.

20. *Ibid.*, 1661/1/144.

21. Gillian H. MacIntosh, *The Scottish Parliament under Charles II, 1660–1685* (Edinburgh, 2007), p. 25.

22. D.B. Quinn, 'The Early Interpretation of Poynings' Law, 1494–1534', *Irish Historical Studies*, 2 (1941), 241–54.

23. Kevin McKenny, 'The Restoration Land Settlement in Ireland: A Statistical Interpretation', in Coleman A. Dennehy (ed.), *Restoration Ireland: Always Settling and Never Settled* (Aldershot, 2008), p. 39

Table 3.1; Connolly, *Divided Kingdom*, p. 137 and n. 27. This is an inevitably unsatisfactory merging of various sets of figures calculated by different means.

24. Pearse Street Library, Dublin, Gilbert MS 207, f. 1.

25. McKenny, 'The Restoration Land Settlement in Ireland', in Dennehy (ed.), *Restoration Ireland*, p. 39 Table 3.1.

26. Coleman A. Dennehy, 'The Restoration Irish Parliament, 1661–6', in *ibid.*, p. 64.

27. *EHD*, pp. 744–5.

28. *An Antheme Sung at the Consecration of the Arch-bishops and Bishops of Ireland, On Sunday the 27 of January 1660 [i.e. 1661] at St Patricks in Dublin* (1661).

29. HMC, *Ormonde*, new series, VI, 482: [Rev.] John Humble to bishop of Derry, 24 November 1682.

30. Raymond Gillespie, 'The Presbyterian Revolution in Ulster, 1660–1690', in W.J. Sheils and Diana Wood (eds), *The Churches, Ireland and the Irish* (SCH, 25, 1989), pp. 159–70.

31. MacIntosh, *Scottish Parliament*, p. 39.

32. Quoted in John Patrick, 'The Origins of the Opposition to Lauderdale in the Scottish Parliament of 1673', *SHR*, 53 (1974), 2.

33. Quoted in Clare Jackson, *Restoration Scotland, 1660-1690: Royalist Politics, Religion and Ideas* (Woodbridge, 2003), p. 79.

34. Quoted in MacIntosh, *Scottish Parliament*, p. 49.

35. Quoted in Jackson, *Restoration Scotland*, p. 117.

36. Patrick, 'The origins of the opposition to Lauderdale', 1–21.

37. Quoted in K.H.D. Haley, *The First Earl of Shaftesbury* (1968), pp. 510–11.

38. J.R. Jones, 'The Scottish Constitutional Opposition in 1679', *SHR*, 37 (1958), 37–41.

39. J.I. McGuire, 'Why was Ormond Dismissed in 1669?', *Irish Historical Studies*, 18 (1973), 295–312.

40. This is the core argument of what remains the most detailed and perceptive coverage of Irish political life at this time: Séan Egan, 'Finance and the Government of Ireland 1660–85' (Trinity College Dublin, PhD thesis, 2 vols, 1983).

41. National Library of Scotland MS 548, ff. 23v, 25v: narrative of Robert Landess of Robroyston, minister of Blantyre 1662–1703.

42. Quoted in Jacqueline R. Hill, 'Dublin Corporation, Protestant Dissent, and Politics, 1660–1800', in Kevin Herlihy (ed.), *The Politics of Irish Dissent 1650–1800* (Dublin, 1997), p. 31.

43. HMC, *Ormonde*, new series, VII, 102: Duke of Ormond to Earl of Arran, St. James's Square, London, 9 August 1683.

44. Quoted in Haley, *Shaftesbury*, p. 584.

45. Jonathan Scott, 'England's Troubles: Exhuming the Popish Plot', in Tim Harris, Paul Seaward, and Mark Goldie (eds), *The Politics of Religion in Restoration England* (Oxford, 1990), pp. 114–15.

46. Patrick Little, *Lord Broghill and the Cromwellian Union with Ireland and Scotland* (Woodbridge, 2004), esp. ch. 6; John Kerrigan, *Archipelagic English. Literature, History, and Politics 1603–1707* (Oxford, 2008), ch. 8.

47. Edward MacLysaght (ed.), *Calendar of the Orrery Papers* (Irish Manuscripts Commission, Dublin, 1941), p. 192: Earl of Orrery to [?Duke of Ormond], Castlemartyr, 25 January 1677/8.

48. *An Accompt of the Bloody Massacre in Ireland: Acted by the Instigation of the Jesuits, Priests, and Friars . . .* (1678), pp. 4, 6, 8.

49. Quoted in Mark Knights, *Politics and Opinion in Crisis, 1678–81* (Cambridge, 1994), p. 307.

50. *An Account of the Publick Affairs in Ireland, Since the discovery of the Late Plot* (1679), unpaginated.

51. *RPS*, 1681/7/18. Date accessed: 3 September 2008.

52. *RPS*, 1681/7/23.

53. *RPS*, 1681/7/29.

54. Reresby, *Memoirs*, p. 228.

55. BL, Add. MS 37981, f. 66v: William Carr to Earl of Conway, Amsterdam, 5 September 1681; BL, Add. MS 37986, ff. 134, 136: Edmund Poley to William Blathwayt and Earl of Conway, Berlin, 3/13 and 6/16 September 1681; Sir Richard Bulstrode, *Memoirs and Recollections Upon the Reign and Government of King Charles the Ist and K. Charles the IId . . .* (1721), pp. 321–2.

56. NLI, MS 4909, f. 30: Clonmel Assize Records, 14 September 1683.

57. NLI, MS 2993, f. 55: Trim assembly book, 1680–1709 (microfilm P8976).

58. MacLysaght (ed.), *Calendar of the Orrery Papers*, p. 307: [Captain] H[enry] Boyle to the dowager countess of Orrery, [Mar. 1685].

59. John Miller, 'The Earl of Tyrconnell and James II's Irish policy, 1685–1688', *HJ*, 20 (1977), 802–23.

60. MacLysaght (ed.), *Calendar of the Orrery Papers*, p. 322.

61. Quoted in De Krey, *Restoration and Revolution*, p. 225.

62. MacLysaght (ed.), *Calendar of the Orrery Papers*, p. 330: [Captain] H[enry] Boyle to the dowager countess of Orrery, Minehead, 14 June 1687.

63. Morrice, *Entring Book*, III, p. 375; IV, p. 73.

64. Sir William Petty, *The Political Anatomy of Ireland* ... (1691; repr. Shannon, 1970), pp. 38–9; Royal Irish Academy, Dublin, MS 12. I. 12, pp. 22–3, 35: Christopher Crofts to Sir Robert Southwell, Cork, 29 October 1688, 6 November 1688, 8 June 1688.

65. MacLysaght (ed.), *Calendar of the Orrery Papers*, pp. 326–7, 329: R[obert] Smith to the dowager countess of Orrery, Dublin, 9 April 1687, Earl of Burlington to same, Chiswick, 21 May 1687.

66. Alastair J. Mann, ' "James VII, King of the Articles": Political Management and Parliamentary Failure', in Keith M. Brown and Alastair J. Mann (eds), *The History of the Scottish Parliament. Vol. 2: Parliament and Politics in Scotland 1567–1707* (Edinburgh, 2005), p. 190.

67. *Ibid.*, p. 200.

68. Morrice, *Entring Book*, III, p. 221.

69. Mann, ' "James VII, King of the Articles" ', p. 203.

70. Morrice, *Entring Book*, IV, p. 307 and n. 4.

71. *EHD*, 611.

72. NLI, MS 36, no. 650: [Captain] H[enry] Boyle to the dowager countess of Orrery, 4 November 1687.

73. Morrice, *Entring Book*, III, pp. 53, 290.

74. G.H. Jones, 'The Irish Fright of 1688: Real Violence and Imagined Massacre', *Bulletin of the Institute of Historical Research*, 55 (1982), 148–53.

75. HMC, *Eleventh Report*, appendix, part V, p. 34: James to Col. George Legge, Brussels, 28 May [1679].

76. HMC, *Ormonde*, new series, IV, 512: Sir Robert Southwell to Duke of Ormond, 13 May 1679.

77. Bodl., MS Carte 69, f. 455v.

78. Quoted in R.A. Beddard, 'A Whig View of Tory Oxford in 1683: Lord Herbert of Chirbury's Criticism of the University', *Bodleian Library Record*, 15 (1995), 179–80.

79. Quotes in Jackson, *Restoration Scotland*, pp. 61, 161.

80. Public Record Office of Northern Ireland, D162/1: 'The names of ye Mayors & sheryfes of Carrickfergus since ... 1568' (microfilm 533 reel 1).

81. *An Abstract of the Unnatural Rebellion, and Barbarous Massacre of the Protestants in the Kingdom of Ireland, in 1641* ... (1689), pp. 4, 6. Akeldama

was a part of Jerusalem stained with the blood of Judas Iscariot after his betrayal of Christ (Acts 1:19; Matthew 27:7).

82. John Childs, *The Williamite Wars in Ireland 1688–1691* (2007).

Chapter 7: What was the Importance of Politics Out-of-Doors in this Period?

1. Tim Harris, *London Crowds in the Reign of Charles II: Propaganda and Politics from the Restoration until the Exclusion Crisis* (Cambridge, 1987), pp. 82–91, quotation at p. 83.
2. Mark Knights, 'London's "Monster" Petition of 1680', *HJ*, 36 (1993), 43.
3. *Ibid.*, 40.
4. Tim Harris, *Restoration: Charles II and his Kingdoms* (2005), pp. 282, 319–20.
5. J. Habermas, *The Structural Transformation of the Public Sphere: An Inquiry into a Category of Bourgeois Society*, trans. T. Burger with Frederick Lawrence (Cambridge, 1989, 1992), p. 57. Our section on the public sphere is heavily indebted both generally and specifically to Joad Raymond, 'The Newspaper, Public Opinion, and the Public Sphere in the Seventeenth Century', in Joad Raymond (ed.), *News, Newspapers, and Society in Early Modern Britain* (1999), pp. 109–40.
6. Habermas, *Structural Transformation*, pp. 57–9, quotation at p. 58.
7. *Ibid.*, p. xvii.
8. For a strong series of essays setting out the current state of play, see Peter Lake and Steven Pincus (eds), *The Politics of the Public Sphere in Early Modern England* (Manchester, 2007).
9. It is, however, no defence of Habermas to claim that he dated the emergence of the public sphere *as he defined it* correctly: historians have also criticised the idea that Habermas's public sphere existed in the eighteenth century.
10. Raymond, 'The Newspaper, Public Opinion, and the Public Sphere', pp. 109–40, quotations at p. 122.
11. Mark Knights, *Representation and Misrepresentation in Later Stuart Britain: Partisanship and Political Culture* (Oxford, 2005).
12. T. C. W. Blanning, *The Culture of Power and the Power of Culture: Old Regime Europe 1660–1789* (Oxford, 2002), pp. 5–14. Habermas is unclear on whether calling the public sphere 'bourgeois' reflects its actual social make up. In the 1640s and 1650s, of course, politics and

culture were intertwined and many political responses were fuelled by and expressed in cultural material, but Blanning's critique of Habermas stands.

13. Blanning, *Culture of Power*, p. 14.
14. Peter Lake with Michael Questier, *The Antichrist's Lewd Hat: Protestants, Papists and Players in Post-Reformation England* (2002), p. x.
15. For a defence of the continued importance of alehouses, and a perhaps over-strident downplaying of the significance of coffeehouses, see Tim Harris, 'Understanding Popular Politics in Restoration Britain', in Alan Houston and Steve Pincus, *A Nation Transformed: England After the Restoration* (Cambridge, 2001), p. 141.
16. Pepys, *Diary*, X, 357–8; John Dryden, *An Essay of Dramatic Poesy*, in John Dryden, *The Major Works*, ed. Keith Walker (Oxford, 2003), p. 77.
17. This section on coffeehouses is indebted to Steve Pincus, ' "Coffee Politicians Does Create": Coffeehouses and Restoration Political Culture', *Journal of Modern History*, 67 (1995), 807–34 and Brian Cowan, *The Social Life of Coffee: The Emergence of the British Coffeehouse* (New Haven and London, 2005).
18. Cowan, *The Social Life of Coffee*, p. 90.
19. Pincus, ' "Coffee" ', 813.
20. Cowan, *The Social Life of Coffee*, p. 93.
21. Grant Tapsell, *The Personal Rule of Charles II 1681–85* (Woodbridge, 2007), pp. 109–11.
22. Quoted in Martin Dzelzainis, N.H. Keeble, Annabel Patterson and Nicholas von Maltzahn (eds), *The Complete Prose Works of Andrew Marvell* (2 vols, New Haven and London, 2003), I, p. 3.
23. *Ibid.*, I, pp. 3–4.
24. Tapsell, *Personal Rule*, p. 111.
25. On this attempt to regulate the coffeehouses and the reasons for its failure see Pincus, ' "Coffee" ', 822–34.
26. F.S. Siebert, *Freedom of the Press in England, 1476–1776* (Urbana, 1965), pp. 265–7; Keeble, *Restoration*, pp. 150–1; Adrian Johns, *The Nature of the Book: Print and Knowledge in the Making* (Chicago, 1998), pp. 135–6. Twyn also admitted publishing *Mene Tekel: Or the Downfall of Monarchy*; Keeble, *Restoration*, p. 151.
27. 'Charles II, 1662: An Act for preventing the frequent Abuses in printing seditious treasonable and unlicensed Bookes and Pamphlets and for regulating of Printing and Printing Presses', *Statutes of the Realm: Volume 5: 1628–80* (1819), pp. 428–35. http://www.british-history.ac.uk/report.aspx?compid=47336

28. N.H. Keeble, *The Literary Culture of Nonconformity in Later Seventeenth-Century England* (Leicester, 1987), p. 105.

29. Elizabeth R. Clarke, 'Mr Jekyll and Dr Watson' (unpublished paper); Elizabeth R. Clarke, 'John Jekyll', *ODNB*.

30. Johns, *Nature of the Book*, p. 129.

31. Keeble, *Literary Culture*, pp. 110–20 provides a good account of the various techniques by which dissenting works could either be passed through or circumvent the licensing process.

32. For the means by which Quaker literature was produced, see John Stephen Tawhana Hetet, 'A Literary Underground in Restoration England: Printers and Dissenters in the Context of Constraints 1660–1689' (University of Cambridge PhD thesis, 1987), pp. 122–54; Thomas P. O'Malley, ' "Defying the Powers and Tempering the Spirit." A Review of Quaker Control over their Publications, 1672–1689', *JEH*, 33 (1982), 72–88.

33. O'Malley, ' "Defying the Powers" ', 74.

34. *Ibid.*, 73–4. On the importance of writing to the early Quaker movement, see the essays collected in Thomas N. Corns and David Lowenstein (eds), *The Emergence of Quaker Writing: Dissenting Literature in Seventeenth-Century England* (London, 1995); Kate Peters, *Print Culture and the Early Quakers* (Cambridge, 2005).

35. F.J. Levy, 'How Information Spread Among the Gentry', *JBS*, 21 (1982), 11–34; Richard Cust, 'News and Politics in Early Seventeenth-Century England', *P&P*, 112 (1986), 60–90.

36. Andrew Mousley, 'Self, State, and Seventeenth-Century News', *The Seventeenth Century*, 6 (1991), 149.

37. Quoted in Cust, 'News and Politics', 63.

38. Quentin Skinner, *Visions of Politics* (3 vols, Cambridge, 2002), II, *Renaissance Virtues*; Jonathan Scott, *Commonwealth Principles: Republican Writing of the English Revolution* (Cambridge, 2004), ch. 8.

39. Tessa Watt, *Cheap Print and Popular Piety, 1550–1640* (Cambridge, 1991).

40. Patrick Collinson, *The Religion of Protestants: The Church in English Society 1559–1625* (Oxford, 1986), chs 3–4; Felicity Heal and Clive Holmes, *The Gentry in England and Wales 1500–1700* (Basingstoke, 1994), ch. 7.

41. Margo Todd, *The Culture of Protestantism in Early Modern Scotland* (New Haven and London, 2002), ch. 1; Raymond Gillespie, *Reading Ireland: Printing, Reading and Social Change in Early Modern Ireland* (Manchester, 2005); http://www.st-andrews.ac.uk/~sahup/historybackground.htm; Alan Ford, *James Ussher: Theology*,

History, and Politics in Early-Modern Ireland and England (Oxford, 2007), chs 6, 9.

42. Jonathan Barry and Christopher Brooks (eds), *The Middling Sort of People: Culture, Society and Politics in England, 1550–1800* (Basingstoke, 1994); H.R. French, *The Middle Sort of People in Provincial England, 1600–1750* (Oxford, 2007).

43. Fritz Levy, 'The Decorum of News', and Ian Atherton, ' "The Itch Grown a Disease": Manuscript Transmission of News in the Seventeenth Century', in Raymond (ed.), *News, Newspapers and Society*, pp. 12–38, 39–65; Mousley, 'Self, State, and Seventeenth-Century News', 149–68.

44. Ian Archer, 'Social Networks in Restoration London: The Evidence of Samuel Pepys's Diary', in Alexandra Shepard and Phil Withington (eds), *Communities in Early Modern England: Networks, Place, Rhetoric* (Manchester, 2000), pp. 76–94.

45. Pepys, *Diary*, I, p. 13; V, p. 37; X, pp. 416–28; V, p. 348; VI, p. 305 and n. 3.

46. *Ibid.*, VII, p. 269; II, p. 221; IX, p. 397; VII, pp. 150–1.

47. Mark S. Dawson, 'Histories and Texts: Refiguring the Diary of Samuel Pepys', *HJ*, 43 (2000), 407–31, quotation at 422.

48. Paul Seaward, 'The Cavalier Parliament, the 1667 Accounts Commission and the Idea of Accountability', in Chris R. Kyle and Jason Peacey (eds), *Parliament at Work: Parliamentary Committees, Political Power, and Public Access in Early Modern England* (Woodbridge, 2002), pp. 149–68.

49. Pepys, *Diary*, VII, pp. 399–400.

50. Morrice, *Entring Book*, II, p. 446.

51. Samuel Rawson Gardiner, *The Constitutional Documents of the Puritan Revolution 1625–1660* (3rd edn, Oxford, 1906), pp. 83, 98.

52. *EHD*, p. 187.

53. *Vox Angliæ: Or, the Voice of the Kingdom* . . . (1682), second part, p. 4.

54. For a wealth of material on urban conflicts, see Paul D. Halliday, *Dismembering the Body Politic: Partisan Politics in England's Towns, 1650–1730* (Cambridge, 1998); John Miller, *Cities Divided: Politics and Religion in English Provincial Towns, 1660–1722* (Oxford, 2007).

55. For more substantial recent accounts, see Tapsell, *Personal Rule of Charles II*, pp. 102–6; Peter Hinds, 'Roger L'Estrange, the Rye House Plot, and the Regulation of Political Discourse in Late-Seventeenth-century London', *The Library*, 7th ser., 3 (2002), 3–31.

56. Roger L'Estrange, *The Observator* . . . , 1 (13 April 1681).

57. Geoff Kemp, 'Roger L'Estrange and the Publishing Sphere', in Jason McElligott (ed.), *Fear, Exclusion, and Revolution: Roger Morrice and Britain in the 1680s* (Aldershot, 2006), p. 70.
58. Atherton, 'Itch Grown a Disease', pp. 39–65.
59. Morrice, *Entring Book*, I, 98–116; Grant Tapsell, ' "weepe over the ejected practice of Religion": Roger Morrice and the Restoration Twilight of Puritan Politics', *Parliamentary History*, 28 (2009), 266–94.
60. Morrice, *Entring Book*, II, p. 373.
61. West Yorkshire Archive Service, Leeds, MX/R/23/55: 'The Information of Michaell Ann esq. Taken upon Oath the 2d day of August Anno Dom: 1683 before S[i]r John Reresby'.
62. Morrice, *Entring Book*, II, pp. 396, 399, 406–7, 414, 392, 406, 421–2.
63. *CSPD 1 Oct. 1683–30 Apr. 1684*, p. 50: Thomas Rich to 'the Secretary of State', North Cerney [Gloucs.], 22 October 1683.
64. Quoted in Mousley, 'Self, State, and Seventeenth-Century News', 165.
65. J.P. Kenyon, *Halifax: Complete Works* (Harmondsworth, 1969), p. 49.
66. Thomas Hobbes, *Behemoth or The Long Parliament* (ed.) Ferdinand Tönnies, with an introduction by Stephen Holmes (Chicago and London, 1990), p. 16.
67. Mark Knights, *Politics and Opinion in Crisis, 1678–81* (Cambridge, 1994), p. 16.
68. These and other questions are magnificently addressed in Knights, *Representation and Misrepresentation in Later Stuart Britain*.

Chapter 8: Why Study Restoration Culture?

1. BL, Lansdowne MS 95, f. 41v. We are very grateful to Jonathan Fitzgibbons for making his transcription of this manuscript available to us.
2. We first came across the phrase in James Campbell, 'The End of Roman Britain', in James Campbell (gen. ed.), *The Anglo-Saxons* (Oxford, 1982), p. 8.
3. Joad Raymond, *Pamphlets and Pamphleteering in Early Modern Britain* (Cambridge, 2003), p. 89. As Raymond makes clear these statistics probably underestimate the true levels of literacy. Raymond also provides some brief discussion of literacy in Wales, Scotland, and Ireland. An excellent discussion of readers and their relation to pamphlets in particular is provided in *ibid.*, pp. 89–97.

4. N.H. Keeble, *The Literary Culture of Nonconformity in Later Seventeenth-century England* (Leicester, 1987), pp. 136–9.

5. Jessica Munns, 'Theatrical Culture I: Politics and Theatre', in Steven N. Zwicker (ed.), *English Literature 1650–1740* (Cambridge, 1998), p. 87; Edward A. Langhans, 'The Post-1660 Theatres as Performance Spaces', in Susan J. Owen (ed.), *A Companion to Restoration Drama* (Oxford, 2001), p. 15.

6. Bodl., MS Don. b. 8.

7. For more on Haward's miscellany, see Harold Love, *The Culture and Commerce of Texts: Scribal Publication in Seventeenth-Century England* (Amherst, Mass., 1998), pp. 211–17. For more on Haward's use of Wild, see George Southcombe, 'The Responses of Nonconformists to the Restoration in England' (University of Oxford DPhil thesis, 2005), pp. 82–4.

8. John Dryden, *Absalom and Achitophel*, in Paul Hammond and David Hopkins (eds), *The Poems of John Dryden* (5 vols, London and Harlow, 1995–2005), I, p. 450.

9. Susan J. Owen, *Restoration Theatre and Crisis* (Oxford, 1996).

10. For readings of *Absalom and Achitophel* and responses to it which complement the one offered here, see Abigail Williams, *Poetry and the Creation of a Whig Literary Culture* (Oxford, 2005), pp. 58–63; Matthew Jenkinson, 'The Politics of Court Culture in the Reign of Charles II, 1660–1685' (University of Oxford DPhil thesis, 2007), pp. 225–42.

11. Dryden, *Absalom and Achitophel*, in Hammond and Hopkins (eds), *Poems of John Dryden*, I, p. 483 (l. 373).

12. *Ibid.*, p. 510 (ll. 683–93).

13. *Ibid.*, p. 530 (ll. 985–8).

14. *Ibid.*, p. 530 (ll. 1000–3).

15. A useful summary of the context for the poem, including a redaction of Phillip Harth's argument that it was not written to influence the jury can be found in *ibid.*, pp. 445–6.

16. Samuel Pordage, *Azaria and Hushai* (1682), p. 12.

17. *Ibid.*

18. *Ibid.*, p. 33.

19. *Ibid.*, p. 38.

20. Dryden, *Absalom and Achitophel*, in Hammond and Hopkins (eds), *Poems of John Dryden*, I, p. 532 (l. 1026); Pordage, *Azaria and Hushai*, p. 38.

21. *Ibid.*, p. 38.

22. Dryden, *Absalom and Achitophel*, in Hammond and Hopkins (eds), *Poems of John Dryden*, I, p. 532 (ll. 1030–1).

23. Pordage, *Azaria and Hushai*, p. 29.

24. Paul Hammond, 'John Dryden', *ODNB*.

25. This reading of Behn is indebted to the groundbreaking work of Susan J. Owen, although it diverges from her on a few points. See for good introductions to her position: Susan J. Owen, 'Behn's Dramatic Response to Restoration Politics', in Derek Hughes and Janet Todd (eds), *The Cambridge Companion to Aphra Behn* (Cambridge, 2004), pp. 68–82; Susan J. Owen, ' "Suspect my Loyalty when I Lose my Virtue": Sexual Politics and Party in Aphra Behn's Plays of the Exclusion Crisis, 1678–83', in Janet Todd (ed.), *Aphra Behn* (Basingstoke, 1999), pp. 57–72. On patriarchalism, see Robert Filmer, *Patriarcha*, in Johann P. Sommerville (ed.), *Patriarcha and other Writings* (Cambridge, 1991), pp. 1–68; Mark Goldie, 'John Locke and Anglican Royalism', *Political Studies*, 31 (1983), 61–85.

26. Aphra Behn, *The Roundheads*, in Janet Todd (ed.), *The Works of Aphra Behn* (7 vols, 1992–6), VI, p. 374 (I.i.329, 331–2).

27. Owen, ' "Suspect my Loyalty" ', in Todd (ed.), *Aphra Behn*, pp. 64–5.

28. See for example, Mercurius Melancholicus, *Mistris Parliament her Gossipping* (1648); Mercurius Melancholieus, *Mrs. Parliament her Invitation of Mrs London, to a Thanksgiving Dinner* (1648). For discussion of these fears, see David Underdown, *A Freeborn People: Politics and the Nation in Seventeenth-Century England* (Oxford, 1996), ch. 5.

29. Owen, ' "Suspect my Loyalty" ', in Todd (ed.), *Aphra Behn*, p. 64; Eric Salmon, 'John Tatham', *ODNB*.

30. Toby Barnard, 'Roger Boyle', *ODNB*; Patrick Little, *Lord Broghill and the Cromwellian Union with Ireland and Scotland* (Woodbridge, 2004).

31. John Spurr, *England in the 1670s: 'This Masquerading Age'* (Oxford, 2000), pp. 63–9, 72–4; John Kerrigan, *Archipelagic English: Literature, History, and Politics 1603–1707* (Oxford, 2008), p. 264. Kerrigan examines the specifically Irish fears which may have impelled Orrery to write. He also provides a discussion of the poem analysed here, which we have drawn on.

32. West Sussex RO, Petworth House Archives, Orrery Papers MS 13187.

33. Andrew Marvell, *The Last Instructions to a Painter*, in Nigel Smith (ed.), *The Poems of Andrew Marvell* (2003), p. 392 (ll. 915–26).

34. Andrew Marvell, 'An Horatian Ode upon Cromwell's Return from Ireland', in *ibid.*, p. 276 (l.54).

35. Marvell, *Last Instructions*, in *ibid.*, p. 392 (ll. 890–8). This section is heavily indebted to Steven Zwicker's reading of the poem. See Steven N. Zwicker, *Lines of Authority: Politics and English Literary Culture, 1649–1689* (Ithaca and London, 1993), pp. 107–19.

36. Marvell, *Last Instructions*, in Smith (ed.), *Poems of Andrew Marvell*, p. 392 (ll. 900–3).

37. *Ibid.* (ll. 903–6).

38. Zwicker, *Lines*, p. 117; Catherine MacLeod and Julia Marciari Alexander (eds), *Painted Ladies: Women at the Court of Charles II* (2001), p. 98.

39. John Evelyn quoted in Stuart Handley, 'Frances Teresa Stuart', *ODNB*.

40. Zwicker, *Lines*, p. 118. The pun on money refers to Frances Stuart's posing as Britannia for a farthing, which is also alluded to in Marvell's poem.

41. Sonya Wynne, ' "The Brightest Glories of the British Sphere": Women at the Court of Charles II', in MacLeod and Marciari Alexander (eds), *Painted Ladies*, p. 44.

42. Obsessive searches for specific allegorical meaning are critiqued in Robert D. Hume, 'The Politics of Opera in Late Seventeenth-Century London', *Cambridge Opera Journal*, 10 (1998), 15–43. Hume also makes the argument that opera often glorified the monarchy. A useful short survey and critique of other approaches, along with a sensible reading of Blow's opera is Jenkinson, 'The Politics of Court Culture', pp. 318–20.

43. We quote from the most easily accessible contemporary version. This is a facsimile of an original printed text which was produced following or perhaps for a revival of the opera in 1684. It is in Richard Luckett, 'A New Source for "Venus and Adonis" ', *The Musical Times*, 130 (1989), 77–8, quotation at 77 (p. 3 of the original). For the suggestion that this text was given out at the 1684 performance, see James A. Winn, ' "A Versifying Maid of Honour": Anne Finch and the Libretto for *Venus and Adonis*', *Review of English Studies*, 59 (2007), 69, n. 5.

44. Luckett, 'A New Source', 78 (p. 6).

45. Curtis Price, 'Venus and Adonis', http://www.oxford,usiconline.com:80/subscriber/article/grove/music/O905445, our emphasis.

46. MacLeod and Marciari Alexander (eds), *Painted Ladies*, p. 124.

47. *Ibid.*, pp. 124–5.

48. Quoted in *ibid.*, p. 209.

49. Quoted in Harold Love, *English Clandestine Satire 1660–1702* (Oxford, 2004), p. 59.
50. For more on this theme, see *ibid.*, pp. 57–62.
51. John Wilmot, Earl of Rochester, 'Of Marriage', in Harold Love (ed.), *The Works of John Wilmot Earl of Rochester* (Oxford, 1999), p. 40 (l. 8).
52. Rochester, 'Dialogue L:R', in *ibid.*, p. 91 (ll. 13–14). A fuller exploration of the context for this work may be found in *ibid.*, p. 423.
53. *Ibid.*, p. 87 (ll. 11–12).
54. *Ibid.* (ll. 14–15).
55. *Ibid.* (ll. 18–19).
56. Quoted in Munns, 'Theatrical Culture', in Zwicker (ed.), *English Literature*, p. 83.
57. Munns, 'Theatrical Culture', in Zwicker (ed.), *English Literature*, pp. 82–103. Munns provides a useful, concise survey of key developments.
58. A number of the plays are usefully collected in two anthologies: Gillian Manning (ed.), *Libertine Plays of the Restoration* (2001); Deborah Payne Fisk (ed.), *Four Restoration Libertine Plays* (Oxford, 2005).
59. On the ways in which libertinism tested orthodox patriarchy, see Faramerz Dabhoiwala, 'The Construction of Honour, Reputation and Status in Late Seventeenth- and Early Eighteenth-Century England', *TRHS*, 6th ser., 6 (1996), 201–13.
60. Thomas Hobbes, *Leviathan* (ed.) Richard Tuck (rev. edn, Cambridge, 1996), pp. 86–90, quotation at p. 90; Warren Chernaik, *Sexual Freedom in Restoration Literature* (Cambridge, 1995), pp. 22–51.
61. Benjamin Keach, *The Glorious Lover* (1679), p. 70.
62. *Ibid.*, p. 71.
63. *Ibid.*, p. 75.
64. *Ibid.*, p. 242.
65. *Ibid.*, p. 260. A reading which in many ways complements the one offered here may be found in Sharon Achinstein, *Literature and Dissent in Milton's England* (Cambridge, 2003), pp. 196–9. Achinstein too stresses how 'Sexual eroticism may be deployed in the service of evangelical Christianity': *ibid.*, p. 199. We remain less convinced that Keach succeeds in ultimately presenting Christ and the Soul's love as 'properly transvalued away from any earthly objects': *ibid.*
66. For the strongest statement that *Samson Agonistes* should be understood within the context of Restoration dissent, see *ibid.*, pp. 48–58, 138–53.

67. John Milton, *Samson Agonistes,* in John Carey (ed.) *Complete Shorter Poems* (1997), p. 410 (l. 1654).
68. The phrase is John Carey's: 'A Work in Praise of Terrorism?', *Times Literary Supplement* (6 September 2002), 15–16.
69. Milton, *Samson,* in Carey (ed.), *Complete Shorter Poems,* p. 355.
70. *Ibid.,* p. 413 (ll. 1755–8).
71. *Ibid.,* p. 357.
72. *Ibid.,* p. 411 (ll. 1692, 1695–6).

Chapter 9: What were the Main Forces for Change and Continuity in the Post-Revolutionary World, 1688–1714?

1. Quoted in John Kenyon, *The History Men: The Historical Profession in England since the Renaissance* (1993), p. 85.
2. John Morrill, 'The Sensible Revolution', in Jonathan Israel (ed.), *The Anglo-Dutch Moment: Essays on the Glorious Revolution and its World Impact* (Cambridge, 1991), pp. 73–104.
3. Some of the key documents surrounding the controversy over oaths can conveniently be found in E.N. Williams, *The Eighteenth-Century Constitution 1688–1815: Documents and Commentary* (Cambridge, 1960), documents 10, 13, 14.
4. Lord Braybrooke (ed.), *The Autobiography of Sir John Bramston, K.B., of Skreens, in the Hundred of Chelmsford* (Camden Soc., 32, 1845), p. 355.
5. Reresby, *Memoirs,* pp. 574, 569, 566, 571, 575.
6. Braybrooke (ed.), *Autobiography of Sir John Bramston,* p. 357.
7. C.D.A. Leighton, 'The Non-Jurors and their History', *Journal of Religious History,* 29 (2005), 241–57.
8. George Ornsby (ed.), 'The Remains of Denis Graville, D.D., Dean and Archdeacon of Durham...', in *Miscellanea* (Surtees Soc., 37, 1860), p. 40.
9. Williams, *Eighteenth-Century Constitution,* p. 26.
10. Tony Claydon, *William III and the Godly Revolution* (Cambridge, 1996), ch. 1.
11. Morrice, *Entring Book,* V, p. 184.
12. *Ibid.,* 137.
13. Julian Hoppit, *A Land of Liberty? England 1689–1727* (Oxford, 2000), p. 135.
14. Quoted in Tony Claydon, 'William III and II', *ODNB.*
15. Morrice, *Entring Book,* V, p. 181.

16. Hugh Ouston, 'York in Edinburgh: James VII and the Patronage of Learning in Scotland, 1679–1688', in John Dwyer, Roger A. Mason, and Alexander Murdoch (eds), *New Perspectives on the Politics and Culture of Early Modern Scotland* (Edinburgh, 1982), pp. 133–55 and ' "From Thames to Tweed Departed": The Court of James, Duke of York in Scotland, 1679–82', in Eveline Cruickshanks (ed.), *The Stuart Courts* (Stroud, 2000), pp. 266–79.

17. Andrew Murray Scott (ed.), 'Letters of John Graham of Claverhouse', in *Miscellany XI* (Scottish History Soc., 5th ser., 3, 1990), pp. 237–8: Claverhouse to Cluny Macpherson[Strone?], 19 May 1689; same to John Macleod of Macleod, Moy, 23 June 1689.

18. Quoted in Allan I. Macinnes, *Union and Empire: The Making of the United Kingdom in 1707* (Cambridge, 2007), p. 234.

19. The best recent account is John Childs, *The Williamite Wars in Ireland 1688–1691* (2007).

20. J.G. Simms, *The Jacobite Parliament of 1689* (Dundalk, 1966).

21. Morrice, *Entring Book*, V, pp. 171–2, 177, 182–3, 185–7.

22. *Ibid.*, V, p. 26.

23. William Marshall, 'Denis Granville', *ODNB*.

24. The phrase is actually Charles Tilly's quoted in Steven Gunn, David Grummitt, and Hans Cools, 'War and the State in Early Modern Europe: Widening the Debate', *War in History*, 15 (2008), 372.

25. For important interventions into this debate, see Clifford J. Rogers (ed.), *The Military Revolution Debate: Readings on the Military Transformation of Early Modern Europe* (Boulder and Oxford, 1995).

26. Alan Cromartie, *The Constitutionalist Revolution: An Essay on the History of England, 1450–1642* (Cambridge, 2006); Clive Holmes, 'The County Community in Stuart Historiography', *JBS*, 19 (1980), 54–73; Clive Holmes, *Why was Charles I Executed?* (2006), pp. 1–34.

27. For the significance of anti-popery, see Peter Lake, 'Anti-Popery: The Structure of a Prejudice', in Richard Cust and Ann Hughes (eds), *Conflict in Early Stuart England: Studies in Religion and Politics, 1603–1642* (1989), pp. 72–106.

28. For a clarion call to an integrated study of state formation, see Gunn, Grummitt, and Cools, 'War and the State'.

29. The impact of William's Protestantism on attitudes to the granting of financial support is a central theme of the final chapter of Jonathan Scott, *England's Troubles: Seventeenth-Century English Political Instability in European Context* (Cambridge, 2000), pp. 474–96. For the argument

that a key outcome of the mid seventeenth-century English revolution was its demonstration that previously unimaginable sums could be obtained from the English populace, see Holmes, *Why was Charles I Executed?*, pp. 198–201.

30. The idea that Elizabeth's reign was militarily glorious was obviously a fabrication. We are grateful to Gabriel Glickman for discussion of the conceptualisation of late seventeenth-century foreign policy.

31. *A Kind Congratulation between Queen Elizabeth and the late Queen Mary II* (1695). For the continued importance of religion in both foreign policy and its representation, see Tony Claydon, *Europe and the Making of England, 1660–1760* (Cambridge, 2007).

32. Figures from Craig Rose, *England in the 1690s: Revolution, Religion and War* (Oxford, 1999), p. 132.

33. Tim Harris, *Revolution: The Great Crisis of the British Monarchy, 1685-1720* (2006), p. 494.

34. For much more on this theme, see Michael J. Braddick, *State Formation in Early Modern England, ca. 1550–1700* (Cambridge, 2000).

35. For important arguments that party remained key to the structure of politics in the period, see the classic account Geoffrey Holmes, *British Politics in the Age of Anne* (rev. edn, 1987); and Tim Harris, *Politics under the Later Stuarts: Party Conflict in a Divided Society, 1660–1715* (1993), pp. 147–207.

36. Quoted in Rose, *England in the 1690s*, p. 95, see also the discussion pp. 94–8. Some deployed more radical arguments, see Mark Goldie, 'The Roots of True Whiggism 1688–94', *History of Political Thought*, 1 (1980), 195–236.

37. Charles-Edouard Levillain, 'Cromwell Redivivus? William III as Military Dictator: Myth and Reality', in Esther Mijers and David Onnekink (eds), *Redefining William III: The Impact of the King-Stadholder in International Context* (Aldershot, 2007), pp. 159–76.

38. The terminology of the 'war state' and the 'law state' is used in relation to a much earlier period in R.W. Kaeuper, *War, Justice and Public Order: England and France in the Later Middle Ages* (Oxford, 1988).

39. Good short accounts of the Sacheverell controversy, on which we have drawn, are Hoppitt, *Land of Liberty?*, pp. 233–4; W.A. Speck, 'Henry Sacheverell', *ODNB*. The essential account remains Geoffrey Holmes, *The Trial of Dr Sacheverell* (1973).

40. Quoted in Speck, 'Henry Sacheverell'.

41. Hoppitt, *Land of Liberty?*, p. 233.

42. John England quoted in Holmes, *Trial of Dr Sacheverell*, p. 234.

43. Nicholas Tyacke (ed.), *England's Long Reformation 1500–1800* (1998); Andrew Starkie, 'Contested Histories of the English Church: Gilbert Burnet and Jeremy Collier', in Paulina Kewes (ed.), *The Uses of History in Early Modern England* (San Marino, CA, 2006), pp. 329–45.
44. Brendan Simms, *Three Victories and a Defeat: The Rise and Fall of the First British Empire* (2007), p. 37.
45. *Ibid.*, p. 75.
46. Geoffrey Holmes, *The Electorate and the National Will in the First Age of Party* (Kendal, 1976), pp. 14–15; Hannah Smith, *Georgian Monarchy: Politics and Culture, 1714–1760* (Cambridge, 2006); John Cannon, *Aristocratic Century: The Peerage of Eighteenth-century England* (Cambridge, 1984).
47. Quoted in John Cannon, *Samuel Johnson and the Politics of Hanoverian England* (Oxford, 1994), p. 110.
48. Holmes, *British Politics in the Age of Anne*, p. 8.
49. David Hayton's researches have been particularly important: *Ruling Ireland, 1685–1742: Politics, Politicians and Parties* (Woodbridge, 2004), ch. 2; 'Traces of Party Politics in Early Eighteenth-century Scottish Elections', *Parliamentary History*, 15 (1995), 74–99.
50. Rose, *England in the 1690s*, p. 67; Goldie, 'Roots of True Whiggism', 196; Blair Worden, *Roundhead Reputations: The English Civil Wars and the Passions of Posterity* (2001), pp. 36–7, 87–8, 103–4, 115–17.
51. Quoted in Rose, *England in the 1690s*, p. 95.
52. On the way in which Ludlow's reputation was constructed, see Worden, *Roundhead Reputations*, pp. 21–121.
53. Quoted in Henry Horwitz, 'The 1690s Revisited: Recent Work on Politics and Political Ideas in the Reign of William III', *Parliamentary History*, 15 (1996), 376.
54. For thoughtful older studies that reproduce much primary material, see J.A.W. Gunn, *Factions No More: Attitudes to Party in Government and Opposition in Eighteenth-Century England – Extracts from Contemporary Sources* (1972); Geoffrey Holmes and W.A. Speck (eds), *The Divided Society: Parties and Politics in England, 1694–1716* (1967).
55. Eveline Cruickshanks, 'Religion and Royal Succession: The Rage of Party', in Clyve Jones (ed.), *Britain in the First Age of Party, 1680–1750: Essays Presented to Geoffrey Holmes* (1987), pp. 19–43.
56. G.V. Bennett, *The Tory Crisis in Church and State, 1688–1730: The Career of Francis Atterbury, Bishop of Rochester* (Oxford, 1975) remains indispensable for an understanding of the Tory perception of events.

57. For accounts focusing on the centre and the localities, respectively, see Clyve Jones, 'Debates in the House of Lords on "the Church in Danger", 1705, and on Dr Sacheverell's Impeachment, 1710', *HJ*, 19 (1976), 759–71 and Donald Spaeth, *The Church in an Age of Danger: Parsons and Parishioners, 1660–1740* (Cambridge, 2000).

58. R. Astbury, 'The Renewal of the Licensing Act in 1693 and its Lapse in 1695', *The Library*, 5th ser., 33 (1978), 296–322.

59. Mark Knights, *Representation and Misrepresentation in Later Stuart Britain: Partisanship and Political Culture* (Oxford, 2004).

60. Gary S. De Krey, *A Fractured Society: The Politics of London in the First Age of Party, 1688–1715* (Oxford, 1985), p. 214.

61. Jeremy Black, *The English Press 1621–1861* (Stroud, 2001), ch. 6; G.A. Cranfield, *The Development of the Provincial Newspaper 1700–1760* (Oxford, 1962), esp. chs 1, 6.

62. One of the greatest of Geoffrey Holmes's achievements was to recover the importance of politicians' principles from the condescension of a sceptical posterity: D.W. Hayton, 'In No One's Shadow: *British Politics in the Age of Anne* and the Writing of the History of the House of Commons', *Parliamentary History*, 28 (2009), 7–8.

63. Alastair MacLachlan, 'The Road to Peace', in Geoffrey Holmes (ed.), *Britain after the Glorious Revolution* (1971), pp. 161–89; Simms, *Three Victories and a Defeat*, ch. 2; Claydon, *Europe and the Making of England*, chs 3–4.

64. For this important relationship, see Frances Harris, *A Passion for Government: The Life of Sarah, Duchess of Marlborough* (Oxford, 1991).

65. Quoted in D.W. Hayton, *Introductory Volume* to Eveline Cruickshanks, Stuart Handley, and D.W. Hayton (eds), *The House of Commons, 1690–1715* (5 vols, Cambridge, 2002), I, p. 67.

66. Linda Colley, *In Defiance of Oligarchy: The Tory Party 1714–60* (Cambridge, 1982); R.C. Richardson, *The Debate on the English Revolution* (3rd edn, Manchester, 1998), ch. 3; H.T. Dickinson, 'The Eighteenth-century Debate on the "Glorious Revolution"', *History*, 61 (1976), 28–45.

Further Reading

This list is necessarily highly selective and concentrates on the most recent literature and a few key earlier works. More detailed literature searches can be undertaken through the superb Bibliography of British and Irish History online on Brepolis. Readers interested in visual images from this period can now consult British Printed Images to 1700: http://bpi1700.org.uk/index.html.

General

David Allan, *Scotland in the Eighteenth Century* (Harlow, 2002).

Toby Barnard, 'Scotland and Ireland in the Later Stewart Monarchy', in Steven G. Ellis and Sarah Barber (eds), *Conquest and Union: Fashioning a British State 1485–1725* (Harlow, 1995).

Toby Barnard, 'Restoration or Initiation?', in Jenny Wormald (ed.), *The Seventeenth Century* (Oxford, 2008).

Brendan Bradshaw and John Morrill (eds), *The British Problem, c. 1534–1707: State Formation in the Atlantic Archipelago* (Basingstoke, 1996) – chs by Goldie and Smyth.

S.J. Connolly, *Religion, Law and Power: The Making of Protestant Ireland, 1660–1760* (Oxford, 1992).

S.J. Connolly, *Divided Kingdom: Ireland 1630–1800* (Oxford, 2008).

Gary S. De Krey, *Restoration and Revolution in Britain: A Political History of the Era of Charles II and the Glorious Revolution* (Basingstoke, 2007).

Coleman A. Dennehy (ed.), *Restoration Ireland: 'Always Settling and Never Settled'* (Aldershot, 2008).

Lionel K.J. Glassey (ed.), *The Reigns of Charles II and James VII & II* (Basingstoke, 1997).

217

Tim Harris, *Restoration: Charles II and His Kingdoms, 1660–85* (2005).

Tim Harris, *Revolution: The Great Crisis of the British Monarchy, 1685–1720* (2006).

David Hayton, 'Contested Kingdoms, 1688–1756', in Paul Langford (ed.), *Short Oxford History of the British Isles: The Eighteenth Century* (Oxford, 2002).

Julian Hoppit, *A Land of Liberty? England 1689–1727* (Oxford, 2000).

Alan Houston and Steve Pincus (eds), *A Nation Transformed: England After the Restoration* (Cambridge, 2001).

Ronald Hutton, *The Restoration: A Political and Religious History of England and Wales, 1658–1667* (Oxford, 1985).

Clare Jackson, *Restoration Scotland, 1660–1690: Royalist Politics, Religion and Ideas* (Woodbridge, 2003).

N.H. Keeble, *The Restoration: England in the 1660s* (Oxford, 2002).

Alan Marshall, *The Age of Faction: Court Politics, 1660–1702* (Manchester, 1999).

John Miller, *After the Civil Wars: English Politics and Government in the Reign of Charles II* (Harlow, 2000).

Craig Rose, *England in the 1690s: Revolution, Religion and War* (Oxford, 1999).

Jonathan Scott, *England's Troubles: Seventeenth-Century English Political Instability in European Context* (Cambridge, 2000).

David L. Smith, *A History of the Modern British Isles, 1603–1707: The Double Crown* (Oxford, 1998), chs 8–11.

Jim Smyth, *The Making of the United Kingdom, 1660–1800: State, Religion and Identity in Britain and Ireland* (2001).

W.A. Speck, *The Birth of Britain: A New Nation 1700–1710* (Oxford, 1994).

John Spurr, *England in the 1670s: 'This Masquerading Age'* (Oxford, 2000).

Politics

Robert Beddard (ed.), *The Revolutions of 1688* (Oxford, 1991).

Glenn Burgess (ed.), *The New British History: Founding a Modern State 1603–1715* (1999) – chs by Jackson and Claydon.

C.D. Chandaman, *The English Public Revenue 1660–1688* (Oxford, 1975).

John Childs, '1688', *History*, 73 (1988), 398–424.

Tony Claydon, *William III and the Godly Revolution* (Cambridge, 1996).

Tony Claydon, *William III* (2002).

Gary S. De Krey, *London and the Restoration, 1659–1683* (Cambridge, 2005).

Edward Gregg, *Queen Anne* (New Haven and London, rev. edn, 2001).

Paul D. Halliday, *Dismembering the Body Politic: Partisan Politics in England's Towns, 1650–1730* (Cambridge, 1998).

Tim Harris, *London Crowds in the Reign of Charles II: Propaganda and Politics from the Restoration until the Exclusion Crisis* (Cambridge, 1987).

Tim Harris, *Politics under the Later Stuarts: Party Conflict in a Divided Society 1660–1715* (Harlow, 1993).

Tim Harris, 'The British Dimension, Religion and the Shaping of Political Identities during the Reign of Charles II', in Tony Claydon and Ian McBride (eds), *Protestantism and National Identity: Britain and Ireland, c.1650–c.1850* (Cambridge, 1998).

D.W. Hayton, *Ruling Ireland, 1685–1742: Politics, Politicians and Parties* (Woodbridge, 2004).

Geoffrey Holmes, *British Politics in the Age of Anne* (rev. edn, 1987).

Ronald Hutton, *Charles II: King of England, Ireland, and Scotland* (Oxford, 1989).

Jonathan I. Israel (ed.), *The Anglo-Dutch Moment: Essays on the Glorious Revolution and its World Impact* (Cambridge, 1991).

Anna Keay, *The Magnificent Monarch: Charles II and the Ceremonies of Power* (2008).

Mark Knights, *Politics and Opinion in Crisis, 1678–81* (Cambridge, 1994).

Mark Knights, *Representation and Misrepresentation in Later Stuart Britain: Partisanship and Political Culture* (Oxford, 2004).

Mark Knights, 'Public Politics in England c. 1675–c. 1715', in Nicholas Tyacke (ed.), *The English Revolution c.1590–1720: Politics, Religion and Communities* (Manchester, 2007).

Mark Knights, 'How Rational was the Later Stuart Public Sphere?', in Peter Lake and Steven Pincus (eds), *The Politics of the Public Sphere in Early Modern England* (Manchester, 2007).

Allan I. Macinnes, *Union and Empire: The Making of the United Kingdom in 1707* (Cambridge, 2007).

Gillian H. MacIntosh, *The Scottish Parliament under Charles II 1660–1685* (Edinburgh, 2007).

Joyce Lee Malcolm, 'Charles II and the Reconstruction of Royal Power', *HJ*, 35 (1992), 307–330.

Alastair J. Mann, ' "James VII, King of the Articles": Political Management and Parliamentary Failure', in Keith M. Brown and Alastair J. Mann (eds), *The History of the Scottish Parliament: Vol. 2: Parliament and Politics in Scotland, 1567–1707* (Edinburgh, 2005).

John Miller, *Charles II* (1991).

John Miller, *James II* (New Haven and London, rev. edn, 2000).
Jonathan Scott, *Algernon Sidney and the Restoration Crisis, 1677–83* (Cambridge, 1991).
Paul Seaward, *The Cavalier Parliament and the Reconstruction of the Old Regime, 1661–1667* (Cambridge, 1989).
W.A. Speck, *Reluctant Revolutionaries: Englishmen and the Revolution of 1688* (Oxford, 1988).
Grant Tapsell, *The Personal Rule of Charles II, 1681–85* (Woodbridge, 2007).
Robert Willman, 'The Origins of "Whig" and "Tory" in English Political Language', *HJ*, 17 (1974), 247–64.

Religion

R.A. Beddard, 'James II and the Catholic Challenge', in Nicholas Tyacke (ed.), *The History of the University of Oxford, Volume IV: Seventeenth-Century Oxford* (Oxford, 1997).
Julia Buckroyd, *Church and State in Scotland 1660–1681* (Edinburgh, 1980).
Justin Champion, *The Pillars of Priestcraft Shaken: The Church of England and Its Enemies, 1660–1730* (Cambridge, 1992).
Gary S. De Krey, 'The First Restoration Crisis: Conscience and Coercion in London, 1667–1673', *Albion*, 25 (1993), 565–80.
Gary S. De Krey, 'Rethinking the Restoration: Dissenting Cases for Conscience, 1667–1672', *HJ*, 38 (1995), 53–83.
Gabriel Glickman, *The English Catholic Community, 1688–1745: Politics, Culture and Ideology* (Woodbridge 2009).
Mark Goldie, 'Sir Peter Pett, Sceptical Toryism and the Science of Toleration in the 1680s', *SCH*, 21 (1984), 274–73.
Mark Goldie, 'The Theory of Religious Intolerance in Restoration England', in O.P. Grell, Jonathan Israel, and Nicholas Tyacke (eds), *From Persecution to Toleration: The Glorious Revolution and Religion in England* (Oxford, 1991).
Mark Goldie (gen. ed.), *The Entring Book of Roger Morrice 1677–1691* (6 vols, Woodbridge, 2007), *Volume I: Roger Morrice and the Puritan Whigs* (Woodbridge, 2007).
Jeremy Gregory and Jeffrey S. Chamberlain (eds), *The National Church in Local Perspective: The Church of England and the Regions, 1660–1800* (Woodbridge, 2003).
Tim Harris, Paul Seaward, and Mark Goldie (eds), *The Politics of Religion in Restoration England* (Oxford, 1990).

Henry Horwitz, 'Protestant Reconciliation in the Exclusion Crisis', *JEH*, 15 (1964), 201–17.

Ronald Hutton, 'The Religion of Charles II', in R. Malcolm Smuts (ed.), *The Stuart Court and Europe: Essays in Politics and Political Culture* (Cambridge, 1996).

Douglas R. Lacey, *Dissent and Parliamentary Politics 1661–89: A Study in the Perpetuation and Tempering of Parliamentarianism* (New Brunswick, 1969).

John Miller, *Popery and Politics in England, 1660–88* (Cambridge, 1973).

John Spurr, *The Restoration Church of England 1646–1689* (New Haven and London, 1991).

John Spurr, 'Later Stuart Puritanism', in John Coffey and Paul Chang-Ha Lim (eds), *The Cambridge Companion to Puritanism* (Cambridge, 2008).

John Spurr, 'From Puritanism to Dissent, 1660–1700' in Christopher Durston and Jacqueline Eales (eds), *The Culture of English Puritanism, 1560–1700* (Basingstoke, 1996).

Culture

Sharon Achinstein, *Literature and Dissent in Milton's England* (Cambridge, 2003).

Jerry Brotton, 'The Art of Restoration: King Charles II and the Restitution of the English Royal Art Collection', *Court Historian*, 10 (2005), 115–35.

Anne Dunan-Page and Beth Lynch (eds), *Roger L'Estrange and the Making of Restoration Culture* (Aldershot, 2008).

Robert D. Hume, 'The Politics of Opera in Late Seventeenth-Century London', *Cambridge Opera Journal*, 10 (1998), 15–43.

N.H. Keeble, *The Literary Culture of Nonconformity in Later Seventeenth-Century England* (Leicester, 1987).

John Kerrigan, *Archipelagic English: Literature, History, and Politics 1603–1707* (Oxford, 2008).

Harold Love, *The Culture and Commerce of Texts: Scribal Publication in Seventeenth-Century England* (Amherst, Mass., 1998).

Harold Love, *English Clandestine Satire 1660–1702* (Oxford, 2004).

Catharine MacLeod and Julia Marciari Alexander (eds), *Painted Ladies: Women at the Court of Charles II* (2001).

Catharine MacLeod and Julia Marciari Alexander (eds), *Politics, Transgression, and Representation at the Court of Charles II* (2007).

Susan J. Owen (ed.), *A Companion to Restoration Drama* (Oxford, 2001).

Joad Raymond, *Pamphlets and Pamphleteering in Early Modern Britain* (Cambridge, 2003).

Andrew Walkling, 'Politics and Theatrical Culture in Restoration England', *History Compass*, 5/5 (2007), 1500–1520 [http://www3.interscience.wiley.com/cgi-bin/fulltext/118491930/PDFSTART].

Abigail Williams, *Poetry and the Creation of a Whig Literary Culture* (Oxford, 2005).

Steven N. Zwicker, *Lines of Authority: Politics and English Literary Culture, 1649–1689* (Ithaca and London, 1993).

Steven N. Zwicker (ed.), *English Literature 1650–1740* (Cambridge, 1998).

Index